Praise for *Capitalism*

'A superbly erudite excursion through the theory and practice of market economies down the ages.'
– Dominic Lawson, *Sunday Times*

'*Capitalism* does a better job of bringing together all the key issues facing today's global economy than any other book I've read ... a delight to read.'
– Tim Montgomerie, *The Times*

'In this thoughtful and stimulating intervention, John Plender [...] offers a tour d'horizon of the debate, enlivened by a deep knowledge of the global economy and an interest in history, together with an open-minded willingness to place capitalism on the scales of justice and see which way they tip.'
– David Priestland, *Financial Times*

'John Plender is one of capitalism's more thoughtful observers. His erudition and lifelong curiosity come together beautifully in this wise and wide-ranging book.'
– Stephanie Flanders

'[John Plender] approaches the quandaries of capitalism with a shrewd eye for detail.'
– *The Economist*

'John Plender's splendid book takes us through the mistrust of profit and money lending through the ages – from the ancient Greeks to Karl Marx and beyond.'
– Vicky Pryce, *Prospect*

'Plender is neither dogmatic nor prescriptive; if you like to read something that furnishes ideas for deba͗ ͗ n this book is for you.'
– Richard Walk͗

· CAPITALISM ·

MONEY,
MORALS AND
MARKETS

JOHN PLENDER

Biteback Publishing

This edition published in Great Britain in 2016 by
Biteback Publishing Ltd
Westminster Tower
3 Albert Embankment
London SE1 7SP
Copyright © John Plender 2015, 2016

ISBN 978-1-78590-020-4

10 9 8 7 6 5 4 3 2 1

A CIP catalogue record for this book is available from the British Library.

Set in Sabon

Printed and bound in Great Britain by
CPI Group (UK) Ltd, Croydon CR0 4YY

To Stephanie, Tom, Olivia, Celia, Richard and Robin

CONTENTS

ACKNOWLEDGEMENTS

This book draws on the wisdom of so many people and so much reading over the years that it would be impossible to thank all my sources individually. What I can do is acknowledge the long-standing support and stimulus from my colleagues at the *Financial Times*, the enthusiastic encouragement of David Marsh, managing director of the Official Monetary and Financial Institutions Forum, and of Andrew Hilton, director of the Centre for the Study of Financial Innovation. Anyone who writes about capitalism from a historical and cultural perspective also has to acknowledge a debt to Jerry Z. Muller, whose book *The Mind and the Market: Capitalism in Western Thought* has been an inspiration and a delight. I offer heartfelt gratitude to my old friend Brian Reading of Lombard Street Research, who read the manuscript. He saved me from numerous errors and made characteristically thoughtful suggestions, most of which I have taken up. I am hugely grateful to my agents, Leslie Gardner and Gabriele Pantucci of Artellus, who believed from the outset in a book that did not fit neatly into any category with which publishers could feel naturally at ease. To the publisher who did take it on board, Iain Dale of Biteback and his enthusiastic team, I am likewise profoundly grateful. Above all I am indebted to my beloved wife Stephanie, who was both a wonderful supporter-in-chief through some very difficult times during the gestation of the book, and a superbly perceptive subeditor. My debt to her in everything is beyond enumeration.

INTRODUCTION

The great financial crisis that began in 2008 with the collapse of Lehman Brothers, the US investment bank, has been the worst since the Wall Street Crash of 1929. Unlike that earlier crisis, it has not put the survival of the capitalist system in doubt. Indeed, the Great Recession that began shortly before the Lehman debacle was the first modern crisis in which no systemic alternative to capitalism was on offer. No one, after all, is looking to North Korea for an alternative vision of the future. Since the fall of the Berlin Wall, the only question has been about the extent of the market orientation of capitalism. What the crisis did do was provoke intense soul searching about the merits and defects of an entrenched capitalist system.

The merits are clear enough. Capitalism, by which I mean a market-based system where predominantly private ownership of industry and commerce is supported by property rights, has lifted millions out of poverty thanks to its remarkable capacity to raise output per worker – the miracle of productivity growth. Since the start of the industrial revolution in the eighteenth century, living standards in the West have been transformed. And since the mid-twentieth century, the process of industrialisation and urbanisation that holds the key to raising rates of economic growth has spread to the developing world. The trail blazed first by Japan, then by the Asian Tiger economies such as South Korea, Taiwan, Hong Kong, Thailand and Singapore, has been followed by other emerging market countries across the globe. As they go through one industrial revolution after another, these countries' growth rates have accelerated to levels far beyond anything achieved through industrialisation in Europe and North America – most spectacularly so in the case of China, where the Communist Chinese leader Deng Xiaoping signalled a milestone in capitalism's slow march towards respectability by declaring that 'to get rich is glorious'.

China's economy grew at 10 per cent per annum on average during the 1990s and 2000s, while the three decades to 2010 saw an eightfold increase in per capita gross domestic product. That rate of growth is not exceptional by recent Asian standards. What is exceptional is the breathtaking scale on which poverty has been reduced. According to the World Bank, the number of people living at or below $1.25 a day, after adjusting for the purchasing power of the dollar in different countries, has fallen from 52 per cent in 1981 to 21 per cent in 2010 – a transformation in living standards without precedent in human history. Small wonder that, while globalisation ensures that the developed and the developing countries are increasingly interdependent, the balance of economic power is shifting towards the latter. A further consequence of this series of industrialisations is that global inequality has lessened.

As Karl Marx rightly perceived, industrial capitalism has always been inherently unstable, which is the first and most palpable defect of the system. The cycle of profit, speculation, irrational exuberance, stock market panic and recession has been an endemic feature of capitalism since the industrial revolution began. Creative destruction, the process identified by the Austrian-American economist Joseph Schumpeter as the essential dynamic of capitalism, has long been trouble-some for those thrown out of work as a result of increasing competition and technological innovation. It also subverts the sense of community. And today, not only is the business cycle made worse by ill-judged monetary policies and manic bankers – there have been more than 100 major banking crises worldwide in the past three decades – but globalisation and economic interdependence have caused basic manufacturing industries to evacuate wholesale from the developed to the developing world, at a high cost in lost jobs. Some jobs have been repatriated since the financial crisis as business leaders discovered that their supply chains were over-extended. Yet it remains an open question whether capitalist innovation can continue to generate new jobs in the way it has done over the past two centuries.

At the same time, globalisation and increased concentration in the banking system since the crisis mean that the scale of any future global financial crisis and subsequent recession will be greater than ever before. Moreover, the environmental cost of bringing emerging market countries up to the per capita income levels of the advanced countries is rising all the time and is hazardous for the planet in a way that the fallout from early industrialisation was not. It follows from all this that the rising living standards for which capitalism deserves credit are accompanied by a high degree of insecurity – an insecurity that is exacerbated at the time of writing by tight fiscal policies in the US and Europe. These were designed to address the government deficits and debt burdens incurred to finance the welfare safety nets that were installed to mitigate that insecurity.

The other key discontent about capitalism concerns its ethical basis. The centrality of the money motive in driving the market economy has long been a worry for many. In the aftermath of the financial crisis, that concern has been heightened by extreme levels of inequality within both developed and developing countries. A particular focus is boardroom pay. Few can see any justification, economic or moral, for the enormous widening of the gap between boardroom and workplace rewards, which is why the Occupy Wall Street movement and comparable protests around the world attracted such sympathy in 2011–12. Most feel absolutely sure that the pay awarded to bankers is wildly excessive. While global inequality has decreased, inequality in many countries of the developed world has soared, partly as a result of the explosion in boardroom pay. There is also a clear sense of unease in the English-speaking world at the increasing financialisation not only of the economy, but of everything from public services to the arts.

These discontents have been a source of fascination to me since the outset of my career. When I left Oxford University in 1966, I embarked on what I confidently expected to be the great twentieth-century novel. With about a third of it written, it dawned on me that it was horrendously devoid of literary merit. When I binned the incomplete manuscript, I had no Plan B and thus succumbed to parental pressure to join one of the big firms of chartered accountants in the City of

London, where a great uncle of mine had been the dominant figure through most of the first half of the century. Three years there left me with a profound distaste for accountancy and a qualification that I did not expect to be of much use. Yet I acquired a growing interest in the workings of the global economy and an enduring concern about the ethical basis of capitalism. These are subjects that I pursued in my subsequent career in journalism, which was later to be informed by practical experience as, among other things, a non-executive director and chairman of a quoted company, and pro bono work on corporate governance around the globe for the World Bank Group and the Organisation for Economic Cooperation and Development.

This book contains the fruits of that experience. It explores current discontents in a historical context, looking at many of the great debates about money, business and markets not just through the eyes of economists and business people, but through the views of philosophers, politicians, novelists, poets, divines, artists and sundry others. It is, in effect, a discursive and opinionated probe around the grumbling bowels of the capitalist system. In it, I have sought to explain the paradox whereby this extraordinarily dynamic mechanism, which has done far more than armies of politicians and bureaucrats to alleviate global poverty, commands such uneasy support. I conclude by explaining why the world is still on the edge of an abyss despite all the efforts of politicians, central bankers and financial watchdogs to strengthen the global financial system. Sadly, there is every likelihood that we will experience a further and more damaging crisis in due course.

CHAPTER ONE

THE ROOT OF ALL EVIL
(OR NOT, AS THE CASE MAY BE)

Capitalism is unloved. Since the collapse of Lehman Brothers, the American investment bank, in September 2008, it has become commonplace to refer to it as broken. Certainly its legitimacy is being questioned more than at any time since the Wall Street Crash of 1929 and the subsequent Great Depression. Few find it easy to live with the turbulent nature of the capitalist market economy, with its constant fluctuations in output and employment, accompanied by recurring financial crises. Many have concerns about the ethical basis of capitalism and the role of the money motive in driving economic growth.

In fact, ambivalence towards moneymaking pre-dates capitalism by centuries. Not only has money throughout the ages had a terrible press on ethical grounds; nothing, apart from religion, has so divided the human race as the issue of how to regard money, wealth and markets. Over millennia, an assorted band of critical ascetics, divines, philosophers, artists and poets has had the best of the moral argument, while exerting minimal influence on human behaviour. For the apologist of the capitalist ethos, the list of antagonists is formidable. Plato set the tone in *The Republic*, where he had Socrates tell Adeimantus that 'the more they [men] think of making a fortune, the less they think of virtue; for when riches and virtue are placed together in the scales of the balance, the one always rises as the other falls'.[1] In the *Laws*, his Athenian speaker accused business of 'breeding in men's souls knavish and tricky ways'.[2] Aristotle lent support in his *Politics*, frowning on trade, which he regarded as ignoble: 'There are two sorts of wealth-getting … one is a part of household management, the other is retail trade: the former necessary and honourable, while that which consists in exchange is justly censured; for it is unnatural, and a mode by which men gain from one another.'

As for finance, he declared that 'of all the modes of getting wealth this is the most unnatural' – a sentiment that resonates down the ages in the light of recurring financial crises.[3] Then came the New Testament, with its low view of worldly goods and its uncompromising assertion that it was impossible to serve both God and Mammon. Jesus had no time for the rich, suggesting that it was well-nigh impossible for them to enter the kingdom of heaven. And then, of course, there was the apostle Paul, that terrible old curmudgeon, who launched the definitive anti-materialist assault in his letter to Timothy, where he declared that the love of money was the root of all evil.

Business people have had as bad a press as business itself. From antiquity to the present day, the vulgarity and pretention of the nouveau riche businessman has been ruthlessly satirised by novelists and dramatists, the supreme examples being the repulsive guests at Trimalchio's banquet in Petronius's *Satyricon* and Molière's Monsieur Jourdain, who delighted in the discovery that he had spent a lifetime speaking prose. Nineteenth-century novelists have been particularly harsh. Balzac, Dickens, Dostoyevsky, Trollope and Zola excelled in the portraiture of miserly ogres and business rogues while showing a lesser inclination to celebrate the creation of wealth. In the modern age, D. H. Lawrence articulated more clearly even than Karl Marx the view that capitalist industry debased mankind. In his essay 'Democracy', he wrote:

> The great crime which the moneyed classes and promoters of industry committed in the palmy Victorian days was the condemning of the workers to ugliness, ugliness, ugliness: meanness and formless and ugly surroundings, ugly ideals, ugly religion, ugly love, ugly clothes, ugly furniture, ugly houses, ugly relationship between workers and employers. The human soul needs actual beauty even more than bread.[4]

As for poets, Robert Graves probably spoke for most of them when he said, 'There's no money in poetry, but then there's no poetry in money either' (although there are some notable exceptions to this rule, as we shall see in Chapter Ten).

All of which is discomfiting for those of us who are business people or, like the author of this book, make a living from writing about economics, business and finance. We have to recognise that for much of history, anti-business sentiment has been a given of the political and social structure. And history provides a big clue as to why capitalism has been such an uncomfortable implant into the cultures of both the West and East, and why it is so hard for people to accept the values that the capitalist system introduces into society.

Consider Europe in the feudal era. At that time, power and wealth came from land, while aristocrats looked down on commerce. For them, arms, estate management and the Church were the only careers suitable for nobles, while the values they ostensibly prized were honour, loyalty and disinterested self-sacrifice. Not for them the bourgeois virtues of thrift and enterprise, although they clearly did have a natural, self-interested desire to preserve their own wealth and status within society. Much the same was true of Asia, where the anti-business ethos was deep seated. In China, early Confucian scholars taught that there was a hierarchy of callings – the Four Occupations – which started with gentleman scholars at the top and ran via rural peasants, then artisan craftsmen, down to lowly merchants and traders. In the similarly stratified feudal society that existed in Japan over many centuries before the Meiji restoration of 1868, the social hierarchy descended from samurai, to farmer, to artisan and finally to the merchant. At best, the merchant was regarded as a necessary evil; at worst, a dangerous and corrupting parasite. India was similarly hierarchical. The precise categories of the Hindu caste system are controversial and confusing, but, broadly speaking, Brahmin priests came first, warriors second, merchants and farmers third and labourers fourth. Untouchables were excluded from these four formal categories.

Happily for the merchants, history did not leave them on the lower rungs of the social ladder for ever. I would argue that the first great landmark on business's long march to semi-respectability came in China, where the progressive commercialisation between the tenth and seventeenth centuries, under the Song and Ming dynasties, saw a loosening of the four occupational categories and the absorption of rich merchants into the ranks of the landowning gentry – though China's bureaucracy, educational system and self-imposed isolation still acted as a powerful brake on modernisation and the development of a capitalist economy. A similar loosening took place in Europe in the course of the feudal period, although this was not thanks to any revisionism on the part of the Catholic Church. The tension between moneymaking and Christian doctrine arguably suited the interests of the clergy because the guilty feelings of those who had money ensured ample donations, while for everyone else the Church was an all-powerful gatekeeper on the path to compensatory riches beyond the grave. Yet, for kings, this tension was less helpful. If the pariah status of business started to erode in Europe, it was chiefly because medieval monarchs needed to tax and borrow. Increasingly, they accepted tax in lieu of military service from the landed class. And they turned initially for credit to the Jews, whose religion had a less party-pooping attitude to wealth than Christianity. It was also less hostile to lending at interest, a practice excoriated by thinkers such as Thomas Aquinas, who recycled Aristotle's view that making money out of money was unnatural.

Yet, to the legalistic Jews, it was more unnatural to lend – at least to Christians – without interest, as Shakespeare's Shylock made clear in casting anathemas on Antonio in *The Merchant of Venice*:

How like a fawning publican he looks.
I hate him for he is a Christian;
But more, for that in low simplicity
He lends out money gratis, and brings down
The rate of usance here with us in Venice.[5]

Why the Christian antipathy towards lending at interest? It is, after all, a core function of the capitalist economy and appears to most modern Christians to be morally neutral. In part, it was because extending credit was seen as an act of friendship and trust, so there was a moral and social dimension to the activity. Lending was often a form of help to a neighbour in distress. Charging interest could thus be seen as a breach of trust. From a more economic perspective, the bias against charging interest is perfectly logical if you bear in mind the context. The mindset stems not so much from a failure to grasp the time value of money as from the nature of a world where minimal or non-existent growth in per capita income was the norm. As the earlier quotation from Aristotle's *Politics* implied, without growth, trade struck people as a zero-sum game where it was felt that one man's profit could only be earned at the cost of inflicting loss on another man. The moral basis of trade thus appeared dubious, while usury, or making money out of money, was still worse. Even the Jews were constrained by their religion in lending to each other at interest, while being permitted to lend to non-Jews. 'Unto a stranger thou mayest lend upon usury,' says Deuteronomy, 'but unto thy brother thou shalt not lend upon usury...' Muslims, of course, continue to be prohibited from lending at interest to the present day. Yet in terms of anti-business sentiment, Islam is a special case in that the Islamic anti-business bias is limited to finance. Muhammad, who was himself a trader before his religious revelation, regarded trade and commerce as lawful. Arab literature, notably in the *Arabian Nights*, even glorifies entrepreneurship in the shape of Sindbad the Sailor, the trader-hero. Note, too, that traders played an important part in disseminating Islam around the world. Some argue that it was contact with Islamic traders that set the medieval Italian city states on their path to an early form of capitalism.

There is a more bizarre and ruthless logic in the cynical way the Catholic Church tolerated usury on the basis that the Jews who carried out the business were going to hell anyway. (In Dante's *Inferno*, usurers were consigned to the seventh circle of hell in the company of sodomites.) As time progressed, both Jewish and Christian merchants also became adept at finding ways around the Church's usury laws through what would now be called regulatory arbitrage. For example, interest could be disguised if the lender issued an IOU, or a bill of exchange, at a discount while insisting on being paid back at face value. In some countries, the laws themselves also ceased to be enforced as the pre-Reformation Catholic Church became more lax. So, like the bank robber Willie Sutton, who reputedly said he robbed banks 'because that's where the money is', the asset-rich, cash-poor European feudal elite went to such merchants because they were the only available source of money for the pursuit of war, grand projects or conspicuous consumption. The evolution of a more market-oriented economy, pre-figuring modern market capitalism, thus freed monarchs from dependence on feudal retainers, while making it possible to run paid bureaucracies and standing armies. For Christians, the Reformation sounded the death knell of absolute prohibitions on usury, although there are still some European countries and a number of US states that maintain usury laws to impose caps on interest rates. So, too, does modern Japan.

It was in the Italian city states that business took its next landmark advance towards greater social acceptability. Merchants and bankers made an existential leap to become the pre-eminent

figures in society. As they melded into a powerful ruling aristocracy, the link between power and land was severed. Their
economies became money-based and proto-capitalist in the
sense that they were based on market exchange and supported
by reasonably clear property rights. With urbanisation and the
establishment of the market economy, Cosimo de' Medici of
Florence provided a model of the cash-rich merchant banker
oligarch, providing patronage to an extraordinary galaxy of
scholars, architects and artists. The change in merchants' status
in the course of the fourteenth century, before Cosimo came
to power, was noted by Boccaccio in *The Decameron*, where
he declared: '*I mercatanti son netti e dilicati uomini*' – merchants are cleanly and refined men. Unfortunately for them,
as they became more refined, the seductions of court life led
to increased lending to monarchs. This was the undoing of the
Medici bank, among many others, which collapsed in 1494,
having lent too lavishly to the English king Edward IV.

Across Europe, the dividing line between aristocracy and business became similarly fluid thanks to one of the ancient social
verities. As Trollope later so nicely put it in *The Way We Live
Now*, trade purchases rank by re-gilding its splendour. That is
to say, rich bankers and merchants married off their daughters
to aristocrats. Anti-money snobbery nonetheless proved exceptionally durable. One of the greatest put-downs in history was
François I of France's description of King Manuel I of Portugal
as the Grocer King, a devastating snub that no doubt reflected
envy of the vast riches amassed by the Portuguese crown from the
spice trade in the Orient. That anti-business prejudice survived
in France until the revolution and beyond, in a society where
hierarchy was more rigidly maintained than in more libertarian

countries such as England. Yet even in England, anti-money prejudice was part of the culture. Alexander Pope reflected this in his 'Epistle to Bathurst', the satirical poem that discusses 'whether the invention of Money has been more commodious, or pernicious to Mankind' and illustrates Pope's conviction that 'we may see the small value God has for riches by the people he gives them to'.

A truly decisive landmark in the balance of the argument over money and markets came with Enlightenment thinkers, who promoted the notion that self-interest was good and that Christian hostility to materialism was pure hypocrisy. Nowhere was the accusation of double standards more powerfully, entertainingly and controversially put than by Bernard Mandeville. Mandeville was a Dutch-born physician who wrote widely on philosophy and economics during an adult life spent mainly in London. His best-known work is the satirical poem *The Fable of the Bees*. In it, the bees did their busy stuff. But high motives had nothing to do with it.

> *The Root of Evil, Avarice,*
> *That damn'd ill-natur'd baneful Vice,*
> *Was Slave to Prodigality,*
> *That noble Sin; whilst Luxury*
> *Employ'd a Million of the Poor,*
> *And odious Pride a Million more:*
> *Envy itself, and Vanity,*
> *Were Ministers of Industry;*
> *Their darling Folly, Fickleness,*
> *In Diet, Furniture, and Dress*
> *That strange ridic'lous Vice, was made*
> *The very Wheel that turned the Trade.*[6]

But then the bees discovered the path of virtue and their frugality had disastrous consequences for the economy.

> *As Pride and Luxury decrease,*
> *So by degrees they leave the Seas.*
> *Not Merchants now, but Companies*
> *Remove whole Manufactories*
> *All Arts and Crafts neglected lie;*
> *Content, the Bane of Industry,*
> *Makes'em admire their homely Store,*
> *And neither seek nor covet more.*

This was as shocking a development in economic thinking as
that of Machiavelli in political thought in the mid-sixteenth
century, when the Florentine diplomat and historian declared
that, in the interests of maintaining the state, a prince 'is often
obliged to act against his promises, against charity, against
humanity and against religion'. Yet Dr Johnson, for one, was
not shocked, remarking that every young man had *The Fable
of the Bees* on his shelves in the mistaken belief that it was
a wicked book. He passionately believed, with Mandeville,
that luxury could be socially beneficial. James Boswell, his
biographer, records him saying: 'You cannot spend money in
luxury without doing good to the poor. Nay, you do more
good to them by spending it in luxury than by giving it; for by
spending it in luxury you make them exert industry, whereas
by giving it you keep them idle.'[7]

Men of letters took sides in this great eighteenth-century
debate on luxury, with Swift and Smollett leading the hair-
shirts while Pope hopped from one side of the fence to the

other. Meantime, the philosopher David Hume took the nu-
anced view that luxury could be morally innocent provided
it was aesthetically refined. The eighteenth-century argument
about the usefulness of luxury is really a version of what is
now known as the trickledown theory. It suffered from the
flaw that in a society marked by an uneven distribution of
income favouring a numerically small elite, the rich had plenty
of spending power to satisfy their desires, but not enough
buying power to dynamise the economy to its full potential
to raise real incomes.[8] The German sociologist and economist
Werner Sombart nonetheless argued two centuries later that
luxury played an important part in the development of capitalism.[9] And Mandeville's point has trickled down through
history. To name just one example, Gordon Gekko's 'greed is
good' speech in the film *Wall Street* clearly descends in a direct
line from the author of the fable.

The Fable of the Bees was not universally admired by other
Enlightenment thinkers. Adam Smith could not bring himself
to accept the extremity of Mandeville's paradox, in which vice
was a necessary condition of prosperity. In his justly celebrated
redefinition of the boundaries of the argument about business
and morality, he emphasised self-interest rather than vice, with
his statement in *The Wealth of Nations* that 'it is not from the
benevolence of the butcher, the brewer or the baker that we
expect our dinner, but from their regard for their own interest'.[10] In much the same vein, he added: 'I have never known
much good done by those who affected to trade for the public
good.'[11] Yet, as the author of *The Theory of Moral Sentiments*,
he also emphasised the need for markets to operate within a
moral context and believed that the act of engaging in market

exchange entailed a discipline that encouraged good individual behaviour as well as the good of wider society.

Such sentiments reflected the intellectual climate of eighteenth-century England and Scotland, an ethos in which the great French writer and *philosophe* Voltaire rejoiced. In *Les Lettres Philosophiques*, which was informed by a long stay in England, he argued that commerce was what made the English citizen free, and lauded the readiness of younger sons of peers of the realm to go into business. This he contrasted unfavourably with France in a rhetorical question larded with irony:

> I do not know ... which man is more useful to a State, a well powdered Lord who knows the precise hour at which the King rises and goes to bed, and who puts on grand airs as he plays the role of slave in the antechamber of a Minister, or a Businessman who enriches his country, gives orders from his office to Surat and Cairo, and contributes to the happiness of the world.[12]

Voltaire also believed that economic self-interest was a less dangerous motive than religious zealotry. A flavour of the argument can be gleaned from his verdict on the Royal Exchange, the predecessor of the London Stock Exchange:

> Come into the London Exchange, a Place more respectable than many a Court. You will see assembled there representatives of every Nation for the benefit of mankind. Here, the Jew, the Mahometan and the Christian deal with one another as if they were of the same Religion and reserve the name 'infidel' for those who go bankrupt. Here the Presbyterian

puts his trust in the Anabaptist, and the Anglican accepts
the Quaker's promissory note. On leaving these peaceful and
free assemblies, some go to the Synagogue, others go for a
drink; another goes to have himself baptised in a large tub in
the name of the Father through the Son to the Holy Ghost;
another has his son's foreskin cut off and has some Hebrew
words muttered over the Infant that he doesn't understand at
all; some others go to their Church to await the inspiration
of God with their hat on their head. And all are content.[13]

Voltaire's brilliant inversion of traditional assumptions about
religion and money – and this was very grubby money since
exchanges were then regarded as thoroughly disreputable –
was on a par with Mandeville's in *The Fable of the Bees*. It was
also a case of exaggerating to make a point. Despite their commercial inclination, the English still managed to look down on
people who were 'in trade' – think only of the anti-trade snobbery that permeates the otherwise highly money-conscious
novels of Jane Austen. Yet the point was still a good one to
lob at the ruling class of Voltaire's more sclerotic homeland
and at those, like his contemporary Jean-Jacques Rousseau,
who thought that the pursuit of material gain led to moral
impoverishment.

Yet for all that, Voltaire in his own life did a great deal to
give money a bad name. He left England in disgrace, accused
of reneging on debts, forging banknotes and other financial
skulduggery. He was forever trying to corner markets and find
insider dealing opportunities. When invited to the court of
Frederick the Great as the resident Enlightenment intellectual,
he rewarded the Prussian monarch's hospitality by engaging

in an illegal bond market scam that would, if successful, have cost the Prussian exchequer dear. (Frederick had his revenge, but that is another story.)

Adam Smith, while admiring Voltaire's extraordinary talents, thought he set 'the most pernicious example'. Nonetheless, Voltaire's entrepreneurial activities, of which the most important was lending money to royalty, made him a vast fortune. He spent the last two decades of his life in a chateau at Ferney on the Swiss border where his income from rent was so great that he was reckoned on his death in 1778 to be one of the twenty greatest landlords in France, despite being a mere commoner. Yet Voltaire's venal behaviour points to one of the perennial problems of business and, indeed, of the wider capitalist system. The centrality of the money motive means that many of the winners in the system are often profoundly flawed or unattractive people. The successful capitalist is not always a great advertisement for capitalism, which is not helpful in convincing people of the merits of the system, as we shall see in later chapters.

In this increasingly secular world, there followed a dramatic change in the context of the debate on money, a final landmark that radically tilted the odds in favour of a more materialist view. The industrial revolution that began in the late eighteenth century and embodied to the full the workings of what we now know as capitalism was ultimately to lift millions out of grinding poverty. The economist Angus Maddison calculated that in the period from 1500 to 1820, world gross domestic product per capita grew at an annual average compound rate of just 0.04 per cent – one-thirtieth of what has been achieved since 1820. Put another way, in Western Europe between 1820 and 1992, per capita growth increased thirteen-fold. Maddison's work is an extraordinary statistical marathon. While some economists quibble about his methodology, few doubt that the broad picture is correct.[14]

The move towards a capitalist market economy that had started in the late medieval period thus became truly transformational. Economic activity was no longer perceived as a zero-sum game in which one man's profit was another's loss and thus morally questionable. It became easier to make great fortunes from industry and commerce than from the land, even if many landed aristocrats in Europe showed a remarkable tenacity in hanging on to their inherited assets. Wealth became increasingly intangible and the rich were rarely powerful in the military sense. War, from which so much evil had stemmed throughout history, began to lose its status as the primary means through which monarchs and states sought to enrich themselves. The owners of great business fortunes provided benefits to society chiefly through the provision of an array of new goods and services, paying their taxes and engaging in large-scale philanthropy. And for the working classes, salvation was no longer exclusively to be sought in the afterlife.

In Victorian Britain, industrialists were even lauded by some men of letters. Thomas Carlyle, who invented the phrase 'captains of industry' and dubbed economics 'the dismal science', was a virulent critic of money worship and the commercialisation of society. Yet he saw businessmen as a potential new warrior class, capable of leading the country out of the grasping materialism and squalid working conditions of the early industrial revolution:

To be a noble Master, among noble Workers, will again be the first ambition with some few; to be a rich Master only the second. How the Inventive Genius of England, with the whirr of its bobbins and billy-rollers shoved somewhat into the backgrounds of the brain, will contrive and devise, not cheaper produce exclusively, but fairer distribution of the produce at its present cheapness! By degrees, we shall again have a Society with something of Heroism in it; something of Heaven's Blessing on it; we shall have again, as my German friend asserts, 'instead of Mammon-Feudalism with unsold cotton shirts and Preservation of the Game, noble just Industrialism and Government by the Wisest'.[15]

Some of that vision, outlined in Carlyle's *Past and Present*, finds its way into the Victorian novel, most notably in the shape of Mrs Gaskell's northern textile manufacturer John Thornton in *North and South*, a self-made man who is persuaded by the heroine of the novel to adopt a more humane attitude to his workers after a violent strike at his factory.

Impressive though the economic and industrial achievements of the Victorians were, it has to be acknowledged that those of the Americans were even greater. In the twentieth century, the United States emerged as the ultimate capitalist economy, combining strong religious roots with a greater commitment to the profit motive than any other country. The intensity of this potent combination no doubt explains what the historian Simon Schama has called 'a pulsing vein of American insecurity about the moral character of money'. Yet the country also had the lowest quotient of anti-business snobbery. This found expression most famously, or notoriously, in President Calvin

Coolidge's declaration in 1925 that 'the chief business of the American people is business'. Also much quoted is his declaration that 'the man who builds a factory builds a temple ... the man who works there worships there'. Because of his belief in minimal regulation in the period of corporate and securities market abuses before the 1929 Wall Street Crash, Coolidge has been roughly treated by many historians. And there is, I feel, a delightful irony in a President named Calvin presiding over an era of licence known as the Roaring Twenties.[16]

That said, the verdicts on Coolidge often overlook his more reflective side. In his Memorial Day address shortly before becoming President in 1923, he gave a notably more measured view of the conflict between Christian values and the profit motive:

> There are two fundamental motives that inspire human action. The first and most important, to which all else is subordinate, is that of righteousness. There is that in mankind, stronger than all else, which requires them to do right. When that requirement is satisfied, the next motive is that of gain. These are the moral motive and the material motive. While in some particular instance they might seem to be antagonistic, yet always, when broadly considered or applied to society as a whole, they are in harmony. American institutions meet the test of these two standards. They are founded on righteousness, they are productive of material prosperity. They compel the loyalty and support of the people because such action is right and because it is profitable.[17]

While there is something uniquely American about Coolidge's small-town Republican belief in righteousness, hard work and small government, the respect for the money motive was not, by that time, confined to the United States. In 1905, George Bernard Shaw, whose Fabian politics were utterly remote from the beliefs of Coolidge, produced his play *Major Barbara*, in which an arms manufacturer is portrayed as morally superior to his Salvation Army daughter, and Mammon triumphs over God. In the play's preface, he declared:

> The universal regard for money is the one hopeful fact in our civilisation, the one sound spot in our social conscience. Money is the most important thing in the world. It represents health, strength, humour, generosity and beauty as conspicuously as the want of it represents illness, weakness, disgrace, meanness and ugliness.

Shaw even went so far as to say that the lack of money was the root of all evil. Shaw's fellow Irishman Oscar Wilde was less of a windbag, but of much the same conviction: 'There is only one class in the community that thinks more about money than the rich, and that is the poor. The poor can think of nothing else. That is the misery of being poor.'

A further dimension to the argument is provided by the great economist John Maynard Keynes. Like Dr Johnson, who declared that 'there are few ways in which a man can be more innocently employed than in getting money', Keynes thought that moneymaking was a socially productive way of channelling the basest instincts:

> Dangerous human proclivities can be canalised into comparatively harmless channels by the existence of opportunities

for money making and private wealth, which, if they cannot be satisfied in this way, may find their outlet in cruelty, the reckless pursuit of personal power and authority, and other forms of self-aggrandisement. It is better that a man should tyrannise over his bank balance than over his fellow citizens.[18]

I think this is an intriguing insight, but it somewhat stretches the pro-money case, with its seeming implication that if only Hitler, Stalin and Mao Zedong had each been given a textile factory to run at an early age, we might have been spared the worst horrors of the twentieth century.

Note, too, that despite Britain's traditional dependence on trade, it retained an impressive snobbery about business. Ogden Nash caught this neatly when he remarked:

England is the last home of the aristocracy, and the art of protecting the aristocracy from the encroachments of commerce has been raised to quite an art.

Because in America a rich butter-and-egg man is only a rich butter-and-egg man or at most an honorary LLD of some hungry university, but in England, why before he knows it he is Sir Benjamin Buttery, Bart.

(One of the ways, of course, that the English aristocracy protected itself from encroaching commerce was to follow the maxim of Trollope referred to earlier, by encouraging its sons to marry American industrial magnates' daughters.) Not that rampant materialism has always gone uncriticised in America. US literature has its fair share of business villains and snake-oil peddlers, most notably F. Scott Fitzgerald's Jay Gatsby, whose

fortune came from bootlegging. *The Great Gatsby* was both
a disillusioned exploration of the Roaring Twenties before the
1929 crash and a jaundiced verdict on the American dream.
Equally critical of American materialism is Sinclair Lewis's
1920s satirical novel *Babbitt*, about a successful realtor who
undergoes a mid-life crisis, goes bohemian and subsequently
returns to the bourgeois fold.

Yet US literature also produced one of the few great novels
that look at a particular business in depth, in the shape of
Herman Melville's *Moby-Dick*. This tells you all you need
to know (and more) about the catching and butchering of
whales. And then there is Upton Sinclair, whose description of
the Chicago slaughterhouses in the campaigning anti-business
novel *The Jungle* was instrumental in bringing about the 1906
Pure Food and Drug Act, and whose novel *The Moneychang-
ers* demonises Wall Street in a way that has taken on a new
resonance in the light of the financial debacle of 2007–09.

So Americans did have their misgivings about capitalism,
though their feelings were mixed, for reasons explained by
John Micklethwait and Adrian Wooldridge of *The Economist*
in discussing the behaviour of the robber barons:

> Most Americans were ambivalent about business. They dis-
> liked concentrations of corporate power – the United States,
> after all, is based on the division of power – but they ad-
> mired the sheer might of business. They disliked the wealth
> of businessmen, but they admired the fact that so many of
> them came from nothing – that Rockefeller was the son
> of a snake-oil salesman and Carnegie began his career as
> a telegraph messenger. In 1867, E. L. Godkin produced an

explanation of why America lacked the intense class consciousness of Europe that probably remains true to this day:
'The social line between the labourer and the capitalist here
is very faintly drawn. Most successful employers of labour
have begun by being labourers themselves; most labourers
... hope to become employers.'[19]

In the new, industrialised, market environment, the backlash
against capitalism in Europe came in many forms. Some, like
Karl Marx and Friedrich Engels, were pleased at the removal
of feudal restraints on enterprise, but railed at the glorification
of self-interest and what they saw as the morally scandalous
foundations of capitalism. For them, the conflict of interest
between rich bourgeois capitalists and poor exploited workers
was irreconcilable. Others, following Rousseau, worried that
the individualistic nature of a capitalist society was destroying
a shared sense of community. Oliver Goldsmith's poem *The
Deserted Village* is an eloquent attack on the shortcomings of
modernity and the impact on the country of mass migration to
industrial cities induced by capitalism:

> *Ill fares the land, to hastening ills a prey,*
> *Where wealth accumulates and men decay;*
> *Princes and lords may flourish, or may fade;*
> *A breath can make them, as a breath has made;*
> *But a bold peasantry, their country's pride,*
> *When once destroyed, can never be supplied.*[20]

In like vein, the German playwright, poet and philosopher
Friedrich Schiller emphasised the anti-spiritual, anti-aesthetic

tendency of contemporary political economy. In his *Letters on the Aesthetic Education of Mankind* of 1794, he wrote:

> But in our day it is necessity, neediness, that prevails, and bends a degraded humanity under its iron yoke. *Utility* is the great idol of the time, to which all powers do homage and all subjects are subservient. In this great balance of utility, the spiritual service of art has no weight, and, deprived of all encouragement, it vanishes from the noisy Vanity Fair of our time. The very spirit of philosophical inquiry itself robs the imagination of one promise after another, and the frontiers of art are narrowed, in proportion as the limits of science are enlarged.[21]

Anticipating Marx, he was equally concerned with the dehumanising nature of work in the modern economy. In an apparent reference to the division of labour – that fundamental characteristic of capitalist production – he said that a time had come when

> enjoyment was separated from labour, the means from the end, the effort from the reward. Man himself, eternally chained down to a little fragment of the whole, only forms a kind of fragment; having nothing in his ears but the monotonous sound of the perpetually revolving wheel, he never develops the harmony of his being; and instead of imprinting the seal of humanity on his being, he ends by being nothing more than the living impress of the craft to which he devotes himself, of the science that he cultivates.

Observing the upheavals wrought by the capitalistic market economy, the German philosopher Hegel argued that a more powerful state would be needed to cope with the disruptive tendencies of the market. Meantime, the British art critic and social thinker John Ruskin provided an aesthetic and environmental critique of the workings of capitalism as well as attacking the dehumanisation inflicted on workers by the division of labour. In *Fors Clavigera*, a series of pamphlets addressed to working men in the 1870s, he delivered this splendid blast:

You think it a great triumph to make the sun draw brown landscapes for you! That was also a discovery, and some day may be useful. But the sun had drawn landscapes before for you, not in brown, but in green, and blue, and all imaginable colours, here in England. Not one of you ever looked at them, then; not one of you cares for the loss of them, now, when you have shut the sun out with smoke, so that he can draw nothing more, except brown blots through a hole in a box. There was a rocky valley between Buxton and Bakewell, once upon a time, divine as the vale of Tempe; you might have seen the Gods there morning and evening, — Apollo and all the sweet Muses of the Light — walking in fair procession on the lawns of it, and to and fro among the pinnacles of its crags. You cared neither for Gods nor grass, but for cash (which you did not know the way to get); you thought you could get it by what *The Times* calls 'Railroad Enterprise'. You Enterprised a Railroad through the valley — you blasted its rocks away, heaped thousands of tons of shale into its lovely stream. The valley is gone, and the gods with it; and now, every fool in Buxton can be at Bakewell in half-an-hour, and every fool in Bakewell at Buxton; which

you think a lucrative process of exchange — you Fools
Everywhere.[22]

Yet despite such reservations, the followers of Marx, an intellectual heir of Hegel, were not entirely clear in their convictions
about the capitalist system. As the writer Geoffrey Wheatcroft
puts it:

> Just as the labour movement had never been quite sure
> whether the capitalist system was on its last legs and needed
> only a final push to be toppled, or was healthy enough to be
> milked over and again, so the cultural-intellectual left had
> never quite decided whether it liked increasing prosperity
> or not.[23]

Donald Sassoon, a historian of the European left, has commented in similar vein:

> Socialism's appeal, when it had one, was to say, at one and
> the same time, that its mission was to transcend capitalism
> while improving it; that everyone was equal but that the
> proletariat was the leading class; that money was the root of
> all evil but that the workers needed more of it; that capital-
> ism was doomed but that capitalists' profits were as high
> as ever; that religion was the opium of the people but that
> Jesus was the first socialist; that the family was a bourgeois
> conspiracy but that it needed defending from untrammelled
> industrialisation; that individualism was to be deplored but
> that capitalist alienation reduced people to undifferentiated
> atoms; that there was more to politics than voting every few

years while demanding universal suffrage; that consumerism beguiles the workers but they should all have a colour television, a car and go on holidays abroad.[24]

Perhaps the more legitimate heirs of the tradition of Goldsmith and Ruskin are today's anti-globalisation and environmental activists who fear that a by-product of the capitalist pursuit of profit in a global free market will be ecological catastrophe.

A curious thing about the source-of-all-evil debate is how many business people have combined religiosity with money-making. In part, that reflects the multiplicity of conflicting moral messages in the Bible, the Koran and other religious texts. Not all religious business people would go as far as the twentieth-century British venture capitalist Harley Drayton, who told the journalist Anthony Sampson: 'The twenty-fifth chapter of Ecclesiasticus is the only economic system which ever worked. It tells you how to run a sinking fund, how to manage a business, how to make an issue [of shares on the stock market].' But the parable of the talents has undoubtedly given many an entrepreneur a sense of moral justification and self-worth.

At a deeper level, Max Weber, one of the founders of modern social science, argued in *The Protestant Ethic and the Spirit of Capitalism* that the more puritanical Protestants, such as the followers of Calvin, were disproportionately represented in the ranks of rich industrialists because their religion favoured the rational pursuit of economic gain in a way that Catholicism did not. He also argued that there were good reasons why capitalism had not developed in Asia. Beliefs such as Confucianism and Taoism, he thought, fostered a bias against technical innovation, while the Chinese were motivated to covet official positions, not profit. Together with China's strong emphasis on kinship, which inhibited the development of legal institutions and laws that were fundamental to the property rights on which a capitalist system depends, these factors constituted a big barrier to capitalist development. Weber believed that the Hindu caste system in India operated similarly to prevent the adoption of capitalism and that these religious and cultural constraints in Asia gave Protestant northern Europe a global competitive advantage.

Weber was curiously downbeat about the Jewish contribution to the development of capitalism, a bias that his contemporary Werner Sombart sought to remedy in his *Die Juden und das Wirtschaftsleben* (*The Jews and Modern Capitalism*). Weber's theory also sits oddly with history. Calvinist Scotland has always performed less well economically than England with its more comfortable, state-sponsored Anglicanism. The Catholic parts of Belgium industrialised in the nineteenth century well before the Calvinist-tinged Netherlands. In the second half of the twentieth century, Catholic Italy produced a spectacular economic growth miracle. And some argue that the origins of capitalism really date back anyway to the pre-Protestant Italian city states rather than the industrial revolution. A larger question for Weber's thesis, though, comes from the explosive recent development of Japan, the Asian Tiger economies and finally China. These have seen the fastest rates of economic growth in history without any help from the Protestant religion.

Yet, before writing off Weber it is important to remember that his concern here related to the very specific question of whether non-European traditions had religious and cultural characteristics that were capable of giving rise spontaneously to capitalist development in the way that Protestantism had done. The fact that non-Europeans subsequently borrowed the capitalist means of production from Europeans is not, in itself, a refutation of his thesis.

The ultimate watershed on business's long march from pariah status towards semi-respectability came when the Chinese leader Deng Xiaoping declared, after starting to open up China's economy in 1978, that 'to get rich is glorious'. Nuances may have been lost in the translation, but this embrace of capitalist values by a hardened veteran of the Communist struggle definitively put the big battalions behind the materialist side of the moral argument and appeared to draw down the curtain on the socialist backlash. It is no coincidence that Deng's conversion broadly coincided with the ascendancy of the Chicago school of economics and the presidency of Ronald Reagan, who oversaw the conclusion of the Cold War. Reagan lauded 'the magic of the market'. Like Margaret Thatcher in Britain, he ushered in an era of liberalisation and neo-conservatism, policies favoured by economists at the University of Chicago. Other intellectual champions of this ethos included Ayn Rand, mentor of the subsequent chairman of the Federal Reserve Alan Greenspan. Rand, a true inheritor of Mandeville's shock-and-awe approach to philosophical issues, trumpeted free markets, argued the merits of selfishness in all things, including sexual relations, and called for a radical reduction in the role of the state. In her novel *Atlas Shrugged*, she did her best to turn the entrepreneur into the ultimate heroic figure and to offer a polemical glorification of moneymaking and unbridled capitalism.

Sadly, this dystopian fantasy, in which society's wealth-creating entrepreneurs decide to opt out of an increasingly anti-business society, which then disintegrates for want of enterprise, cannot be considered a plausible runner in the Great American Business Novel stakes. Despite a compelling narrative, which appeals particularly strongly to today's Silicon Valley entrepreneurs, the characters are made of cardboard and the plot is too zany to make the literary grade. That said, the book undoubtedly satisfies the market test, since it remains one of the publishing world's outstanding bestsellers.[25]

If there is now a more widespread acceptance that the money motive is not invariably reprehensible, there are caveats. For some, like Keynes, the motive could still be highly distasteful. In forecasting how the world might look to his generation's grandchildren, he wrote that the love of money would ultimately be recognised as 'a somewhat disgusting morbidity'. For others, such as Joseph Schumpeter, the economist best known for identifying creative destruction as the motor of capitalism, there remained a question as to how far the profit-maximising business person could be regarded as an admirable role model. He argued that something was lost in the transition from a society governed by aristocrats, whose values were essentially military, to an industrial age; and, unlike Thomas Carlyle, he saw the businessman as woefully unheroic:

> With the utmost ease and grace the lords and knights metamorphosed themselves into courtiers, administrators, diplomats, politicians and into military officers of a type that had nothing whatever to do with that of the medieval knight. And – most astonishing phenomenon when we come to think of it – a remnant of that old prestige survives even to this day, and not only with our ladies.

Of the industrialist and merchant the opposite is true. There is surely no trace of any mystic glamour about him, which is what counts in the ruling of men. The stock exchange is a poor substitute for the Holy Grail. We have seen that the industrialist and merchant, as far as they are entrepreneurs, also fill a function of leadership. But economic leadership of this type does not readily expand, like the medieval lord's military leadership, into the leadership of nations. On the contrary, the ledger and the cost calculation absorb and confine.

I have called the bourgeois rationalist and unheroic. He can only use rationalist and unheroic means to defend his position or to bend a nation to his will. He can impress by what people may expect from his economic performance, he can argue his case, he can promise to pay out money or threaten to withhold it, he can hire the treacherous services of a condottiere or politician or journalist. But that is all and all of it is greatly overrated as to its political value. Nor are his experiences and habits of life of the kind that develop personal fascination. A genius in the business office may be, and often is, utterly unable outside of it to say boo to a goose – both in the drawing room and on the platform.[26]

Somehow I doubt that the Japanese, who emerged relatively recently from feudalism, would understand that argument. Businessmen in Japan, who were originally despised by the samurai warrior class, are now seen as inheritors of the samurai tradition and regarded by many, in the spirit of Carlyle, as genuinely heroic. Certainly they are less prone to greed than their English-speaking counterparts and cultivate a work ethic that is intended to promote the corporate and national interest rather than individualistic self-gratification. In fact, the Japanese version of capitalism is uniquely egalitarian, with companies being run in the interests of managers and employees, rather than shareholders. In effect, Japan has tried to solve the ethical dilemma at the core of capitalism by turning capitalism into corporate communism.

As for Schumpeter's description of business faint-hearts, it does not square at all with my experience, which is that people in the West who run large companies nowadays are the very opposite of timid. Leading a life that is increasingly remote from the rest of the population, they find their confidence bolstered by outsized bonuses that tend to confirm their high estimation of their own worth. And there, of course, is the rub. To the extent that there is an ethical basis for capitalist accumulation, it is rooted in utilitarianism, or the principle of the greatest happiness of the greatest number. This can entail rough justice for minorities, with the notable exception of the rich, and makes no moral judgement about greed and the money motive. For many people, such flawed justice detracts from the system's otherwise morally attractive feature of generating far higher living standards than were common through most of human history. How can it be right, they ask, for an American chief executive to earn 500 times the average wage on the shop floor, especially if corporate performance is not up to much? And even where corporate performance is spectacular, I believe that many people will continue to feel ill at ease with the paradox whereby capitalism converts vices such as greed and vanity – or, in the more innocuous version, self-interest – into virtue.

As outlined earlier, most of us also find the rigours of the un-tamed economic cycle, along with manic financial markets that lead to painful fluctuations in income and employment, hard to handle. And while some of the virtues that Calvin Coolidge prized, such as hard work and inventiveness, survive, those of thrift and self-restraint disappeared from the very heart of the Anglo-American capitalist edifice, the financial system, in the first decade of the new millennium. For individuals, they have been squeezed out by the arrival of the credit card. Thrift and self-restraint appear to have migrated to Asia, while dallying a little in Germany en route. Nor is it a coincidence that the powerful populist backlash against globalisation is essentially moralistic as well as nostalgic, harking back, as it does, to the critique of Oliver Goldsmith in *The Deserted Village*.

There is, in fact, something curiously Manichean about the way the capitalist political economy works, as the chapters that follow will show. Things that are in themselves a benefit to society – banking, debt, speculation, animal spirits – become damaging when taken to excess. And excess seems to be a recurring feature of economic cycles and of capitalism itself. After the long period of market fundamentalism introduced by Ronald Reagan and Margaret Thatcher, and after the worst re-cession since the 1930s, people are understandably resentful of huge boardroom pay awards, fat bank bonuses and rising in-equality. How far society's waning tolerance of these excesses will lead to a much more heavily regulated, lower growth form of capitalism turns heavily on these difficult issues about the moral character of money. Certainly money and business have suffered a major setback on the path towards respectability as a result of the great financial crisis that struck in 2008.

CHAPTER TWO

ANIMAL SPIRITS

Few understood better than John Maynard Keynes the importance of enterprise for the workings of the capitalist system. Yet the great economist had a poor view of entrepreneurs. His celebrated reference to their so-called animal spirits in the *General Theory of Employment, Interest and Money* is a lofty implicit put-down and he regarded the money motive as a form of morbidity. That view may well have been influenced by Karl Marx, who saw the urge to accumulate capital as the sole motivation of the entrepreneurial capitalist. It is a powerful perception that still colours thinking today and it has been reinforced as the populist backlash against the banks since the financial crisis spilled over into the wider corporate sector. Many regard entrepreneurs as greedy, unethical people who can be relied on to take shortcuts and break all the rules of society on the path to fortune. It is an ancient prejudice that throws up a big challenge for the legitimacy of the capitalist system. The challenge appears in its most extreme form, as we saw in Chapter One, in Mandeville's notion of vice as the mainspring of wealth creation. I will nonetheless argue in this chapter that entrepreneurs, for all the failings that many have displayed, deserve a more sympathetic hearing – not by appealing to economic theory, but by looking at the nature of the beast.

What is entrepreneurship about? For a century or so, students of economics have been taught that enterprise is one of the four factors of production – resources that go into the production of goods and services. Unlike the other three – land, labour and capital – it sits rather oddly with the conventional economist's view of the world, in which *homo economicus* engages in the rational, orderly pursuit of well-defined goals. Entrepreneurs belong to the world of messy, disorderly reality and their motives are many and various. Downright mavericks abound in this neck of the economic woods. Vladimir Gusinsky, the Russian media baron who, with a handful of other oligarchs, made billions in murky transactions with Boris Yeltsin's government after the disintegration of the old Soviet Union, explained his personal philosophy to the journalist Chrystia Freeland – now a Canadian Member of Parliament – in this wonderfully over-the-top and no doubt tongue-in-cheek statement:

I always risk everything. A man must regularly, every five or seven years, change his life. If he doesn't do that, he becomes internally boring. Girls stop loving him, and his own children stop respecting him. Even dogs no longer come up and sniff him. Don't laugh, it is true – a man must be loved by women, children and dogs. Those three categories are the essentials of life.[27]

Gusinsky's egoism and attention seeking would, of course, have confirmed Keynes's prejudice. Yet a large ego is one of the dominant, probably essential, features of entrepreneurial energy, as is reliance on gut instinct when considering new ventures. Dogged persistence is equally important, since anyone who tries to start a business will constantly be rebuffed, especially by financiers, who make a speciality of giving a firm and repeated no to business proposals. Europeans are particularly prone to nay-saying about new ventures. Having been a director of two successful start-up companies, I know from experience the relish with which people will explain why a new venture cannot possibly get off the ground. If and when it does get off the ground, many of the nay-sayers will still explain even more earnestly why the business has no future. When its future is secure, they then often have no difficulty convincing themselves that they were supportive from the outset and thought the business would succeed all along.

This was something that Dr Johnson understood well in his essay on projectors, a word which in the eighteenth century described not just inventors and entrepreneurs, but all those who applied vaulting ambition to a great undertaking, whether for a military, political or business purpose. The great doctor talks of

> projectors, whose rapidity of imagination and vastness of design raise such envy in their fellow mortals, that every eye watches for their fall, and every heart exults at their distress: yet even a projector may gain favour by success; and the tongue that was prepared to hiss then endeavours to excel others in loudness of applause.[28]

Small wonder that entrepreneurs tend to be driven people and that high optimism is another absolute prerequisite for survival, not least because the statistics for failure rates of business start-ups are daunting. In the US, for example, a quarter of all new businesses are reckoned to fail within the first year. For those that live longer, the perennial hazards of undercapitalisation and over-expansion all too often lead to sudden death.

Many entrepreneurs have been impatient with formal education. Thomas Edison, inventor of the light bulb and founder of the company that turned into the modern General Electric, only managed three months at school, where his teacher referred to him as 'addled' – a misjudgement that might rank in history with Emperor Joseph II of Austria telling Mozart that *The Marriage of Figaro* had too many notes. Edison was taught at home by his formidable mother, evidently to great effect. Alexander Graham Bell, inventor of the telephone, left school in Edinburgh at fifteen, having achieved poor grades and been notable for frequent bunking off. More recently, in the computer age, Bill Gates, founder of Microsoft, famously dropped out of Harvard University, while Michael Dell, who started his personal computer business in a dormitory room at the University of Texas at Austin, never completed his degree course. Steve Jobs, co-founding genius of Apple, dropped out of Reed College in Portland, Oregon. The same is true of countless others in the industry.

As befits practitioners of the dismal science, economists have sought to downplay the idea of the fearless, ambitious, difficult, larger-than-life entrepreneur. There is a body of academic research suggesting that becoming an entrepreneur has more to do with ready access to capital, for example through a handy bequest, which is an accident of fate, than any particular psychological make-up. The evidence also points to people with a self-employed parent being more likely to become self-employed themselves. This is no doubt true. Yet, having known and worked with a number of entrepreneurs who have built large businesses from scratch, I share the view of the British serial entrepreneur Luke Johnson, who argues that some people simply cannot stand being dependent employees and want to take control of their own destiny, often relishing all the obstacles put in the way of those who dare to start a business. He rightly says: 'The buck stops with an owner in a way that it never does with a hired hand. And that is why resilience in an entrepreneur is more important than brilliance – grit trumps almost every other trait.'[29]

Nowadays there is what I would call grudging assent to the proposition that entrepreneurship has a vital role in generating economic growth, an idea that was first given its proper due by the Austrian school of economists in the twentieth century. Joseph Schumpeter, in particular, lauded the role of entrepreneurs in the capitalist process of creative destruction, whereby inefficient businesses are wiped out in the downturn of the economic cycle, and new, more competitive businesses emerge. The Austrians were bested in argument by Keynes in the 1930s on the question of whether to rely on *laissez-faire*, or on the monetary and fiscal activism that Keynes preferred, as a remedy for unemployment in the Great Depression. They were consequently out of fashion for decades afterwards. Yet their views have had a revival since the Thatcherite 1980s, and most modern politicians, whether aware of the Austrian school or not, now have some notion of the contribution of entrepreneurs to job creation.

Despite their social utility, entrepreneurs have nonetheless been prone throughout history to give wealth creation a bad name, a phenomenon already touched on in Chapter One. There is a widespread belief, for example, that they have to be rule breakers or rogues to succeed, a view reflected in Balzac's alleged remark that behind every great fortune there is a great crime. This is nonsense, but it remains true that history has a full quotient of unsavoury entrepreneurs. One who seems to me to exemplify perfectly Mandeville's view of the dynamics of wealth creation is a contemporary of the author of *The Fable of the Bees*, Nicholas Barbon, whose economic ideas influenced Mandeville's thesis in the poem discussed in Chapter One. This seventeenth-century economist, physician and property developer is a figure of enduring historical interest who left a mark on the London landscape that remains visible today. His full name, imposed on him by a strongly puritan father, was Nicholas If-Jesus-Christ-Had-Not-Died-For-Thee-Thou-Hadst-Been-Damned Barbon.[30] Yet little in his life appears to have been guided by religious principle. He was an early advocate of free markets and a critic of the mercantilists. They were the folk who believed that trade was a zero-sum game and that the way to enhance the prosperity and strength of a country was to boost exports and restrain imports in order to accumulate reserves of gold. His economic writings, of which *A Discourse of Trade* was the most important, were admired by Keynes, Schumpeter and Marx. He was also a pioneer of fire insurance after the Great Fire of London in 1666 and helped found England's first mortgage bank.

Barbon combined these remarkable financial innovations with a role as the biggest speculative builder in London,

creating the districts around what is now the Strand, and rebuilding the Temple after a fire in 1678. He also developed
much of London's Bloomsbury. His building activities relied
heavily on credit, yet he was notoriously reluctant to pay his
creditors, even stipulating in his will that his debts should not
be met. He ignored restrictions imposed by Acts of Parliament
on new building and often demolished existing structures
without permission. And he cut corners in his building work
as well as with the law. So cheap were the materials in the
houses he built in Mincing Lane in the City of London that
they collapsed soon after construction.

Barbon's modus operandi in clearing and assembling sites
for development is nicely caught by Roger North, Barbon's
architect for the rebuilding of the Temple, who describes him
turning up, invariably late, to deal with the occupants of potential development land:

> He would make his entry, as fine and as richly dressed as
> a lord of the bedchamber on a birthday. I have often seen
> him so dressed, not knowing his design, (to charm and im-
> press his victims) and thought him a coxcomb for so doing.
> Then hard-headed fellows that had prepared to give him all
> the affronts and opposition that their brutal way suggested,
> seeing such a brave man, pulled off their hats and knew
> what not to think of it. The Doctor, (Barbon) being much of
> a gentleman, proposed his terms, which were ever plausible,
> and terminated in their interest. It mattered not if a litigious
> knave or two did stand out, for the first thing he did was to
> pull down their houses about their ears, and build upon the
> ground and stand it out in law until their hearts ached, and

at last they would truckle and take any terms for peace and a
quiet life.[31]

In the period when Barbon was Member of Parliament for
Bramber in Sussex, he used parliamentary privilege to ward off
legal suits. So much litigation was pending against him when
he died that it was unclear whether his assets were sufficient
to cover his liabilities. Whether his way of doing business was
genuinely novel at that time I do not know, but it has certainly been much followed by later property developers, while
predatory litigation has become a widely used weapon in
big business.

In short, Barbon is Mandeville's theory personified, being
both vicious and economically creative. But that does not
make him a stereotypical entrepreneur. In practice, individual
entrepreneurs are to be found at all points of the ethical spectrum. At the virtuous end are people like the English entrepreneur Matthew Boulton, who, with the Scottish engineer
James Watt, developed the steam engine that was central to
the industrial revolution that began in the second half of the
eighteenth century. As well as being a leader in modern production methods, Boulton, a high-minded non-conformist like
so many early English industrial innovators, was a model employer who pioneered a workers' insurance scheme. Steeped
in the scientific inquisitiveness that is the mark of the really
creative entrepreneur, he was a founder member of the Lunar
Society, a famous discussion group that included Joseph Priest-
ley, discoverer of oxygen, Josiah Wedgwood, the ceramics
entrepreneur, and Erasmus Darwin, whose views prefigured
the evolutionary thinking of his grandson Charles. The very

opposite of Gradgrind, the monster-industrialist in Charles Dickens's *Hard Times*, Boulton was closely involved, among other charitable works, in the Birmingham Dispensary, which provided medicine and medical care for the poor.

A similar ethical impulse can be found among entrepreneurs who have founded cooperatives or given their companies to their customers or workers. The early socialist and cooperative pioneer Robert Owen was a model employer and promoter of workers' education at his New Lanark textile mills in Scotland. That tradition survives into the twentieth and twenty-first centuries, with such outstanding examples as Gottlieb Duttweiler (1888–1962), founder of the Swiss retail group Migros, which was a pioneer of own branding and discounting. As well as handing over the ownership to the customers in 1941, Duttweiler insisted that a fixed percentage of the revenues should go into cultural, athletic and hobby-type activities. In a similar league was Britain's John Spedan Lewis, who turned the John Lewis department store group over to its employees in the late 1920s. The group now owns one of Britain's leading supermarket chains, Waitrose, as well as twenty-eight department stores around the country.

Having suggested that there is a moral spectrum in entrepreneurship, I would still accept that there can be long periods when rogues and robber barons are in the ascendant, which is why there is enduring public scepticism about the social utility of entrepreneurs. There is, I think, an identifiable historical pattern in this, relating to the natural rhythm of capitalist activity. Such periods are usually the result of policies of business or financial liberalisation that lead to booms in which ethical standards fall and sharp practice flourishes. When the boom collapses, public outrage then prompts a political backlash in the shape of re-regulation.

Consider the late seventeenth century. In Nicholas Barbon's day, joint stock companies were a rarity, because incorporation required a Royal Charter or private Act of Parliament. Since incorporation was usually accompanied by the grant of privileges such as trading rights, monarchs and governments were very careful with their largesse. Yet, after the Glorious Revolution of 1688, when London was experiencing a big expansion of trade, especially with India, a more liberal attitude to incorporation prevailed. The formation of the South Sea Company in the new century, together with the stellar performance of its stock, accelerated an already powerful slew of incorporations, with 195 joint stock companies being formed in the year to August 1720. These were popularly known as 'bubbles'.

A central feature of incorporation was that it increased the scope for fraud, because the people running the bubble companies had access to other people's money. In the modern jargon, there was a principal–agent problem. The agents, or managers, were not properly accountable to the principals, or stockholders, because corporate governance was rudimentary. Trading in the shares was frenetic and often fraudulent, as Daniel Defoe, author of *Robinson Crusoe*, explained in a tract entitled *The Anatomy of Change-Alley*, in which he said:

There is not a man but will own 'tis a complete system of knavery; that 'tis a trade founded in fraud, born of deceit, and nourished by trick, cheat, wheedle, forgeries, falsehoods, and all sorts of delusions; coining false news, this way good, that way bad; whispering imaginary terrors, frights, hopes, expectations and then preying upon the weakness of those whose imaginations they have wrought upon, whom they have either elevated or depressed.[32]

When the South Sea Company collapsed, fraud was revealed on the part of directors, who had corrupted members of the cabinet, using shares in the company as bribes. Some of the perpetrators of the fraud were thrown into jail, while the directors' estates were expropriated and used to compensate victims of the fraud. More to the point, from our perspective here, there was a tough regulatory response in the Bubble Act of 1720, which severely restricted company incorporations for more than 100 years.

This pattern of liberalisation and re-regulation was then repeated in the nineteenth century. As so often happens, changes in the structure of the economy made the Bubble Act increasingly restrictive and damaging to economic growth. The rise of new, capital-intensive industries such as railways made capital demands that could only be satisfied by large numbers of investors. Entrepreneurs responded to legislative restraints in England by setting up companies in the US and in France to conduct operations in their home country. In recognition of the needs of industry and the reality of cross-border regulatory arbitrage, the Bubble Act was repealed in 1824. There followed another flurry of incorporations approved by Parliament.

These stock promotions were all too often accompanied by fraud, as the temptation to make off with other people's money became overwhelming. Anyone who wishes to understand this phenomenon should turn not to economic historians but to Dickens and, more specifically, *Nicholas Nickleby* (of which more in Chapter Five). There, he describes the flotation of a company whose promoters lure outsiders into a stock market bubble and discreetly take their leave before the whole thing pops.

While this nineteenth-century corporate party was already going with a swing, it enjoyed a further boost from generalised incorporation, which was introduced in English law along with limited liability under statute, in mid-century. The party was at its most frenetic in the rail industry, where George Hudson, known as 'the railway king', was the leading entrepreneur. At his peak, when he became Tory MP for Sunderland in 1846, Hudson controlled over a quarter of all the railways then built in England. He was a visionary who created the first modern rail network, helped by his friend George Stephenson, builder of the early steam locomotive the *Rocket*. Yet his methods were crooked. In 1848 he was found to have bribed MPs, manipulated share prices and defrauded his creditors, resulting in his imprisonment in York Castle for debt. Among the indignities he felt most acutely was hearing that his wax effigy at Madame Tussauds had been melted down.

In the railway mania of the time, Hudson was far from being the only fraudster. The requirement to obtain parliamentary consent for the building of railways meant that there was a constant temptation to bribe MPs, while the increasing ease with which companies could be set up and floated was an encouragement to play fast and loose with other people's money. Then, as with the Bubble Act in 1720, came re-regulation. The Companies Act 1862 set out the duties of directors, requirements for the conduct of the company, its accounts and audit, together with penalties for malpractices of the kind described by Dickens. The Act was further amended in response to successive corporate scandals and banking crises over the best part of 150 years as this pattern of liberalisation and re-regulation repeated itself across the developed world. (I have a particular interest, having been a member of the steering group of the British company law review that provided a blueprint for the latest update in the UK: the Companies Act 2006.)

While Britain was the pioneer of the company as the dominant organisational form for economic activity, similar corporate development soon followed in continental Europe, and also in the US, which spawned the so-called robber barons – the likes of Jay Gould and Cornelius Vanderbilt in rail, Andrew Carnegie and Henry Clay Frick in steel, John D. Rockefeller in oil and John Pierpont Morgan in banking. As well as indulging in various forms of business malpractice – Henry Frick famously employed armed Pinkerton detectives to break a strike, leaving many workers dead – the robber barons were accused of being monopolists. The regulatory backlash came in the Sherman Antitrust Act of 1890, which, with subsequent amendments, remains one of the toughest competition laws in the world.

Here is one of the great paradoxes of capitalism. However dubious their business practices, the robber barons indisputably drove one of the fastest periods of economic growth in US history, perfectly illustrating Mandeville's law of positive unintended consequences. Yet the fact that these archcapitalists played fast and loose with the rules accounts for another recurring feature in the history of entrepreneurship: the suspicion among politicians and the public of business. As I implied earlier, it is a suspicion that wanes and waxes with business booms and busts in much the same way that the stock of moral capital does. And despite the accumulation of company laws and financial regulations, it never seems to go away, leaving a nagging question about the moral character of capitalism. No doubt this reflects the tension explored earlier between conventional morality and the money motive. But it may be exacerbated because so much modern entrepreneurial activity is devoted to financial engineering and paper shuffling that is often devoid of perceptible social utility.

That said, I would argue that the greatest entrepreneurs tend to be remote from the morbidity syndrome identified by Keynes. Greatness, in this context, means people who combine a phenomenal capacity for innovation with powerful business acumen, so that they make a marked difference to the lives of the population at large. Such people are usually motivated less by money than by a passionate interest in the potential of their innovative products or services to satisfy human wants. Profits are a happy by-product of this activity. In effect, the best entrepreneurs obey Ruskin's injunction in *Unto This Last* that 'it is no more [the merchant's] function to get profit for himself out of that provision than it is the clergyman's function to get his stipend'.[33] A good illustration is provided by the entrepreneur who I believe stands out above all others in history: Thomas Edison.

Edison was the ultimate combination of boffin and business brain. In the course of his early career as a telegraph operator, he worked night shifts so that he could read and conduct experiments in tandem with his work. On one occasion, he was working with a lead-acid battery and spilled sulphuric acid on the floor, which leaked onto his boss's desk in the room below. He was fired in the morning. That would not unduly have upset a man who later remarked: 'If I find 10,000 ways something won't work, I haven't failed. I am not discouraged, because every attempt discarded is another step forward.'

The sheer multiplicity of Edison's inventions beggars belief. Everyone knows about the light bulb, where he was the first to find a practicable, commercial application for a technology that others were busy working on at the time. Then he pioneered electric power generation and its distribution to homes, factories and businesses, which allowed him to capitalise on the success of his bulbs. Numerous inventions of his contributed to the arrival of mass communications, most notably telecoms, while he played a key role in the development of sound recording, motion pictures, radiography, batteries, and mining and cement technologies. No fewer than 1,093 US patents were filed in his name. He even discovered the original Falconbridge iron ore body in Canada, though he failed to bring it into successful commercial production, and abandoned his claim. This setback was remedied by others at a later date.

Part of the key to his success was that he was one of the first to see the potential for applying mass production techniques and teamwork to the process of invention. His laboratory at Menlo Park in New Jersey is generally reckoned to have been the first industrial research laboratory. Others made a substantial contribution to his innovations, which he acknowledged, saying, 'I am quite correctly described as more of a sponge than an inventor.' This probably overstates the case, but it contains a large grain of truth.

Edison's ability to translate such inventiveness into business success is surely unparalleled. For him, unlike Alexander

Graham Bell, business was as important as inventing, and his tenacity in promoting innovations was legendary. The most striking evidence for this was the epic battle he fought against George Westinghouse in electricity, where he championed direct current (DC) against alternating current (AC), which had been developed by his former employee Nikola Tesla. The problem with DC was that its range was much shorter than AC, which could carry high-voltage electricity hundreds of miles with only marginal loss of power.

So Edison tried to demonstrate that AC was too dangerous to provide a realistic alternative to DC. To support his argument, he helped develop the electric chair, despite being against capital punishment, in order to demonstrate the lethal nature of AC. His attempts to have it banned included having his employees electrocute Topsy, a rogue elephant at Luna Park near Coney Island which had killed several men. In the end, AC won the battle, but DC has its uses to this day, notably in subway systems, which are still mostly powered by this means.

Edison left behind not just innovations but several well-known companies. Most noteworthy was Edison General Electric, which ultimately became today's General Electric, a company that is rarely far from the top of the global league tables on most measures of corporate size and achievement. Other still-familiar names are Commonwealth Edison, Consolidated Edison and the Motion Picture Patents Company, which ran nine studios in the early days of the film industry.

What secures Edison's claim to be the greatest entrepreneur of all time is the extent to which he transformed the way people lived all across the globe. The opening of the *New York Times*'s obituary in 18 October 1931 goes to the heart of it:

Thomas Alva Edison made the world a better place in which to live and brought comparative luxury into the life of the working man. No one in the long roll of those who have benefited humanity has done more to make existence easy and comfortable. Through his invention of electric light he gave the world a new brilliance; when the cylinder of his first phonograph recorded sound he put the great music of the ages in reach of everyone; when he invented the motion picture it was a gift to mankind of a new theatre, a new form of amusement. His inventions gave work as well as light and recreation to millions.

His inventive genius brooded over a world which at night-fall was engulfed in darkness, pierced only by the feeble beams of kerosene lamps, by gas lights or, in some of the larger cities, by the uncertainties of the old-time arc lights. To Edison, with the dream of the incandescent lamp in his mind, it seemed that people still lived in the Dark Ages. But his ferreting fingers groped in the darkness until they evoked the glow that told him that the incandescent lamp was a success, and that light for all had been achieved. That significant moment occurred more than fifty years ago – on 21 October 1869.

One of Edison's own verdicts on his life was equally hearten-ing: 'I never did a day's work in my life. It was all fun.' Nothing morbid about that.

There is a risk, at this point, that I am making entrepreneur-ship sound like an Anglo-American phenomenon. Yet the word entrepreneur is of course French, despite former US President George W. Bush's assertion to the contrary. Both Europe and Asia produced remarkable entrepreneurs before Europeans first set out for America, most notably Johannes Gutenberg, the German who developed moveable-type printing technology in the mid-fifteenth century, and the even earlier printing innovator Bi Sheng in eleventh-century China. (This technology was arguably more vital to human development than the innovations of Edison, but if I put Edison first in my pantheon, it is because his inventions did more to improve the comfort and quality of life of ordinary people than the availability of printed material, which was of greater benefit to the elites of society.)

I also wonder – but remain uncertain – whether in continental Europe and Asia there may have been more entrepreneurs whose interest in money was a less powerful motivator. Werner von Siemens and his brothers in mid-nineteenth-century Germany, for example, were impressive both as inventors and businessmen, giving the world the first electric elevator, the first electric train and the first international deep-sea telegraph cable, as well as being leaders in developing dynamos for electricity generation. As quirky entrepreneurs go, Werner takes some beating. He carried out many of his electrical experiments in prison, having been put away for acting as a second in a duel. He was reputedly annoyed to be let out because of the potentially deleterious impact on his work. Yet, unlike Edison, Werner von Siemens's efforts were part of a family endeavour and continued to be so into the twentieth century. The motivation differed from Edison's in being more dynastic. Werner wrote to his brother Karl: 'I regard our business only secondly as a source of wealth; for me it is rather a kingdom that I hope to leave intact to my successors for further creative work.'

That sentiment could equally have come from Sakichi Toyoda (1867–1930), founder of the Toyoda Automatic Loom Works, the great industrial entrepreneur who remains something of a national hero in Japan. Often referred to as the father of the Japanese industrial revolution and the Japanese Thomas Edison, Toyoda, the son of a poor carpenter, was a pioneer in automation, inventing an internationally competitive power loom that would immediately cease production if it detected an error. Such radical innovation in a developing country is an extraordinary achievement. In the catch-up phase of industrialisation, high rates of growth are usually generated by following the example of more developed countries without necessarily fostering radical domestic innovation. Yet Toyoda showed himself capable of transforming industrial processes that had been developed in the advanced countries of the West. His system became part of the production process of Toyota Motor Company, which was spun off from Toyoda Automatic Loom Works after Sakichi Toyoda's death, while his descendants continue to work in what is now the world's biggest car company.

The post-war period was particularly rich in creative entrepreneurs, who rebuilt the devastated landscapes of Europe and Japan. Among the most dogged and successful of those who defied the Keynesian stereotype was France's Marcel Dassault, whose company was at the forefront of the European aerospace industry. In the First World War, Marcel Bloch, as he was then called, had just started producing reconnaissance planes for the French air force when the war came to an end, killing off his promising venture. He responded by diverting his efforts into real estate, until Lindberg's transatlantic flight

to Paris in 1927 fired his imagination on the potential for civil
aviation. Having gone back into manufacturing, he then saw
his company nationalised in 1936. Undaunted, he set up afresh
while simultaneously working in the now state-owned concern
to help power the country's re-armament programme.

Come the German occupation, Bloch, a Jew, refused to collaborate with the Germans on aircraft production and was
imprisoned by the Vichy regime. He ended up in Buchenwald
in 1944. Yet even in the concentration camp he was fixated
with the potential for a huge expansion of commercial aviation after the war. When peace came, as he rebuilt his empire
he was nonetheless urged by the French government to focus
primarily on military aviation, both for national use and for
export. This he did to great effect, attracting global attention when his Mirage fighter planes played a crucial part in
the Israeli victory in the 1967 Six Day War. He also had the
distinction of producing Europe's first supersonic plane, the
Mystère. Towards the end of this wildly chequered career, and
now renamed Dassault (the *nom de guerre* of his brother Paul
Bloch, a leader of the French resistance), he became a successful, if controversial, newspaper baron and politician.

That rugged quality of the post-war entrepreneurs is lacking
in the great information technology entrepreneurs of our own
time. Yet technology giants such as Bill Gates have a record in
philanthropy that harks back to that of the more enlightened
industrial pioneers like Matthew Boulton. And while rugged is
not quite the adjective to apply to most women entrepreneurs,
it is hard not to be impressed by those, like billionaire TV host
Oprah Winfrey, who have broken away from conventional
areas of female entrepreneurship such as cosmetics to thrive in

hitherto male-dominated industries such as the media and to make substantial philanthropic efforts.

Most of the people mentioned in this chapter made enormous contributions both to economic growth and, ultimately, to the quality of people's lives. At the same time, entrepreneurs in the developing world are actively engaged in lifting millions out of poverty, even if that is not their direct intention or motivation. And in failing states such as North Korea, entrepreneurs have emerged to create a private parallel economy in the midst of chaos. Some of these people were undoubtedly vicious; others were morally admirable. So the conclusion has to be that there is truth in the views of both Mandeville and Keynes. Yet the Marxian view of the entrepreneur as a ruthless accumulator of capital is surely anachronistic.

In the early stages of the industrial revolution, many entrepreneurs, perhaps a majority, were indeed ruthless in their greedy pursuit of profit. The same phenomenon is visible today in countries such as China, where the industrialisation process is both young and frequently brutal. Yet the developed world has largely moved beyond such unrestrained capitalism. And the greatest entrepreneurs, such as Thomas Edison, simply do not fit the Marxist or the Keynesian stereotype. Given the importance of entrepreneurship for economic growth and its centrality in the workings of the capitalist system, the Keynesian view is, to my mind, seriously anti-social.

CHAPTER THREE

HIJACKED BY BANKERS

Voltaire, the great all-purpose Enlightenment intellectual, is said to have remarked that if you see a banker jump out of the window, jump after him – there is sure to be a profit in it. That neatly encapsulates the deep-seated popular conviction that bankers are among capitalism's most self-seeking, devious and unfathomable creatures. It is a view that has been greatly reinforced by the recent financial crisis, and has its roots in antiquity. According to Aristotle:

> The most hated sort [of wealth-getting], and with the greatest reason, is usury, which makes a gain out of money itself, and not from the natural object of it. For money was intended to be used in exchange, but not to increase at interest. And this term interest, which means the birth of money from money, is applied to the breeding of money because the offspring resembles the parent. Wherefore of all modes of getting wealth this is the most unnatural.[34]

Few outside the Muslim world share Aristotle's view on the unnaturalness of lending at interest today, although the rise of payday lenders charging annualised rates of interest of up to

5,000 per cent or more has revived justifiable public concern about usury. And there is no question that since modern banking first emerged in medieval Italy, the hatred referred to by Aristotle has waned. Indeed, by the twentieth century, bankers had succeeded in acquiring a degree of respectability. In the post-war period, when financial conditions were relatively stable, they were even regarded as pillars of the community. Then there was a turning of the tide. Towards the end of the century, many bankers suffered the indignity of being replaced by computers, which played an increasing role in the allocation of credit. And for those who retained their jobs, it was a chastening experience to discover that the financial crisis not only turned them into social pariahs; they were also perceived to be a threat to the free market system. Indeed, a central lesson of the financial crisis and the Great Recession is that the world economy and the capitalist system are now hostage to over-sized, over-complex and unmanageable financial behemoths. Banking thus remains profoundly problematic.

Not that there was ever much chance that people would learn to love the banking fraternity. Bankers naturally gravitate towards the rich because they are more creditworthy than the poor. Even for rich borrowers, the obligation owed to the banker can feel oppressive, and to those who have been denied credit, the lack of an obligation feels worse. For good measure, populist anti-bank sentiment is invariably fuelled when banks inflict bankruptcies on their clients in economic downturns. And in the financial crisis, bankers did nothing to help their case by continuing to take fat bonuses while also taking government rescue money. Once again, this syndrome of populist anti-bank sentiment was known to antiquity.

Cicero, the Roman politician and orator, remarked in his *De officiis*: 'Now in regard to trades and employments, which are to be considered liberal and which mean, this is the more or less accepted view. First, those employments are condemned which incur ill will, as those of collectors of harbour taxes and money lenders.'[35]

Yet there is a more fundamental reason, albeit not well understood, why bankers will always incur ill will – namely that their business model is a confidence trick. An important characteristic of banking is that only a fraction of a bank's deposits are kept in reserve, available in case depositors want their money back. The bank treats the rest as its own money. And by employing these excess cash reserves to extend credit to customers, the bank transfers temporary ownership of the money to borrowers despite the depositors retaining the right to claim back these same funds and despite the bank providing a guarantee that all deposits can be withdrawn on demand. This leads to a curious position where both depositor and borrower are entitled to control over the same funds simultaneously. If depositors lose confidence in the bank and demand their money back all at once, the bank will be unable to meet its obligations. A run on deposits will follow.

Such crises of confidence started in northern Italy in the late Middle Ages when this so-called fractional reserve banking became the norm. A vivid description of how bank runs arose comes from a contemporary Venetian account in the sixteenth century:

The following year, 1584, I heard of the failure of the Pisani and Tiepolo bank for a very large sum of money. This was caused chiefly by the bankruptcy of one Andrea da l'Osta, a Tuscan, a Pisan, and a very rich merchant, who had lived in our city for many years. He had built up much credit by his many business transactions, but in truth it was based on his reputation alone and not upon his capital, for this market and the city of Venice are naturally very much inclined to love and trust in appearances. Hence, heaping business upon business, his reach exceeding his grasp [*abbracciando molti ne esso tutto stringendo*], he suffered the fate of almost all those who want to be bigger than other men. With his fall came the fall of the bank, because its creditors believed that he owed it more than he really did, because he could call upon it at will, and so they all wanted to be satisfied at the same time. The bank kept going for a few days, paying them off as best it could, but in the end the crowd of creditors increased and the bank collapsed and failed, to the detriment of numberless people and great damage to this market, which was without a bank for four years, so that business shrank to an unbelievable extent. The Republic felt the effects of this, and took very extensive measures, but to no avail.[36]

Today, bank runs usually take a different form. Big depositors such as companies, pension funds and other financial institutions simply decide not to renew lending lines or certificates of deposit, so an ailing bank finds that its sources of funds dry up. Notwithstanding that, the British bank Northern Rock actually experienced in 2007 an old-style run in which worried retail depositors queued up outside branches to withdraw their money. Either way, the reality is that all money lenders that operate on the basis of fractional reserve banking are inherently technically bankrupt. Hence the quip generally attributed to Henry Ford: 'It is well enough that people of the nation do not understand our banking and monetary system, for if they did, I believe there would be a revolution before morning.'

Bankers are well aware of this fundamental flaw in their business model, which is why appearances are so important in banking, as the account of the rise and fall of Andrea da l'Osta emphasised. They have always taken great care to don the visual trappings of solidity and respectability. Ogden Nash made the point in his poem 'Bankers Are Just Like Anybody Else, Except Richer':

> *Most bankers dwell in marble halls*
> *Which they get to dwell in because they encourage deposits*
> *and discourage withdralls.*
> *And particularly because they all observe one rule which*
> *woe betides the banker who fails to heed it,*
> *Which is you must never lend money to anybody unless*
> *they don't need it.*[37]

All that marble is intended to inspire awe and respectful acquiescence, though marble is by no means a sine qua non. The partners in Tellson's Bank in Dickens's *A Tale of Two Cities* had a very different way of conveying an impression of probity:

Tellson's Bank by Temple Bar was an old-fashioned place, even in the year one thousand seven hundred and eighty. It was very small, very dark, very ugly, very incommodious. It was an old-fashioned place, moreover, in the moral attribute that the partners in the House were proud of its smallness, proud of its darkness, proud of its ugliness, proud of its incommodiousness. They were even boastful of its eminence in those particulars, and were fired by an express conviction that, if it were less objectionable, it would be less respectable. This was no passive belief, but an active weapon which they flashed at more convenient places of business ... When they took a young man into Tellson's London house, they hid him somewhere till he was old. They kept him in a dark place, like a cheese, until he had the full Tellson flavour and blue-mould upon him. Then only was he permitted to be seen, spectacularly poring over large books, and casting his breeches and gaiters into the general weight of the establishment.

Tellson's was modelled on Child & Co., whose fusty image served it in good stead since it survives to this day in London's Fleet Street, albeit as a subsidiary of the Royal Bank of Scotland. The aim of this careful image-making was once again to stun the public into credulous submission.

Why, you might ask, does society tolerate what amounts to a fraud against depositors and a powerful force for economic instability? The short answer is that there is a widespread belief that if banks were required to keep 100 per cent of depositors' money on hand to be paid instantly, less credit would be available to finance industry and commerce and facilitate economic growth. As long as that remains the majority view – there is a dissenting minority of economists who have yet to persuade policymakers otherwise – the flawed business model will continue to be regarded as a necessary evil.

A further difficulty with the way the banking system works is that the banks have become more dangerous over time. One reason is that, from the nineteenth century, banks began to abandon partnership and adopt limited liability. This was a big step because the unlimited liability associated with partnership acted as a tight control on imprudent behaviour. If a bank failed, creditors had recourse to all the personal assets of the individual partners. Once partnerships turned themselves into joint stock companies, the shareholders still enjoyed unlimited potential for gain but could never lose more than the amount they spent buying shares in the bank. This asymmetry was morally hazardous in that it encouraged greater risk taking. And in the nineteenth and twentieth centuries, commercial banks took more risks by extending their traditional deposit-taking and lending operations into investment banking and securities trading. Investment banking, which consists of issuing and distributing shares on behalf of corporate clients and making markets in shares, has a buccaneering culture wholly different from that of commercial banking. Michael Lewis, in one of the few really witty books written on high (or low) finance – *Liar's Poker* – caught the essence of it neatly:

A commercial banker was reputed to be just an ordinary American businessman with ordinary American ambitions. He lent a few hundred million dollars each day to South American countries. But really, he means no harm. He was only doing what he was told by someone higher up in an endless chain of command. A commercial banker wasn't any more a troublemaker than Dagwood Bumstead. He had a wife, a station-wagon, 2.2 children and a dog that

brought him his slippers when he returned home from work
at six...

   An investment banker was a breed apart, a member of a
master race of deal makers. He possessed vast, almost unim-
aginable, talent and ambition. If he had a dog it snarled. He
had two little red sports cars yet wanted four. To get them,
he was, for a man in a suit, surprisingly willing to cause
trouble.[38]

After the Wall Street Crash in 1929, lawmakers decided that
depositors' funds should not be used in speculative investment
banking activity. A rigid firewall was erected between commercial and investment banking by the Glass–Steagall Act of
1933. The legislation that imposed the division was repealed
in 1999, when the world's biggest banks were enthusiastical-
ly expanding while taking on more risk. Between 1990 and
2007, global bank balance sheets increased fourfold in size.
On the eve of the crisis they had reached $75 trillion, or 1.5
times the output of the entire planet.[39] At the same time, the
amount of capital in those balance sheets – the cushion banks
need to protect themselves from losses – was shrinking. In the
second half of the nineteenth century, it was normal for banks
to maintain a capital buffer of 20 to 40 per cent of the total
balance sheet. In the interwar years, this was down to 10 per
cent. By the 1990s, around 5 per cent was the norm.[40] When
the crisis erupted, some big banks were operating with as little
as 2 or 3 per cent. In other words, the banks' assets had only
to fall in value by 2 or 3 per cent for the bank to be wiped
out. In a world where the stock market can fall by around
20 per cent or more in a day, as it did on Black Monday in

1987, that is an absurdly fragile base on which to maintain a financial system.

While capital was shrinking, bankers' pay was soaring. In 1989, chief executives of the largest US banks earned 100 times the median US household income. By 2007, the multiple was 500.[41] Nothing in the operating performance of the banks had taken place to justify this stratospheric increase. As William McDonough, a former chief executive of the Federal Reserve Bank of New York, once pointedly remarked of the wider tendency towards inequality in the workplace:

> It is hard to find somebody more convinced than I of the superiority of the American economic system, but I can find nothing in economic theory that justifies this development. I am old enough to have known both the CEOs of twenty years ago and those of today. I can assure you that we CEOs of today are not ten times better than those of twenty years ago.
>
> What happened? Sadly, all too many members of the inner circle of the business elite participated in the over-expansion of executive compensation. It was justified by a claimed identity between the motivation of the executives and share-holder value. It is reasonably clear now that this theory has left a large number of poorer stockholders, especially including employee stockholders, not only unconvinced, but understandably disillusioned and angry.
>
> The policy of vastly increasing executive compensation was also, at least with the brilliant vision of hindsight, terribly bad social policy and perhaps even bad morals.[42]

A similar if less spectacular progression was under way in Europe. The escalation coincided with a power shift within banking whereby traders replaced conventional bankers at the top. They genuinely believed that financial innovations that involved packaging products such as subprime mortgages into bundles of securities that could be sold to investors were both useful and lucrative, as did the credit rating agencies that awarded triple-A status to these securitised products. So, too, did a growing band of mathematicians and scientists who left other research-intensive industries to share in the banking bonanza. At the same time, financial and human resources were diverted away from retail banking, which provides services for households and small businesses, into investment banking. Paternalistic bank managers and regional loan officers were replaced, as mentioned earlier, by impersonal computerised credit assessments based on credit risk models.

Yet despite all this excitement, the return on bank assets over the period was stagnant. While the bankers pointed to a rising return on the equity capital in justification, this was simply a reflection of how much banks were borrowing. If equity capital shrinks, the return on equity will increase for any given volume of business. In other words, the high return reflected very high risks, and when the subprime mortgage fiasco erupted in 2007, it became clear that much of the return was illusory, as was the social utility of all the complex financial innovation that had been going on. And because banks had been offloading securitised loans from their balance sheets, the quality of the loans they made was of decreasing importance to them. Nor was there any incentive for the banks to monitor the loans once they had been peddled to investors and shunted into what came to be known as the shadow banking system.

Why did the shareholders not cry wolf? Economists who note the asymmetric payoff that comes from limited liability speculate that many fund managers thought they could profit from the boom and make their exit before it imploded. Perhaps there were some who did this. My own view is that there was a huge analytical failure during the bubble period. Most investors simply failed to recognise that the rising return on bank equity was just a reflection of the shrinkage of the equity capital.[43] Much the same was true of stock market analysts. Bubbles induce myopia and a tendency to believe that all is for the best in the best of all possible worlds. Muddled thinking seems a more plausible explanation than a conspiracy between shareholders and bankers to make a quick buck at the expense of the taxpayer, who ended up bailing out banks that were too big to be allowed to fail.

What, too, of the central bankers? Historically, the central banks have had a vital role in addressing the confidence trick problem and preventing financial crashes. Long before they acquired their monetary policy role – tightening and relaxing monetary conditions by, for example, raising or reducing interest rates – they acted as lenders of last resort to solvent banks that might otherwise have failed as a result of a contagious financial panic. Given the moral hazard arising from the reduction of market discipline implicit in last-resort lending and the similar moral hazard arising from the introduction of deposit insurance from the 1930s onwards, the central banks also acquired a role in regulating and supervising banks. Yet when Alan Greenspan was chairman of the Federal Reserve as the housing bubble inflated, he conspicuously failed to fulfil the Fed's mandate to supervise the subprime mortgage market. He was convinced that the market process was so benign – 'efficient', in economists' argot – that supervision was a waste of time. At the Bank of England, Mervyn (now Lord) King was notoriously uninterested in financial stability issues before the crisis. In the period ineptly dubbed 'the Great Moderation', central bankers were prone to think that if inflation was kept within target, the financial system would look after itself.[44] They also claimed credit for this apparent stability. In 2004, Ben Bernanke, governor of the Fed and later its chairman, said: 'My view is that improvements in monetary policy, though certainly not the only factor, have probably been an important source of the Great Moderation.'[45]

This plaudit for central bankers included by implication a pat on the back for Bernanke himself.

The approach to central banking outlined here was in marked contrast to the days before academics and professional economists took over from banking practitioners at the head of leading central banks. David Kynaston quotes, in his colourful history of the City of London, a paper prepared in 1962 at the Bank of England for a course on central banking. The authors, Maurice Allen and Humphrey Mynors, economic adviser and deputy governor respectively, assembled a list of propositions circumspectly called 'Opinions Attributed to Central Bankers'. Among the more revealing were these:

A central banker needs a sense of smell. Analysis is only theorising but may be encouraged when it confuses critics.

No civil servant understands markets.

Politicians do not sufficiently explain the facts of life to the electorate.

Central bankers should always do what they say and never say what they do.

Taxes are too high.

Bankers are people who do, in the main, what you wish. The rest are fringe institutions. They do not exist.

Wave the big stick if you like, but never use it; it may break in your hand. Better still, try wagging your finger.

In banking, the essence of solidity is liquidity.

Never spit into the wind.

Always lean against the wind.[46]

The modern reader will be struck by the arrogance implicit in many of these sayings. Yet that, historically, has been the culture of this mandarin profession. As the economist Karl Brunner once put it, central bankers were

> traditionally surrounded by a peculiar and protective political mystique [that] thrives on a pervasive impression that central banking is an esoteric art. Access to this art and its proper execution is confined to the initiated elite. The esoteric nature of the art is moreover revealed by an inherent impossibility to articulate its insights in explicit and intelligible words and sentences.[47]

In their book on central banking, Howard Davies and David Green, two former central bankers, commented on the psyche of members of this priestly caste thus:

Central bankers often congratulate each other at their frequent international gatherings on how remarkably well they
get on together by comparison, say, with their finance minis-
try colleagues or even their friends in the supervisory world.
They believe they think the same way and have the same
reactions in the face of a rather hostile, uncomprehending
non-central banker world. There is a distinct sense of a central bankers' club, bound together by a common psyche that
seems to transcend differences in history, functions, degrees
of independence, size, or importance.

This attitude has a number of characteristics, which can
be seen to bring both advantages and handicaps. They include secrecy, a belief in quasi-papal infallibility, caution,
over-analysis and 'constructive ambiguity'.

Central bankers have traditionally been secretive and not
averse to cultivating a sense of mystery.[48]

Since the financial crisis, the ethos has been tarnished and
there is greater emphasis on transparency and accountability.
Yet despite the less attractive features of the Bank of England
paper, it is worth noting that it contains considerable wisdom,
starting with the emphasis on liquidity, which means retaining
a sizeable cash cushion as a protection against a loss of confidence among depositors. The international regulatory regime,
framed since the 1980s at central bankers' gatherings in Basel,
did not impose liquidity ratios before the crisis. The assumption was that if banks had a sufficient cushion of capital – the
funds originally advanced by shareholders and subsequently
enhanced by the bank's retained profits – there would be no
problem with liquidity. That might be true, but given that the

banks had run down their capital to a negligible sliver, the assumption was both heroic and irrelevant.

A growing discussion is taking place, too, about the case for leaning against the wind – that is, raising interest rates more than would be necessary to maintain price stability in the short and medium term in order to curb a dangerous increase in banks' risk appetite or to dampen overheating asset prices. As for waving sticks and spitting into the wind, the points show a realistic appreciation of the difficulty of influencing markets. This is a salutary warning for central bankers in the aftermath of the crisis, since they are now committed to macro-prudential policymaking, which entails imposing counter-cyclical increases and decreases in banks' capital buffers, as well as other forms of intervention such as quantitative controls on lending. The timing of such action is exceptionally difficult to judge.

As for the regulators – whether sitting in central banks or existing independently outside them – they were struggling in the run-up to the crisis to understand huge changes in the structure of the financial system. Paid far less than the rocket scientists in the big banks who were devising new and complex financial instruments, they were, as always, one step behind the people they were trying to regulate. In the case of the British, they were also being urged by government ministers not to be too tough on the City of London, which appeared to have a unique capacity for creating employment and generating tax revenue in an industry where Britain appeared to enjoy a remarkable comparative advantage.

The regulators will continue to struggle because they are locked in a vicious circle. Every time there is a financial crisis, a political backlash ensures a raft of ever more complex re-regulatory measures. Financial market practitioners react to these by engaging in regulatory arbitrage, which is relatively easy in a world of global capital flows without a global regulator – banks simply put their business through markets in countries that have less draconian rules. There is always some jurisdiction, after all, in which the rules are looser than in most of the countries where a given bank is domiciled. As risk accumulates in areas that watchdogs find hard to monitor, the seeds of another crisis are sown. Come the crash, another round of imperfect re-regulatory measures is imposed. And so on, indefinitely. This vicious circle, when combined with morally hazardous bailouts when banks go bust, helps explain why there have been more than 100 major banking crises worldwide over the past three decades.[49]

This process of regulatory escalation can be clearly seen in the Basel capital accords, the international agreements referred to earlier governing the amount of capital banks must maintain. From the capital standards of Basel I in 1988 to the Basel II agreement in 2004, the number of calculations that a large, representative international bank had to make to determine its regulatory capital ratio rose from single figures to over 200 million.[50] Much the same has been going on with more detailed re-regulation. In a paper to the central bankers' annual jamboree at Jackson Hole, Wyoming, in 2012, Andy Haldane and Vasileios Madouros of the Bank of England described the Kafka-esque process thus:

Contrast the legislative responses in the US to the two largest financial crises of the past century – the Great Depression and the Great Recession. The single most important legislative response to the Great Depression was the Glass–Steagall Act of 1933. Indeed, this may have been the single most influential piece of financial legislation of the twentieth century. Yet it ran to a mere thirty-seven pages. The legislative response to this time's crisis, culminating in the Dodd–Frank Act of 2010, could not have been more different. On its own, the Act runs to 848 pages – more than twenty Glass–Steagalls. That is just the starting point. For implementation, Dodd–Frank requires an additional almost 400 pieces of detailed rule making by a variety of US regulatory agencies.

As of July this year, two years after the enactment of Dodd–Frank, a third of the required rules had been finalised. Those completed have added a further 8,843 pages to the rulebook. At this rate, once completed, Dodd–Frank could comprise 30,000 pages of rule making. That is roughly a thousand times larger than its closest legislative cousin, Glass–Steagall. Dodd–Frank makes Glass–Steagall look like throat-clearing.

The situation in Europe, while different in detail, is similar in substance. Since the crisis, more than a dozen European regulatory directives or regulations have been initiated, or reviewed, covering capital requirements, crisis management, deposit guarantees, short-selling, market abuse, investment funds, alternative investments, venture capital, OTC derivatives, markets in financial instruments, insurance, auditing and credit ratings.

These are at various stages of completion. So far, they cover over 2,000 pages. That total is set to increase dramatically as primary legislation is translated into detailed rule writing. For example, were that rule making to occur on a US scale,

> Europe's regulatory blanket would cover over 60,000 pages.
> It would make Dodd–Frank look like a warm-up Act.[51]

There has been a similar escalation in the number of watch-dogs. In the same paper, Haldane and Madouros point out that in the UK, for example, there was one regulator in 1980 for roughly every 11,000 people employed in the UK financial sector. By 2011, there was one for every 300 people employed in finance. This manic escalation in regulatory enthusiasm – nonetheless referred to as 'light-touch' regulation before 2007 – was wholly ineffective in preventing the financial crisis. It also leads to manic escalation in the number of bankers en-gaged in compliance activities. In September 2013, Jamie Dimon, chief executive of JPMorgan Chase, America's biggest bank, sent a memo to staff revealing that the bank had added a whopping 3,000 employees to bolster controls, devoted 500 people to fulfilling the Federal Reserve's stress tests, and given staff 750,000 hours of training on compliance matters.

Whether all this effort will be productive is moot. A fail-ure of internal controls at JP Morgan that led in 2012 to the loss of around $6 billion in a London trading operation – the so-called London whale scandal – demonstrated that neither Jamie Dimon nor his fellow top executives knew what was going on inside the bank. Given that Mr Dimon is generally reckoned to be the most accomplished banker of his genera-tion, there could be no clearer indication that today's financial behemoths are too big and too complex to manage. At the same time, the revelation in 2013 that JP Morgan had been obliged to put aside a $23 billion reserve for litigation arising from mis-selling mortgages – a euphemism for duping people

– underlined the depressing fact that the culture of the banking industry was fundamentally rotten. The biggest banks in the US and Europe appear to have suffered an extraordinary collapse of ethical standards in the light not only of widespread mis-selling but of the numerous criminal charges brought against them for rigging the interbank lending rates used in global financial markets such as the London Interbank Offered Rate; rigging the foreign exchange market; criminal violations of the US sanctions regime against Iran; criminal drug money laundering; and facilitating tax evasion.

The economist J. K. Galbraith had an interesting theory on morality in financial markets:

> At any given time there exists an inventory of undiscovered embezzlement in – or more precisely not in – the country's businesses and banks. This inventory – it should perhaps be called the bezzle – amounts at any moment to many millions of dollars. It also varies in size with the business cycle. In good times people are relaxed, trusting, and money is plentiful. But even though money is plentiful, there are always many people who need more. Under these circumstances the rate of embezzlement grows, the rate of discovery falls off, and the bezzle increases rapidly. In depression all this is reversed. Money is watched with a narrow, suspicious eye. The man who handles it is assumed to be dishonest until he proves himself otherwise. Audits are penetrating and meticulous. Commercial morality is enormously improved. The bezzle shrinks.[52]

Galbraith's insight needs to be expanded to apply to the wider capitalist system. I believe that there is within the corporate sector a stock of moral capital that fluctuates over time. It has both cyclical and structural components. While the moral capital stock evidently shrank in the period before the financial crisis for much the same reason that Galbraith's bezzle increased, there was also a sea change in the way the system worked. The move all across the corporate sector in the English-speaking world towards equity-related bonuses and performance-related pay encouraged a new level of greed among top executives.

Continuing revelations of unethical and criminal behaviour since the financial crisis suggest that the stock of moral capital has fallen to a much lower level than has prevailed in recent decades. The facts that so many big institutions were the subject of morally hazardous bailouts and so few people have gone to jail in the wake of the crisis, along with the persistence of the bonus culture in banking and in the wider corporate sector, mean that the improvement in commercial morality that Galbraith expected to take place in downturns did not happen to the extent it should have during the Great Recession. Despite the protestations of bankers that they are embracing an ethical approach to running the business, little appears to have changed. In the cumbersome bureaucracies of the international banking world it is unbelievably difficult to change a culture that has become so heavily infected by greed. It is probably impossible to change it when the incentive structures that govern executives' behaviour are completely at odds with the demands of an ethical approach to doing business. Certainly the ethical codes promulgated by the big banks – usually cooked up with the aid of outside consultants – are a gigantic fig leaf.

Against that background, I cannot resist quoting from Jonathan Swift's 'The Run upon the Bankers', in which the great eighteenth-century satirist does not rate the bankers' chances of making it to heaven very high:

When Other Hands the Scales shall hold,
And They in Men and Angels Sight
Produc'd with all their Bills and Gold,
Weigh'd in the Ballance, and found Light.[53]

I will nonetheless risk courting opprobrium by arguing that the bankers have been disproportionately blamed for the Great Recession. Yes, some of them were undoubtedly greedy. But it is also important to acknowledge the monetary and financial background. On one view, first advanced by the economist Charles Dumas of Lombard Street Research and subsequently embraced by Alan Greenspan's successor at the Fed, Ben Bernanke, in the run-up to the crisis, the bankers were working in a world of global imbalances. Asia, the petro-economies and much of northern Europe were running up big balance-of-payments surpluses on current accounts and saving far more than they were investing. As a result, these excess savings were depressing yields on all investments around the world. Pension funds and other investors were desperate for income. By creating all those structured products, such as asset-backed securities, collateralised mortgage obligations and the rest, banks were responding to their clients' need for assets that yielded a higher income than that available on conventional government bonds.

At the same time, the Basel capital regime was encouraging them to bump up their mortgage lending by according mortgages an unrealistically low-risk status that called for less capital backing than in, say, small business lending. So the housing bubble in the US and the related property bubbles in the UK and Spain were partly driven by ill-conceived regulation. The politicians were also doing their bit. With real incomes stagnant or falling, the people on Capitol Hill looked to the banks to provide credit so that poorer people could participate in the American dream and existing home owners could continue to enjoy a rising standard of living by borrowing on their property collateral. And had Americans not been prepared to run down their savings and raise consumption, excess global savings would have led to a 1930s-style slump induced by deficient demand. Many powerful groups were thus complicit in the boom and bust. On this view, if the central banks and regulators had been more prescient and if private banks had been better behaved, the financial crisis might have been less extreme. But when monetary forces in the world economy were so markedly out of joint, it was not in their power to prevent a crisis.

An alternative view, advanced most forcefully by economists at the Bank for International Settlements, the central bankers' bank, is that central banks and market participants such as institutional investors simply pushed interest rates too low, thereby contributing to an unsustainable surge in credit and asset prices. The BIS economists were long critical of the asymmetric approach to monetary policy pursued by the Fed since the 1980s, whereby it intervened to underpin asset prices if they collapsed, but failed to do anything to dampen them down if they overheated. It should be added, in passing, that they also foresaw the crisis, but were rebuffed by the central banks that the BIS exists to serve, and told to mind their own business. On that reading, the central bankers have got off too lightly relative to the private bankers.

Tempting though it is to put bankers in the stocks, allocating blame is a less important priority than re-designing the system to prevent a further crisis. And the problem now is that despite its appalling cost in taxpayer bailouts and lost output, the crisis has not – incredibly – delivered a big enough shock to bring about a better, simpler and more fool-proof regulatory system, any more than it has succeeded in restoring the stock of moral capital. Moreover, history suggests that simple structural solutions such as the Glass–Steagall Act, with its clear split between commercial and investment banking, have a more powerful restraining influence on behaviour than detailed rule making. Yet there is a reluctance to return to such clear structural solutions, despite the toxicity, in particular, of the big banks' market-making operations, whereby banks facilitate securities trading and trading in derivative instruments such as swaps and options by acting as an intermediary between buyers and sellers.

Back in the financial crisis of the mid-1970s, a wise City of London banker explained to me that the business model of market makers – then known as stockjobbers – was problematic because it was prone to regular collapses. This is because it has many of the features of a game of poker, which combines skill with random fluctuations due to chance. If the participants have equal skill, their results will be random. The wealth of individual players will fluctuate and every so often one will go bust and withdraw from the game. The most likely loser is the one who starts with the least money. If those going bust are not replaced by new entrants, the average wealth of the remaining players rises as their number falls.

In market making, skill comes from using intelligently the information derived from the orders placed by buyers and sellers. Size provides an advantage: the more of the market you can observe directly, the easier it is to minimise the risk of being wrong-footed by adverse price movements that hit the value of the inventory of securities that the market maker holds to meet the clients' needs. As can happen with poker, the business has become concentrated and much of it now takes place within big banks, most notably in relation to derivatives trading. The risk is that the scale of bankruptcies among market makers rises with each new financial crisis. This, as the London-based economist Andrew Smithers argues, has the makings of a doomsday machine. As crisis follows crisis, each bankruptcy is likely to involve a larger bank and pose a bigger threat of economic and financial disruption.[54]

It follows that it is not enough just to divide low-risk from high-risk business within banks by ring-fencing, as the Vickers Commission in Britain has proposed. And the initiative by Paul Volcker, the former chairman of the Federal Reserve, to prevent banks from engaging in trading on their own account – the Volcker rule – appears to miss the point. It is right that banks should not be allowed to use depositors' money to speculate on their own account in markets. But the much bigger risk of a systemic crisis lies in the banks' market-making activity in derivatives and in excessive exposure to property, which time and again has been at the heart of financial crises.

Market making needs to be taken outside banks and kept as small as possible to ensure that bankruptcies do not bring down the whole system. So far, no country in the developed world has been prepared to contemplate such action. Our chief protection against future crises thus lies in forcing banks to maintain a substantial capital cushion. To be effective, that cushion needs, in my judgement, to be much bigger than any policymaker is now willing to contemplate.

A further snag in safety proofing the system is that the politicians, especially in the US, are beholden to Wall Street and the banking lobbyists because they are dependent on them for campaign finance. So attempts, misconceived or otherwise, to impose structural solutions such as the Volcker rule are being unpicked thanks to the efforts of the banks' lobbyists. Meantime, concentration in the financial system has increased as a result of mergers and acquisitions during the crisis. So a smaller number of bigger banks are perceived to be too big to fail and enjoy lower borrowing costs than other banks. They thus still benefit from a de facto subsidy from the taxpayer that runs into billions of dollars a year. And while significant efforts have been made to make it easier to unwind insolvent banks in an orderly way, the failure of a big, complex international bank could still be chaotic in the absence of a global regulator and watertight international agreements on how to wind it down and distribute the losses across national boundaries.

Sheila Bair, chairman of the Federal Deposit Insurance Corporation between 2006 and 2011, puts the dilemma well. While acknowledging that some regulatory progress has been made, she has said:

Sadly, banks remain too reliant on borrowed money and unstable, short-term funding. Money-market funds still pretend they are banks, risking destabilising runs. Though we have moved a chunk of unlisted over-the-counter derivatives into centralised trading and clearing systems, well over half the market remains in the shadows. A proposed ban on speculative trading languishes. Securitisation is unreformed...

Millions of families that suffered in the Great Recession are only now clawing their way back. For their sake, let us hope the Fed can gradually end this era of cheap money without significant market upheaval. Regrettably, it will have to do so using a financial regulatory base that is, at best, one-third built.[55]

When banks were smaller, the acute flaw in their business model – the confidence trick – was something that society could tolerate thanks to the ability of governments and central banks to stabilise the system. Today, it is quite another matter. The widening and deepening of central bank and government support for the banks is morally hazardous and continues to provide an incentive for big banks to become even bigger. Thomas Jefferson argued that banks were more dangerous to our liberties than standing armies. I would not go that far. But there is no question that they are far more dangerous than they should be and that the big banks remain a potent threat to the world economy and the safe workings of the capitalist system in a way that is not the case with non-financial business. To put it crudely, capitalism has been hijacked by the banks. That is not how it is meant to work. The only question is how long it will take before the system blows up again.

CHAPTER FOUR

INDUSTRIAL SHRINKAGE, FINANCIAL EXCESS

When Karl Marx wrote about the capitalist mode of production in *Das Kapital*, he was concerned primarily with manufacturing. In 1867, when the first volume of that formidably indigestible opus appeared, this was synonymous with what modern Americans call smokestack industry and it was not pleasant for those employed in it. Manufacturing, according to Marx,

> seizes labour power by its very roots. It converts the labourer into a crippled monstrosity by forcing his detail dexterity at the expense of a world of productive capabilities and instincts; just as in the States of La Plata they butcher a whole beast for the sake of his hide or his tallow. Not only is the detail work distributed to the different individuals, but the individual himself is made the automatic motor of a fractional operation, and the absurd fable of Menenius Agrippa, which makes man a mere fragment of his own body, becomes realised.[56]

It is ironic, then, that many, particularly but not exclusively those on the left of the political spectrum, have the conviction that entrepreneurs are greedy, unethical individuals, hell-bent on capital accumulation, while at the same time believing that making things is innately virtuous and much more virtuous than peddling services. Such people see manufacturing as uniquely productive. The purest expression of this prejudice is to be found in the Soviet literary tradition of the production novel, a socialist realist genre whose plot requires a heroic worker to overcome innumerable obstacles in a titanic struggle to create a model workplace and advance Soviet industry.

Many also feel instinctively that a nation's strength can be measured by the amount of swarf on its boots – swarf being the metal chippings found on factory floors. And because this view is so widespread, the decline of manufacturing in countries such as the US and UK is generally perceived to be disturbing, especially when there is high unemployment in 'rustbowl' industries that are conspicuous victims of globalisation and de-industrialisation. According to this school of thought, advanced countries cannot live by services alone, not least because services have less export potential than manufactures. So a shrinking manufacturing base must be equated with national decline, as must the growing financialisation of the economy. No surprise, then, that the decline in manufacturing employment in the UK, from 31 per cent of the workforce in 1975 to 25 per cent in 1983 to 8 per cent in 2014, causes much angst, as does the almost-as-severe percentage fall in the US, where manufacturing employment is down to 9 per cent. Unfavourable comparisons are made with Germany and Japan, where manufacturing constitutes a much bigger part of the economy and contributes consistently to large trade surpluses.

This belief in the intrinsic merits of manufacturing is perhaps understandable, given that manufacturing was – and still is, in the developing world – responsible for raising the great mass of people out of poverty. It is an overwhelmingly powerful truth that manufacturing secured the triumph of capitalism. Yet, as I will show, it is arguable that manufacturing employment *ought* to fall in a mature economy; and one of the safest predictions for the twenty-first century is that in the developed world it will continue to do so without causing a collapse in living standards.

To make this case is admittedly quite a challenge, because the prejudice about the superiority of manufacturing over services has deep historical roots. Adam Smith, still hugely influential across the centuries, showed a bias in *The Wealth of Nations* against services, suggesting that while the labour of a manufacturer added value, the labour of a menial servant did not:

> There is one sort of labour which adds to the value of the subject upon which it is bestowed: there is another which has no such effect. The former, as it produces a value, may be called productive; the latter, unproductive. Thus the labour of a manufacturer adds, generally, to the value of the materials which he works upon, that of his own maintenance, and of his master's profit. The labour of a menial servant, on the contrary, adds to the value of nothing ... A man grows rich by employing a multitude of manufacturers: he grows poor by maintaining a multitude of menial servants ... His [the menial servant's] services generally perish in the very instant of their performance, and seldom leave any trade or value behind them for which an equal quantity of service could afterwards be procured.[57]

Smith's view is shared by many modern historians. Domestic service employed 1.3 million, mainly women, at the start of the twentieth century. Yet the socialist historian E. P. Thompson has scarcely a word to say about them in his celebrated book *The Making of the English Working Class*. Economic historians who claim to write 'history from below' almost invariably exclude history below the stairs, preferring to write about the progress of the labour movement through strikes, demonstrations and socialist politics.[58] For them, domestic service is not 'real work'. Only when they abandoned domestic service for work in munitions factories in the First World War did working-class women become worthy of these historians' consideration.

Equally well entrenched is the obsession with manufacturing decline. In 1903, when the British confronted a serious competitive challenge from the US and Germany, the businessman turned statesman Joseph Chamberlain argued with great rhetorical panache for protectionism as follows:

Your once great trade in sugar refining is gone; all right, try jam. Your iron trade is going; never mind, you can make mouse traps. The cotton trade is threatened; well, what does it matter to you? Suppose you try dolls' eyes ... believe me ... although the industries of this country are very various, you cannot go on for ever. You cannot go on watching with indifference the disappearance of your principal industries, and always hoping that you will be able to replace them by secondary and inferior industries.[59]

Chamberlain was echoing those who, in the debate on luxury in the eighteenth century, feared that the increasing production of goods designed to meet the whims and fancies of fashionable women would cause society to become decadent and effeminate. He in turn was echoed decades later by Lord Weinstock, chief executive of Britain's General Electric Company, before the House of Lords committee on overseas trade in 1985, when Margaret Thatcher's government presided over a painful period of de-industrialisation:

> What will the service industries be servicing when there is no hardware, when no wealth is actually being produced? We will be servicing, presumably, the production of wealth by others. We will supply the Changing of the Guard, we will supply the Beefeaters around the Tower of London. We will become a curiosity. I do not think that that is what Britain is about. I think that is rubbish.

This line of thinking has now been absorbed into the globalisation debate, of which more in a moment. But on Capitol Hill in Washington DC, protectionist remedies are back in fashion, just as they were in Britain in Joseph Chamberlain's time. That is a measure of the potency of the pro-manufacturing argument – though it has to be said that protectionist instincts have never really been wholly absent in the US, which, despite its ostensible commitment to free trade, provides considerable shelter from competition for a number of domestic industries.

A curious feature of this fear of industrial shrinkage is that it exactly mirrors the nineteenth-century panic about agricultural decline. Between 1816 and 1914, agriculture's share of Britain's gross national product fell from 20 per cent to less than 7 per cent. The fear was that shrinking agriculture would enfeeble the nation and leave it vulnerable to the military might of the other Great Powers. Similar worries were felt perhaps even more acutely in France, where Talleyrand, the great (and slippery) French diplomat, echoed an age-old concern about moneymaking when he remarked that 'industry weakens national morality. France must necessarily be agricultural.'[60] Yet, in practice, what was happening in the eighteenth and nineteenth centuries was that increases in the efficiency of agriculture were releasing people from the land to move to the cities, where the industrial revolution was making better-paid jobs available, albeit in often squalid and dangerous conditions. This rural exodus has characterised most major industrialisations and is taking place today most conspicuously in China, with exactly the same social problems but on a scale unimaginably greater than that experienced by Europeans or Americans in the nineteenth century.

Note, in passing, the equally curious way in which contemporary literature mirrored the economic reality of rural decline and the rise of industry. With hindsight, the agricultural debate looks like an after-echo, in the economic sphere, of the waning of the protracted poetic nostalgia for rural life, which goes back to Virgil's *Eclogues* and beyond. The pastoral, the poetic form that idealises the life of shepherds and shepherdesses, was going into decline in Europe, by a neat coincidence, just as the industrial revolution was becoming, in the mid-nineteenth century, a pervasive reality.[61] Perhaps industrialisation bears some indirect responsibility for the weakening grip on the poetic imagination, at least temporarily, of seasonal change and the lives of animals and plants.[62] Such things were of little interest to the likes of Charles Baudelaire, the iconic poet of modernity who idealised the urban dandy. Meantime, some Victorian writers in England filled the place vacated by nymphs and shepherds with an idealised vision of the industrial process, somewhat implausibly turning Manchester, the world's first great manufacturing city, into a new Arcadia, peopled by toiling workers in hobnail boots. Here, for example, is Thomas Carlyle waxing lyrical about the same mills that William Blake found satanic:

> Hast thou heard, with sound ears, the awakening of a Manchester, on Monday morning, at half-past five by the clock; the rushing-off of its thousand mills, like the boom of an Atlantic tide, then-thousand times ten-thousand spools and spindles all set humming there, – it is perhaps if thou knew it well, sublime as a Niagara, or more so.[63]

When you consider what Engels was writing about the dismal plight of the urban poor in Manchester and Dickens was portraying in novels such as *Hard Times* at around the same period, this glorification of industry in Carlyle's pamphlet 'Chartism' spectacularly misses the human dimension of the story. Alexis de Tocqueville, as acute an observer of Anglo-Saxon mores in the nineteenth century as Voltaire was in the eighteenth, was more realistic if still positive with qualifications on his visit to Manchester:

> A sort of black smoke covers the city. The sun seen through it is a disc without rays. Under this half daylight 300,000 human beings are ceaselessly at work. A thousand noises disturb this damp, dark labyrinth, but they are not at all

the ordinary sounds one hears in great cities. The footsteps of a *busy* crowd, the crunching of wheels of machinery, the shriek of steam from boilers, the regular beat of the looms, the heavy rumble of carts, these are the noises from which you can never escape in the sombre half-light of these streets. You will never hear the clatter of hoofs as the rich man drives back home or out on expeditions of pleasure. Never the gay shouts of people amusing themselves, or music heralding a holiday.

You will never see smart folk strolling at leisure in the streets, or going out on innocent pleasure parties in the surrounding country. Crowds are even hurrying this way and that in the Manchester streets, but their footsteps are brisk, their looks preoccupied, and their appearance sombre and harsh. Day and night the street echoes with street noises … From this foul drain the greatest stream of human industry flows out to fertilise the whole world. From this filthy sewer pure gold flows. Here humanity attains its most complete development and its most brutish; here civilisation works its miracles, and civilised man is turned back almost into a savage.[64]

Yet, he also understood – as did Richard Wagner in *The Ring of the Nibelung* – the relationship between manufacturing prowess and military might. While Richard Cobden and the Manchester School of free traders argued idealistically that capitalist industry could be a great material and moral force for peace in a world free of trade barriers (which will be explored further in Chapter Six), harder-headed politicians saw things differently. It was precisely the recognition of this relationship between industry and defence requirements, for example, that prompted the Japanese to put feudal isolation behind them through the Meiji restoration of 1868, having been humbled in 1853 by the American 'black ships' of Commodore Perry. The Japanese elite saw that rapid industrialisation offered the only escape from the threat of colonisation, after this crude naval attempt by the Americans to open up Japan to foreign trade.

In a variation on the same theme, state revenue from manufacturing could also be put to use in financing wars. In mid-nineteenth-century Prussia, cash from substantial state-owned enterprises enabled Bismarck to escape accountability to a democratic parliament that he despised. In our own time, China's decision under Deng Xiaoping to embrace a form of market capitalism from 1978 was driven as much or more by the desire to reassert China's power and influence in the world – and no doubt by the Communist rulers' urge to hang on to office – as by the wish to raise Chinese living standards.

This connection between manufacturing capability and power seems to me to provide a genuine argument for concern about a decline in the manufacturing base, much as it does on the issues of energy and food security. To be dependent on other countries' manufacturers for the nation's defence is a potential vulnerability even if, in the case of the UK, there are no obvious immediate external threats to the country's security. But when it comes to economic as opposed to military arguments, things become more complex. For a start, the economic consequence of the decline of manufacturing in Britain has not been obviously damaging, any more than the earlier decline in agriculture was. Since the industrial revolution, the underlying trend growth rate of the British economy has remained broadly the same at around 2 per cent, despite all the jeremiads. And despite the worries of the late Victorians and early Edwardians about both agricultural and manufacturing decline, Britain did not lose the First World War. The contrast between apparent decline and persistently respectable economic growth rates was already puzzling the social reformer Beatrice Webb in the 1920s, when she wrote in her diary:

> What troubles me is the gross discrepancy between the alarmist views ... about the industrial decadence of Great Britain ... [and] the absence of all *signs* of extreme poverty among the people at large. Compared with the '80s, even the early years of the twentieth century, there is no outward manifestation of extreme destitution: no beggars, few vagrants, no great and spontaneous demonstration of the unemployed, no 'bitter outcries' or sensational description of the sweaters' dens and poverty-stricken homes...[65]

As for Adam Smith's strictures on services and the worry that they make little contribution to increased productivity or the balance of payments, his point remains partly valid in that you can export a hairdryer but not a haircut. But there are also services such as transport that add value even if the service vanishes once performed. Moreover, the world has changed a great deal since the eighteenth century. Some of the most impressive gains in productivity have been achieved by retailers such as Wal-Mart in the US, Metro in Germany and Tesco in the UK.

Sectors such as financial services, communications and business services are not only capable of strong productivity growth;

they are also increasingly traded across national boundaries. In fact, a high service content in trade is nowadays regarded as a sign of economic advancement, as is a large contribution to the balance of payments from royalties and licence fees from various kinds of intellectual property, including music and the arts. Knowledge has become as important an advantage in creating wealth as capital or labour. And in modern industries such as pharmaceuticals, most of the value is created by scientists, not by the actual manufacturing activity that turns out the pills and potions. In the advanced sectors of the economy, such as drug making and information technology, the term capitalism is scarcely appropriate unless you choose to interpret it as a reference to human capital.

Moreover, the distinction between manufacturing and services in the information age is becoming harder to draw. Although a company like IBM still makes computer hardware, its core business consists of selling software solutions. Manufacturing companies like General Electric, Siemens or Rolls-Royce derive much of their profit from servicing the original equipment they sell. And countless manufacturing companies have outsourced functions such as accounting, transport, catering and cleaning to companies that are classed for statistical purposes as service companies. The decline in manufacturing may thus have been exaggerated by the increase in outsourcing.

The reality is that wealth in a modern capitalist economy comes from producing whatever it is that people want to consume. So if they want to consume more and more services, the service sector inevitably becomes a greater source of wealth than manufacturing. Indeed, as countries grow richer, people spend more on labour-intensive services like health care, leisure and education. In the UK, health care, for example, now accounts for a greater proportion of the workforce than manufacturing. And in advanced economies such as the US or UK, it is striking that most of the growth in employment in recent years has been in the non-tradable sector of the economy. It is worth recording, too, that even in the dying days of the old Soviet Union, attitudes to service industries started to change. This was reflected in the literary tradition of the production novel to which I referred earlier. In *The Hotel Manager*, for example, a popular 1970s novella by Irina Grekova, a pen name for the Soviet mathematician and novelist Elena Venttsel, the heroine looks for work at a hotel on the Black Sea after the death of an overbearing husband. Having confronted hostility from all around, she ends up running the hotel and finding true love at a mature age. So a literary genre that had hitherto set out to glorify manufacturing simultaneously embraced feminism and trumpeted the merits of a leading service industry.

More fundamentally, the decline in the manufacturing industry's share of employment and output reflects economic progress in the shape of rapid productivity growth – an increase in the output generated by each individual worker. This is important for reasons outlined by the economist Paul Krugman: 'Productivity isn't everything, but in the long run it is almost everything. A country's ability to improve its standard of living over time depends almost entirely on its ability to raise its output per worker.'[66]

High productivity in manufacturing means that industry may have little or no need for more labour, while the volume of goods produced actually increases even when industry's share of the economy's output is falling. In other words, manufacturing decline can be a sign of higher living standards and quality of life. And because productivity still increases faster in industry than in services, output can go on rising even if industry is shrinking as a percentage of the overall economy, while using decreasing human resources.

The practical implications have been well described by the British journalist Peter Marsh in a book on what he calls the new manufacturing revolution. He cites the case of a British company, R. A. Chilton, based in Cheshire, that has a global near monopoly on a coatings technology that is essential to the workings of air-bearing spindles, devices that allow high-speed drills to operate reliably when punching tiny holes in items of electronic equipment. Without it, companies world-wide making everything from smartphones to oven controls would have to rethink their production methods. Yet despite its strong position, dealing with hundreds of companies in a global market, it employs all of seven people. Nor, inciden-tally, is the reduced capacity of manufacturing to generate jobs purely an advanced-country characteristic. Even in China, where the manufacturing sector contributes 33 per cent of GDP, manufacturing employment is now below its level in the late 1990s.

Perhaps the biggest impetus behind the decline of manufac-turing in the advanced economies is globalisation. In effect, developed countries have been outsourcing their manufactur-ing to China and other emerging markets that are now going through the rapid urbanisation and industrialisation that characterises the early stages of capitalist development, in which very low labour costs create comparative advantage. This is, then, part of a continuing process of international specialisation. If there is a backlash against this transfer of manufacturing activity to the developing countries, it is chiefly because 'structural adjustment', as the economists call it, involves wrenching change. Those whose jobs are lost in old industries may lack the skills or the willingness to migrate to take up jobs in new industries elsewhere, or be reluctant to take on lower-skill jobs than they have previously done. In short, it is not much fun being structurally adjusted. Martin van Buren, who succeeded Andrew Jackson as President of the United States in 1836, highlighted the problem perfectly in a letter he wrote to Jackson while still Governor of New York:

> If canal boats are supplanted by 'railroads', serious unemployment will result. Captains, cooks, drivers, hostlers, repairmen and lock tenders will be left without means of livelihood, not to mention the numerous farmers now employed in growing hay for horses. Boat builders would suffer and tow-line, whip and harness makers would be left destitute ... As you may well know, Mr President, 'railroad' carriages are pulled at the enormous speed of fifteen miles per hour ... by 'engines' which roar and snort their way throughout the countryside, setting fire to the crops, scaring the livestock, and frightening women and children. The Almighty certainly never intended that people should travel at such breakneck speeds.[67]

Throughout history, such creative destruction, in the celebrated phrase of the economist Joseph Schumpeter, has increased economic growth and, ultimately, human welfare, but the transitional human cost as the structure of the economy changes is invariably high. There are also social costs. Many of the newer industries that are replacing manufacturing operate, in salary terms, on a 'winner takes all' basis, so that a lucky few make vast fortunes. This contributes to inequality both inside companies and in society at large, leading to the kinds of discontent and alienation expressed by the Occupy movement across America in 2011 and 2012, along with similar protests around the world.

It is possible to put a case that manufacturing can shrink too far if international specialisation causes economies to suffer from a lack of diversity. That was the case with Britain, which was seriously under-diversified when the credit crunch struck in 2007. Back then, it derived more than 9 per cent of GDP from financial services. Yet it is also possible to suffer from a lack of diversification by dint of excessive exposure to manufacturing, as was the case with Germany at the same time. The Germans' over-reliance on exports to drive economic growth meant that the collapse in world trade after the bankruptcy of Lehman Brothers in 2008 resulted in a greater percentage loss of output than in the US, which was the epicentre of the financial crisis.

Despite these caveats, the conclusion has to be that the decline in manufacturing in so many Western countries is not a catastrophe. We are going through a change in the economic balance from manufacturing to services that precisely mirrors the change from agriculture to manufacturing in the eighteenth and nineteenth centuries. If there is a worry, apart from the economic and social strains of structural adjustment, it is whether the service sector can fill the gap in terms of employment and what the quality of those service jobs will be. No one can be absolutely certain of the outcome on either score, but it has always been dangerous, in forecasting, to underestimate human ingenuity.

In reality, there is nothing innately virtuous about making things. To worry about the decline of manufacturing is to fall into the trap of what the British economist Roger Bootle calls 'thingism', or the notion that wealth is exclusively about the production of tangible things rather than intangible services. But nor is there any justification in the attitude of many modern bankers, hedge fund managers and traders who think that manufacturing is for wimps – although this view has become notably less prevalent since the financial crisis. Manufacturing, as I have explained, has the extraordinary characteristic of being able to use decreasing human resources in producing ever increasing output. That is no mean trick and is an important part of the process whereby millions across the world have increasingly enjoyed the benefit of fast-rising living standards.

One of the more poignant episodes in the afterlife of Lehman Brothers was the auctioning at Christie's in 2010 of memorabilia from the defunct investment bank's London office. These included a fine edition of Gibbons's *The History of the Decline and Fall of the Roman Empire*, which fetched £2,375. Among other things, this event raised the question of whether the rise of finance before the Lehman collapse should have been a greater cause for concern than the decline of manufacturing.

Some economic historians argue that an oversize financial sector is an indication of national decline. Charles Kindleberger, for example, believed in a life cycle, whereby the economic vitality of a nation ultimately runs its course. He and others identified as symptoms of decline such things as: an obsession with consumption at the expense of investment; low savings; resistance to taxation; inequality; corruption; mounting debt; financial services becoming more dominant than industry; and a tendency towards financial manipulation. And certainly there is something counter-intuitive about a financial sector that grows much faster than the underlying economy, because the economic and social function of finance is, after all, to serve the rest of the economy. It might thus be expected to grow in line with gross domestic product.

This has not been the case in the US, where finance as a per-centage of GDP grew from 1.5 per cent in the mid-nineteenth century to 8.3 per cent in 2006 before the financial crisis. What is striking about this progression is that there have been two conspicuous spikes in the level of financial activity and profitability. One was in the Roaring Twenties, which led to a peak contribution by finance to the wider economy of nearly 6 per cent of GDP after the 1929 crash. The other was in the years before the recent credit crunch and subsequent collapse of Lehman Brothers. Even more impressive growth can be seen in the UK, where, over 160 years, financial services outstripped growth in the economy as a whole by 2 percentage points a year, accounting for no less than 9.4 per cent of GDP in 2006. In a less heavily regulated environment, UK bank balance sheets grew much faster than those in the US. Bank assets went from 50 per cent of GDP in the early 1970s to a phenomenal 500 per cent of GDP at the peak of the credit bubble. In both countries, national statistics point to a productivity miracle in the years before the credit crunch.[68]

There are some respectable reasons for the ascendancy of finance during the two spikes in financial activity. In the 1920s, bankers were rising to the challenge of financing the second industrial revolution, in which the emergence of the electricity, auto and pharmaceutical industries made huge demands on capital. It is also true that as countries grow richer, the demand for financial services increases disproportionately. More people have bank accounts and save for pensions, to give two obvious reasons. And from the 1980s, when growth in financial services accelerated onto a markedly higher plain than ever before, the financial system was developing a new role. After the break-up of the post-war fixed exchange rate system and the liberalisation of financial services that began in the 1970s, governments and central banks ceased to protect industry and commerce from the volatility of currency and financial markets. As the task was privatised by default, the whizz-kids of the Chicago, New York and London markets promptly developed derivative instruments such as interest rate and currency swaps, futures and options designed to allow financial institutions and corporations to insure against risk. According to the Bank for International Settlements, the central bankers' bank in Basel, the total market value in June 2013 of derivatives traded over the counter – that is, traded bilaterally between financial institutions, corporations and governments, rather than on formal exchanges – topped $20 trillion.[69]

Yet there are also less savoury reasons for the size of the two historic spikes in financial activity. In both cases there was a high degree of innovation, including new financial instruments of questionable social utility. The economist J. K. Galbraith has rightly pointed out that every new financial instrument 'is, without exception, a small variation on an established design, one that owes its distinctive character to the ... brevity of financial memory'. The world of finance, he added, 'hails the invention of the wheel over and over again, often in a slightly more unstable version'.

Another feature highlighted by Galbraith is the prevalence of leverage – that is, a build-up of borrowing: 'All financial innovation involves, in one form or another, the creation of debt secured in greater or lesser adequacy by real assets ... All crises have involved debt that, in one fashion or another, has become dangerously out of scale in relation to the underlying means of payment.'[70]

In other words, bank profits in the 1920s and 2000s were going up, as we saw in Chapter Three, because banks were taking bigger risks. Moreover, the figures pointing to a productivity miracle were completely misleading. In a bubble, when market prices do not properly reflect the risk inherent in financial products, a flaw in the national statisticians' methodology means that the financial sector's contribution to the economy is systematically overestimated. Modern accounting standards also inflate bank profits in an upswing and shrink them disproportionately in a downswing, while failing to reflect adequately the risks that are being run – especially in the more complex financial products where the banks are writing the equivalent of catastrophe insurance.

As Andrew Haldane and his colleagues at the Bank of England have convincingly demonstrated, the productivity miracle is really a mirage. The great financial bubble that started to deflate in 2007 involved a dramatic misallocation of economic resources, as highly qualified people were rewarded with huge bonuses for trading in products of increasing complexity and questionable social utility. And where a country plays host to banks that are disproportionately large in relation to gross domestic product, such activity can wreck the economy, as Iceland, Ireland and Cyprus know to their cost.

Recent research by Stephen Cecchetti and fellow economists at the Bank for International Settlements has also cast doubt on the notion that financial development is invariably good for economic growth because it allocates scarce resources to their most efficient uses. This work, covering sixteen OECD countries from 1980 to 2009, shows that there is a point where both financial development and the financial system's size, measured by employment and output, turn from good to bad. It also finds that growing financial employment hurts average productivity growth in the wider economy. According to Mr Cecchetti:

> Financial development is not costless. The expansion of finance consumes scarce resources that could be used elsewhere. And finance's large rewards attract the best and the brightest. When I was a student, my classmates dreamed of curing cancer, unifying field theory or flying to Mars. Those in today's cohort want to become hedge fund managers. Given finance's booms and busts, is this the most efficient allocation for such scarce resource? I doubt it ... beyond a certain point, financial development is bad for an economy. Instead of supplying the oxygen that the real economy needs for healthy growth, it sucks the air out of the system and starts to slowly suffocate it. Households and firms end up with too much debt. And valuable resources are wasted.[71]

The theory that a bias towards finance at the expense of industry is a sign of national decadence is less susceptible of easy proof. Yet it remains remarkable that the two great periods of financial dominance in the past 100 years seemed to breed huge inequalities of income and wealth, huge mountains of debt and great social tension, as well as precipitating crises that unleashed the Great Depression and the Great Recession. There are issues here about what is cause and what is effect. But, for me, at least one or two messages are pretty clear. When finance becomes increasingly remote from servicing industry and commerce, it is time to watch out. And when it becomes disproportionately large in relation to the economy, it needs to be cut down to size.

CHAPTER FIVE

SOPHISTERS, ECONOMISTS AND CALCULATORS

A striking feature of the Anglo-American approach to capitalism in the two and a half decades before the great financial crisis was a belief in what Ronald Reagan called 'the magic of the marketplace'. This, the US President declared in a radio address in 1984, would create opportunities for growth and progress, free from the deadweight of government interference. His faith in the unfettered market's ability to deliver the economic and social goods was underpinned by the best efforts of economists at the University of Chicago. These high priests of capitalism have had a potent influence on the behaviour of the financial community. Among the chief strands of their work has been the so-called efficient markets hypothesis, pioneered by Eugene Fama in the 1960s and 1970s. There are differing versions of the thesis, but the most potent of them holds that financial assets are always correctly priced because competition between profit-seeking market participants ensures that any divergence between price and value will be quickly eliminated. Prices in financial markets are said to be an accurate reflection of all available information. In effect, the efficient markets hypothesis asserts that the level of the stock market represents a good forecast of the present value of the future earnings of all the companies quoted there. Implicit in the theory is the notion that capital markets are self-correcting.

Given the twitchy behaviour of stock markets, this seems counter-intuitive. It also sits oddly with the extreme booms and busts that take place in the property market, which are so often the cause of financial crises. The recurring collective memory loss exhibited by bankers in property lending does not look like the result of measured deliberations by *homo economicus*. And how can the efficient markets hypothesis be reconciled with great financial aberrations such as the South Sea Bubble, of which Alexander Pope wrote:

> *At length Corruption, like a gen'ral flood,*
> *(So long by watchful Ministers withstood)*
> *Shall deluge all; and Av'rice creeping on,*
> *Spread like a low-born mist, and blot the Sun;*
> *Statesman and Patriot ply alike the stocks,*
> *Peeress and Butler share alike the Box,*
> *And Judges job, and Bishops bite the town,*
> *And mighty Dukes pack cards for half a crown.*
> *See Britain sunk in lucre's sordid charms...*
> *'All this is madness,' cries a sober sage:*
> *But who, my friend, has reason in his rage?*
> *The ruling Passion, be it what it will,*
> *The ruling Passion conquers Reason still.*[72]

Throughout history there have been periods where asset prices have moved far out of line with economic fundamentals, driven by what Jonathan Swift, in his ballad *The Bubble*, called 'the madness of crowds'. These episodes, ranging from the Dutch tulip mania of the seventeenth century to the Mississippi Bubble in eighteenth-century France, were brilliantly chronicled in *Memoirs of Extraordinary Popular Delusions* by the nineteenth-century journalist Charles Mackay, of which more in a moment.[73]

If this sounds like a narrow academic debate, it is not. For much of the instability that currently afflicts the world economy is a direct reflection of an aberrant turn in the direction taken by academic economics over the past sixty years or so. Consider, first, the huge influence that the efficient markets hypothesis has had over the thinking of central bankers, who have increasingly been recruited from the ranks of academics rather than market practitioners. Before the 1980s, central bankers were deeply concerned about the need to maintain financial stability. William McChesney Martin, chairman of the Federal Reserve from 1951 to 1970, famously summed up this concern when he said that the job of the Fed was 'to take away the punchbowl just as the party gets going' – that is, to tighten policy by, for example, raising interest rates or imposing curbs on bank lending. This concern for financial stability fell victim to academic fashion in the 1980s and 1990s when the rise of professional economists in the central banking fraternity increasingly led to the adoption of inflation targeting as the single objective of monetary policy. The new conventional wisdom held that if the level of consumer or product prices was kept stable, financial crises were unlikely to occur and that intervention to prevent bubbles was unnecessary. Who were central bankers anyway to second-guess efficient markets? As Alan Greenspan, a later chairman of the Fed, remarked to the

US Congress as the dot.com bubble of the late 1990s neared its peak: 'Bubbles generally are perceptible only after the fact. To spot a bubble in advance requires a judgement that hundreds of thousands of informed investors have it all wrong. Betting against markets is usually precarious at best.'[74]

What is remarkable about this statement is that back in 1994, Greenspan and the Federal Reserve had identified an incipient bubble in asset prices which they successfully pricked by raising interest rates. And in 1995 he clearly identified that the technology boom was turning into a bubble, telling the Fed's main policymaking body, the Federal Open Market Committee, in May of that year, 'The way I put it is that I am more nervous about the asset price bubble than I am about product prices.' But he also worried that if the Fed pricked the bubble, it could 'blow the economy out of the water'. At the September 1996 FOMC meeting, he said: 'I recognise that there is a stock market bubble problem at this point ... We do have the possibility of raising major concerns by increasing margin requirements. I guarantee that if you want to get rid of the bubble, whatever it is, that will do it.'

Later that year he made a speech in which he famously referred to 'irrational exuberance' in the stock market. Yet from then on he spent much time justifying the ever increasing level of the market by reference to a productivity miracle. He did this in the face of considerable scepticism on the part of senior Fed staff members. When the market was at its wildest, Michael Prell, a Fed economist, told the FOMC that initial public offerings of dot.com stocks were redolent of the atmosphere in the South Sea Bubble. Yet the chairman had little time for such input. And those members of the FOMC who worried about the bubble were sidelined by Greenspan in the committee's deliberations. He exerted rigid control throughout his tenure.[75]

As the dot.com saga spiralled out of hand, Greenspan's view, which became highly influential, was that since it was impossible for central banks to identify and prick bubbles, all they could do was to clean up after the event. Given the enormity of the financial crisis that followed the credit and housing bubbles of the first decade of the new century, the collapse of Lehman Brothers in 2008 and the gigantic scale of the resulting mess in terms of lost employment and output, the cost of this approach appears to have been astonishingly high. While he has expressed shock and told the US Congress he has come to doubt the models of rational behaviour on which he relied, Greenspan has yet to offer fulsome apologies for the flaws in Fed policy. But he has offered revisionism. In an extraordinary U-turn in a recent interview in the *Harvard Business Review*, he declared: 'You can spot a bubble. They're obvious in every respect.' But he added that it was impossible to quash a bubble in a democratic society because it would lead to the Fed's independence being curtailed.[76] As for efficient market theorists such as Eugene Fama, they, too, remain unrepentant. How do they justify themselves?

Consider this, first, from the perspective of financial history. In an academic paper, the economist Peter Garber has examined three great bubbles in detail: the Dutch tulip mania, in which contract prices for bulbs soared to astronomical heights and then collapsed; the Mississippi Bubble in France, a scheme engineered by the Scottish adventurer John Law which enjoyed a monopoly over French colonial trade and ended in a speculative frenzy fuelled by the issue of paper money; and the South Sea

Bubble in England, where speculation hinged on the South Sea Company's modest trading rights in the West Indies and South America, together with its purchase of the national debt in exchange for an annual payment from the Exchequer.[77]

On the seventeenth-century tulip euphoria, Garber argues that Charles Mackay failed to discuss what the fundamental price of tulips should have been, pointing out that there is a standard pricing pattern for new varieties of flowers that holds even today. When a particularly prized variety is developed, its original bulb sells for a high price. As the bulbs accumulate, the variety's price falls rapidly. After less than thirty years, bulbs sell at their reproduction cost. Their 'bubble' valuations, claims Garber, were therefore perfectly rational, and the collapse of prices merely reflected the fact that once they were bred, they became easy to propagate. So increased supply was responsible for the decline in prices.

As for the two great eighteenth-century bubbles, Garber argues that they were far from an irrational aberration because the rise in asset prices was based on the perception that these schemes would produce large returns. Buyers of the shares did not know until after the event that the economics of the schemes were flawed. Alternatively, buyers may have recognised the flaws but observed repeated waves of share buying at ever increasing prices and sought to profit by jumping on the bandwagon. As for the frenzied atmosphere surrounding all this speculative activity, as described by Mackay, Garber remarks that it was little different from the behaviour of traders in the pit of a Chicago derivatives exchange today.

Some of these criticisms of Charles Mackay are well made and Garber's paper makes interesting reading. Yet, while the pattern of pricing of bulbs he describes clearly makes sense, he does not satisfactorily explain away why prices of ordinary garden-variety tulips went through the roof and then through the floor. As for the eighteenth-century booms and busts, he argues that they could not be considered bubbles if people perceived an increased probability of large returns, whether from good economic news, a novel theory about increased payoffs or fraud by insiders who peddled a persuasive story about a forthcoming bonanza. Yet this is linguistic sleight of hand: it defines a bubble in such a way as to rule out any possibility of bubbles because everyone who participates in a speculative boom is inevitably fired by greed and optimism about the prospect for profits. It does not properly address the conventional understanding of bubbles, which is that they arise when asset prices rise out of line with underlying economic fundamentals.

Research by the British economist Richard Dale has shown that many contemporary observers did see that the South Sea Company, whose main business was the very simple one of owning the equivalent of annuities, was seriously overvalued.[78] The most notable was a Member of Parliament, Archibald Hutcheson, who used well-established valuation techniques, including net present value calculations and price-earnings ratios, to demonstrate that absolute valuations of the company had departed from accepted valuation criteria to an extreme degree that amounted to irrationality. He foresaw the crash:

> If the truth be, as I verily believe it is, that there is no real foundation for the present, much less for the further expected, high price of South Sea stock; and that the frenzy

which now reigns, can be of no long continuance in so cool
a climate; and amongst a people hitherto so justly famed for
wisdom and prudence; I say, if this be the case, is it not the
duty of the British Senate, to take all necessary precautions,
to prevent the ruin of many thousands of families...[79]

As it happened, numerous parliamentarians had been bribed
with equity in the company by the directors and had no wish
to call a halt to market euphoria.

Dale also shows that the new shares issued by the South
Sea Company late in the boom were absurdly overvalued in
relation to the existing stock and also in relation to down payments on other new shares. The fact is that madness was in
the air, combined with a powerful admixture of opportunism
and fraud. This is clear from Charles Mackay's most extreme
bubble company phenomenon, maybe apocryphal – 'the most
absurd and preposterous of all, and which shewed, more completely than any other, the utter madness of the people, was
one started by an unknown adventurer, entitled, "A company
for carrying on an undertaking of great advantage, but nobody
to know what it is".' The point is underlined by the brilliant
quote from Daniel Defoe with which Charles Mackay begins
his book:

> *Some in clandestine companies combine;*
> *Erect new stocks to trade beyond the line;*
> *With air and empty names beguile the town,*
> *And raise new credits first, then cry 'em down;*
> *Divide the empty nothing into shares,*
> *And set the crowd together by the ears.*[80]

Missing from the work of efficient market theorists are the insights of behavioural finance, which brings the disciplines of psychology and sociology to the analysis of behaviour in financial markets. In discussing bubbles, economists such as Robert Shiller and Richard Thaler posit a feedback theory. When prices rise fast, the profits made by investors attract public attention, promoting word-of-mouth enthusiasm and encouraging expectations of further price rises. Commentators fuel the boom with rationalisations such as the idea that the economy has reached a new era of permanently higher returns. If the feedback is not interrupted, the result is a bubble. I find Shiller's definition of a speculative bubble persuasive: 'a situation in which news of price increases spurs investor enthusiasm, which spreads by psychological contagion from person to person, in the process amplifying stories that might justify the price increase'. This attracts 'a larger and larger class of investors who, despite doubts about the real value of the investment, are drawn to it partly through envy of others' successes and partly through a gambler's excitement'.[81]

Implicit in this definition, he adds, is a suggestion as to why it is so difficult for smart money to profit by betting against bubbles: the psychological contagion promotes a mindset that justifies the price increases, so that participation in the bubble might be called *almost* rational. This is intended to address the efficient market theorists' argument that a bubble is an impossibility because market participants would detect any valuation anomaly and immediately bet against it, bringing prices back to 'efficient' levels. Shiller has also produced detailed statistical work on stock prices and dividends going back to 1871, in which he finds that the volatility of prices relative to underlying corporate performance is far more than can be explained by efficient market theory.[82]

Charles Mackay is interestingly in tune with these insights of behavioural finance, even if he is prone to exaggerate. Writing of the tulip mania, he said:

> Many individuals grew suddenly rich. A golden bait hung temptingly out before the people, and one after the other, they rushed to the tulip-marts, like flies around a honey pot. Everyone imagined that the passion for tulips would last for ever, and that the wealthy from every part of the world would send to Holland, and pay whatever prices were asked for them. The riches of Europe would be concentrated on the shores of the Zuyder Zee, and poverty banished from the favoured clime of Holland. Nobles, citizens, farmers, mechanics, seamen, footmen, maid-servants, even chimney-sweeps and old clotheswomen, dabbled in tulips. People of all grades converted their property into cash, and invested it in flowers. Houses and lands were offered for sale at ruinously low prices, or assigned in payment of bargains made at the tulip-mart … At last, however, the more prudent began to see that this folly could not last for ever. Rich people no longer bought the flowers to keep them in their gardens, but to sell them again at cent per cent profit. It was seen that somebody must lose fearfully in the end. As this conviction spread, prices fell, and never rose again.

Note the typical bubble phenomenon that people stopped buying for long-term economic reasons and merely bought to sell on at a short-term profit. This feedback phenomenon, which has been better understood by novelists and poets than many Chicago economists, was also at work in the South Sea Bubble, as we saw in my initial quotation from Alexander Pope. Pope, incidentally, was himself one of those irresistibly charmed by the South Sea Bubble. So, too, was the greatest genius of the day, Isaac Newton. As Master of the Royal Mint and the man who put England onto the gold standard when he was not busy discovering the physical laws of the universe, he was hardly a novice in finance. Having made an initial 100 per cent profit of £7,000 on his shares in the South Sea Company, he was unlucky enough to go back into the market close to the top and lost £20,000, equivalent to £2.5 million in today's money. A rueful Newton clearly grasped the logic of behavioural finance when he famously remarked: 'I can calculate the motions of the heavenly bodies, but not the madness of people.'

Part of the psychology, as Robert Shiller points out, is that news of the profits of others leads people to a sense of futility in doing their relatively unrewarding day-to-day work and to a growing sense of envy. For many, including Pope, the stock market also appeared to hold the answer to their immediate financial problems. Dickens understood all this well. At the start of *Nicholas Nickleby*, which was written with the financial mania of 1825–26 in mind, he expertly catches the feel of how ordinary people can be swept along by the speculative tide:

As for Nicholas, he lived a single man on the patrimonial estate until he grew tired of living alone, and then he took to wife the daughter of a neighbouring gentleman with a dower of one thousand pounds. This good lady bore him two children, a son and a daughter, and when the son was about

nineteen, and the daughter fourteen, as near as we can guess
– impartial records of young ladies' ages being, before the
passing of the new act, nowhere preserved in the registries of
this country – Mr Nickleby looked about him for the means
of repairing his capital, now sadly reduced by this increase in
his family and the expenses of their education.

'Speculate with it,' said Mrs Nickleby.

'Speculate, my dear?' said Mr Nickleby, as though in doubt.

'Why not?' asked Mrs Nickleby.

'Because, my dear, if we *should* lose it,' rejoined Mr Nickleby, who was a slow and time-taking speaker, 'if we *should*
lose it, we should no longer be able to live, my dear.'

'Fiddle,' said Mrs Nickleby.

'I am not altogether sure of that, my dear,' said Mr
Nickleby.

'There's Nicholas, pursued the lady, 'quite a young man –
it's time he was in the way of doing something for himself; and
Kate too, poor girl, without a penny in the world. Think of
your brother; would he be what he is, if he hadn't speculated?

'That's true, replied Mr Nickleby. 'Very good, my dear.
Yes. I *will* speculate, my dear.

Speculation is a round game; the players see little or nothing of their cards at first starting; gains *may* be great – and
so may losses. The run of luck went against Mr Nickleby; a
mania prevailed, a bubble burst, four stockbrokers took villa
residences at Florence, four hundred nobodies were ruined,
and among them Mr Nickleby.

Coming from a habitually discursive author, that passage
reveals a concision and wit that would have done credit to

Voltaire, as well as showing a firm grasp of bubble psychology. Among other things, the story illustrates the implicit assumption made by so many who are caught up in speculative bubbles – to wit, that speculation carries an entitlement to profit regardless of risk, while losses are simply unthinkable.

Today, markets are dominated by professional fund managers. How can we explain the continuing existence of bubbles when professionals rather than inexpert individual savers drive the level of the market? In fact, for prices to be out of line with fundamentals does not require people to be irrational. And there has been a tendency in recent decades for bubbles to become more rational than in earlier periods. Underlying the trend is the fact that there are only two strategies for investing. One is fundamental investing, where decisions are based on expected future earnings and dividends. The other is momentum investing, which boils down to trend following – jumping on bandwagons – whereby the investor considers only short-run price changes and disregards value.

Momentum investing has come to dominate stock markets and, indeed, currency, derivatives and other markets. According to the finance theoreticians in Chicago, trend following, or herding, ought not to happen, because profit-seeking investors would immediately exploit the anomalies in the market's valuation of companies that the bandwagon approach to investing would throw up. Yet it does happen. One reason is that share prices are not set by private investors – the 'representative household', in the economic jargon – but by fund managers to whom savers and pension fund trustees have delegated authority for managing their money. These fund managers, the agents, may have a very different agenda to that of savers and trustees, the principals. They also have more and better information about companies and markets. So there is, as the economists put it, both a principal–agent problem and an information asymmetry problem. These lead to conflicts of interest.

The technology bubble in the second half of the 1990s provides a good example of how the conflict works. Dot.com stocks rose initially on the basis of a conviction that technology had fundamentally changed the way the economy worked, so that expectations of future profits spiralled while conventional methods of company valuation were abandoned. One consequence of this was that funds invested in unglamorous 'value' sectors underperformed the market. It is difficult in these circumstances for savers and pension fund trustees to know whether the value manager is incompetent or likely to be proved right in the long run. In practice, as underperformance in the dot.com era persisted, investors lost confidence in the ability of fund managers who worked on the basis of economic fundamentals. They handed over the money to apparently more successful growth managers. This switch then propelled technology stocks even higher. A similar boost came from value managers who felt obliged to switch from value to growth to avoid being fired by pension fund trustees. Those value managers who stuck to their guns often paid a high price, a conspicuous example being Tony Dye, a fund manager at the big Swiss bank UBS, who saw early on that the dot.com phenomenon was a bubble, and avoided technology stocks. As the market continued to rise, and his underperformance appeared persistent, a growing number of clients abandoned him. UBS, miffed at the apparent threat to the profits of their fund management business, fired him just as the bubble was about to burst. Much the same fate befell Jeffrey Vinik, the star manager of the Fidelity Magellan fund in the US. He dramatically reduced the fund's holding of technology stocks in 1996, which was at least four years too early to assure his job security. Seeing the writing on the wall as the Magellan fund consistently underperformed, he jumped before he was pushed.

What that tells us, among other things, is that rational profit seeking by agents and the investors who appoint them leads to mispricing in the stock market and to volatility. Fund managers inevitably try to minimise the risk to their business and career by staying close to the competition, which in practice means hugging a benchmark based on a stock market index. The need to minimise risk in this way impels the fund manager towards momentum investing. This interpretation of market activity has been developed into a new economic model of financial behaviour by Paul Woolley and Dimitri Vayanos at the London School of Economics' Centre for the Study of Capital Market Dysfunctionality – a title that must cause apoplexy among market fundamentalists at Chicago University.[83] They argue that once momentum becomes embedded in markets, agents then logically respond by adopting strategies that are likely to reinforce trends and contribute to bubbles. The model does not invalidate behavioural finance, but provides a powerful complement. And it poses a serious challenge to the efficient markets hypothesis.

Another reason prices can diverge from fundamentals for a considerable period is that arbitrage, whereby investors simultaneously buy and sell identical or similar financial instruments which are temporarily mis-priced and thus bring prices back into line, is rarely free of risk. This was amply demonstrated by the near-collapse in 1998 of Long-Term Capital Management, a hedge fund run by former Salomon Brothers trader John Meriwether, which counted two distinguished finance academics, Robert Merton and Myron Scholes, on its strength. LTCM used complex mathematical models to exploit minute divergences in the relative value of different bonds. It was betting on the idea that the valuations would inevitably converge by buying the underpriced security and selling the overpriced security in the hope of making a small margin on the trade when convergence took place. Because the margins were thin, the hedge fund borrowed heavily to take very big trading positions in order to magnify profits. And it thereby ignored the maxim attributed to John Maynard Keyes that markets can remain irrational much longer than you and I can remain solvent.

Sure enough, LTCM was wrong-footed when Russia defaulted on its bonds in 1998, which caused panicky flows of capital that prevented the convergence in bond prices from which it had hoped to profit. It had also been taking arbitrage positions in shares listed on more than one stock exchange, such as Royal Dutch Shell and the UK-based Shell, where the Dutch shares traded at a premium to the UK paper. In the turbulent market conditions of 1998, the valuation anomaly worsened and LTCM was forced to unload stock at a particularly unfavourable time because it was under financial pressure on its other over-borrowed trades. According to Roger Lowenstein, in his definitive account of LTCM's rise and fall, the hedge fund's equity, or the net worth of its owners, fell from \$2.3 billion to \$400 million in less than a month.[84] The message here is that the risks in arbitrage trading are so great that unless traders have unlimited equity to sustain a bet on converging prices, they will be wary of exploiting a seeming opportunity. So mispricing will not prompt a sufficient volume of bets on convergence to bring a quick end to the valuation anomaly and prices will continue to deviate from fundamentals for quite some time.

That said, some recent bubbles have undoubtedly incorporated irrational elements, most notably in the case of Japan. The great Japanese bubble of the 1980s made spectacular fools of top bankers, not least at Industrial Bank of Japan, which was the most respected of Japanese financial institutions at that time. In the late stages of the bubble, its senior executives took advice on the stock market from – incredibly – a porcelain toad owned by an Osaka restaurant owner, Onoe Nui. Madame Nui would throw herself into a trance to interpret the toad's tips, after which the bankers returned on the bullet train to Tokyo to act on the toad's advice, which moved the market.

The denouement was unhappy for all, as Alex Kerr, author and long-time resident in Japan, has recorded in a splendid vignette:

When, toward the end of 1987, black limousines began lining up each afternoon in front of Madame Onoe Nui's house in Osaka, the neighbours thought little of it. The cars disgorged blue-suited men carrying brief cases who disappeared inside, sometimes not to emerge until two or three the next morning. Nui operated a successful restaurant, and it appeared that she had expanded her dinner business into earlier daylight hours. Only later did the neighbours learn that Madame Nui's visitors were not coming for the good food. The men in blue suits were coming to pay homage to a shadowy resident of Nui's house, a figure later revealed to be the single most important player in the Japanese stock market at the time. He was Nui's pet ceramic toad.

Toads, as is well known, are magic beings that like badgers and foxes are adept at weaving spells, especially those involving money. People like to have as charms in their gardens ceramic statues of badgers with a jug of wine in one paw and ledgers of receipts in the other. Toads, though less popular, are more mysterious, as they can transform themselves into demon princesses, and they know ancient sorcery from China and India.

The blue-chip Industrial Bank of Japan (IBJ), Japan's JP Morgan, especially favoured Madame Nui's toad. Department chiefs from IBJ's Tokyo headquarters would take the bullet train down from Tokyo to Osaka in order to attend a weekly ceremony presided over by the toad. On arriving at Nui's house, the IBJ bankers would join elite stockbrokers from Yamaichi Securities and other trading houses in a midnight vigil. First they would pat the head of the toad. Then they would recite prayers in front of a set of Buddhist statues in Nui's garden. Finally Madame Nui would seat herself in front of the toad, go into a trance, and deliver the oracle – which stocks to buy and which to sell. The financial markets in Tokyo trembled at the verdict. At his peak in 1990, the toad controlled more than $10 billion in financial instruments, making its owner the world's largest individual stock investor.

Madame Nui was also the world's largest individual bank borrower. 'From the mouth of the toad,' she proclaimed, 'comes money,' and she seems to have called considerable Chinese and Indian sorcery into play, for she parlayed a small initial set of loans made in 1986 into a vast financial empire. By 1991, in addition to IBJ, which lent Nui Y240 billion to buy IBJ bonds, twenty-nine other banks and financial institutions had extended her loans totalling more than Y2.8 trillion, equal to about $22 billion at the time.

Onoe Nui was riding the success of the so-called Bubble, when Japanese investors drove stocks and real estate to incredible heights in the late 1980s. In 1989, the capitalisation of the Tokyo Stock Exchange (TSE) stood slightly higher than that of the New York Stock Exchange; real estate assessors reckoned that the grounds of the Imperial Palace in Tokyo were worth more than all of California; the Nikkei index of the TSE rose to 39,000 points in the winter of 1989, after almost a decade of continuous climb. At that level, the average price to earnings ratios for stock (about twenty to thirty in the United States, the United Kingdom, and Hong Kong) reached eighty in Japan. Yet brokers were predicting that the stock market would soon rise to 60,000 or even 80,000. Euphoria was in the air. Japan's unique financial system – which is based on asset valuation, rather than on cash flow, as is the norm in the rest of the world – had triumphed.

When the crash came, it hit hard. In the first days of January 1990, the stock market began falling, and it lost 60 per cent of its value over the next two years. Ten years later, the Nikkei has still not recovered, meandering in a range between 14,000 and 24,000. When the stock market collapsed, so did real estate prices, which fell every year after 1991 and are now about one fifth of the Bubble-era values or lower.

Many other types of speculative assets also evaporated. Golf club memberships, which during their heyday could cost $1 million or more, today sell for 10 per cent or less of the Bubble price, and bankruptcy looms over many golf club developers, who must return tens of billions of dollars taken in as refundable deposits from members.

Despite the best efforts of Madame Nui's bankers and the toad, her empire crumbled. In August 1991 the police arrested her, and investigators found that she had based her first borrowings on fraudulent deposit vouchers forged by friendly bank managers. Nui's bankruptcy resulted in losses to lenders of almost Y270 billion, the resignation of the chairman of the Industrial Bank of Japan, and the collapse of two banks. The 'Bubble Lady', as the press called her, spent years in jail, along with her bank manager patrons.[85]

When markets reach astonishing heights with the help of a toad, and the bursting of a property bubble precipitates the biggest recession in history, as happened in 2008, it might seem that the efficient markets hypothesis has a problem – namely, that it asserts, like Dr Pangloss in Voltaire's *Candide*, that all is for the best in the best of all possible worlds. Yet in an interview with John Cassidy in the *New Yorker* magazine, Eugene Fama, chief architect of the theory, flatly denies it.[86] He even argues that the financial crisis was not the cause of the recession, while saying he has no idea what the real cause was. That is a macro-economic issue and since Fama claims not to be a macro-economist the admission does not bother him. He merely notes that economics has not been good at explaining swings in economic activity.

As for bubbles, Fama regards the word as meaningless. Like Alan Greenspan in revisionist mode, he claims that most bubbles are 20/20 hindsight:

> Now, after the fact you always find people who said before the fact that prices are too high. People are always saying that prices are too high. When they turn out to be right, we anoint them. When they turn out to be wrong, we ignore them. They are typically right and wrong about half the time.

Meantime, Queen Elizabeth II famously asked at the London School of Economics why no one had predicted the crisis. But many had. Among leading economists Robert Shiller and Raghuram Rajan, a former chief economist at the International Monetary Fund who subsequently became governor of the Indian central bank, had given due warning, as had Nouriel Roubini of New York University's Stern School of Business. And numerous fund managers have a consistently good record in identifying bubbles. Jeremy Grantham of the US fund management group GMO, to take just one example, has an impeccable history on this score and argues that they are, in fact, easy to identify. Indeed, Wall Street's wittiest commentator, Michael Lewis, wrote a bestselling book about fund managers who foresaw the financial crisis and made fortunes out of it. Even I and fellow colleagues at the *Financial Times* had no difficulty identifying the Japanese and dot.com bubbles. I also foresaw to a fair extent the great financial crisis, although I have to admit that I did not identify every one of its multiple causes.[87] To have done so when the structure of the financial system was changing very rapidly would have taken superhuman prescience.

The reason so many people did predict these bubbles was that, on most conventional measures of market valuation observed over decades, the markets were hopelessly overvalued. In Fama's world, when markets are high, investors' expectations of future returns should be low, and they should be high when markets are low. Yet there is now academic evidence from Robin Greenwood and Andrei Shleifer at Harvard University that when markets are close to their peak, investors are most bullish because they tend to extrapolate recent rises in prices into the future when they form their expectations. In short, they expect the highest future returns when markets are close to a cyclical peak. And when markets are down, they are gloomy for the same reason. The Harvard economists reach this conclusion on the basis of several surveys of investor opinion, together with the relevant economic and market data.[88] This chimes with what I have seen repeatedly in bull and bear markets since the 1960s. And on Fama's point about the identifiers of bubbles being wrong half the time, I would simply point to those like Jeremy Grantham who have been consistently right on the really big financial bubbles. The trouble is that they are more readily identified by people who have worked in markets over decades than by academics, or by central bankers who are hostage to Chicago-induced myopia.

There is nonetheless a problem for those who identify a bubble, which is that it is impossible to predict when it will burst. So prescient fund managers are always at risk of selling too early in the period of euphoria, while journalists are accused of crying wolf and are constantly contacted, as I was during the dot.com bubble, by investors and traders attacking them for failing to 'keep the faith' – a phrase that rather gives the efficient market game away, faith being the province of religion, not economics.

Yet it is important not to exaggerate the weaknesses of the efficient market case. There remains an important truth in Fama's original perception, which is reflected in the inability of most fund managers to outperform the market consistently without the help of inside information. This is a very literal sense in which Margaret Thatcher's famous adage – you cannot buck the market – is right. Share prices do tend to incorporate all known information, so it is extraordinarily difficult for individual fund managers to outperform over the long run. And while Paul Woolley's diagnosis of the rationally induced bubble seems plausible, it is hard to know how far, in more stable times, momentum trading is taking the stock market valuation of companies out of line with fundamentals.

It is also important in policy terms to recognise that the activist alternative to the central bankers' recent malign neglect of financial stability is problematic. Even if they identify bubbles, judging the moment at which to prick them is tricky. Because the act of pricking can lead to slower growth or even recession, it is best to prick early, when it is harder to be sure that the bubble is real. Leave it too late and a huge hike in interest rates may prove impotent in the face of epic market euphoria. Either way, pricking involves the central banker in substantial career risk because the logic of incurring a modest recession today to avoid a deeper one tomorrow is lost on politicians. They will simply note the current loss of output and jobs and call for the central banker's head. That, no doubt, was why Alan Greenspan was so terrified of blowing the US economy out of the water with a pre-emptive strike against the technology bubble.

The central banker's dilemma was summed up with characteristic shrewdness by J. K. Galbraith, whose politics and
economics were as far removed from Alan Greenspan's as it
was possible to be, in his book *The Great Crash 1929*:

> Action to break up a boom must always be weighed against
> the chance that it will cause unemployment at a politically
> inopportune moment. Booms, it must be noted, are not
> stopped until after they have started. And after they have
> started the action will always look, as it did to the frightened
> men in the Federal Reserve Board in February 1929, like a
> decision in favour of immediate as against ultimate death. As
> we have seen, the immediate death not only had a disadvan-
> tage of being immediate but of identifying the executioner.[89]

Jeremy Grantham has frequently remarked that the real world
of markets is messy. That is something that theoretical economics and academic market fundamentalists find hard to capture.
The reason is that modern economists have locked themselves
into an intellectual ivory tower. Their mathematical models
are underpinned by extraordinarily long lists of heroically un-
realistic assumptions, some of which border on the absurd.
For example, even after the financial crisis, most models of the
economy do not include debt and asset prices. The financial
system is simply excluded from their calculations.

Going back over a much longer period, economics has
incorporated an extraordinarily crude conception of human
nature, with its belief in a perfectly rational, utility-maximis-
ing, autonomous individual. More recently, the attempt initiated by the American economist Paul Samuelson in the 1940s

to emulate the certainty of the physical sciences led economists to dispense completely with human nature in building their models. They also employ a simplifying concept known as 'the representative agent', which assumes, in effect, that everyone in the economy is the same. Another blind spot lies in economists' tendency to downplay the importance of the institutional context of economies in their model building. The result, as the widely respected British economist John Kay has observed, is that their models resemble the completely artificial worlds found in computer games.

Robert Lucas, doyen of modern macro-economics, has defended mainstream economists for their failure to foresee the crisis, arguing that economic theory predicts that these events cannot be predicted. This side-stepping apologia does not say much for economic theory and there are more salient reasons, which I will come to shortly, that explain why the great majority of mainstream practitioners of economics failed to understand the mechanisms that put the global economy at risk. Such people referred to the period preceding the crisis as 'the Great Moderation' because it was marked by prolonged growth and low inflation. At the same time, Lucas has acknowledged that 'exceptions and anomalies' to the efficient markets hypothesis have been discovered, 'but for the purposes of macro-economic analyses and forecasts they are too small to matter'.[90]

John Kay's verdict on this is scathing:

This is to miss the point: the expert billiard player plays a nearly perfect game, but it is the imperfections of play between experts that determine the result. There is a – trivial – sense in which the deviations from efficient markets are too small to matter – and a more important sense in which these deviations are the principal thing that matters. The claim that most profit opportunities in business or in securities markets have been taken is justified. But it is the search for the profit opportunities that have not been taken that drives business forward, the belief that profit opportunities that have not been arbitraged away still exist that explains why there is so much trade in securities. Far from being 'too small to matter' these deviations from efficient market assumptions, not necessarily large, are the dynamic of the capitalist economy ... The preposterous claim that deviations from market efficiency were not only irrelevant to the recent crisis but could never be relevant is the product of an environment in which deduction has driven out induction and ideology has taken over from observation. The belief that models are not just useful tools but also are capable of yielding comprehensive and universal descriptions of the world has blinded its proponents to realities that have been staring them in the face. That blindness was an element in our present crisis, and conditions our still ineffectual responses.[91]

The economists' quest for the status of physical science for their discipline has also encouraged them to seek to drain their academic discipline of moral content. As Michael Sandel, the Harvard philosopher, recently remarked,

Over the past three or four decades, the public life of our societies has been animated by a faith that market mechanisms can answer all questions and solve all problems. This era of unquestioned faith in markets coincided with the time when political life lost the sense of morality or public purpose. Market reasoning seems to offer a non-judgemental way of allocating goods and incomes, but in many cases we have to make moral judgements. The new economic thinking that is now required has many affinities with the old economic thinking. Classical economists, going back to Adam Smith, did not view economics as a value-neutral science or even as an autonomous discipline. They all understood economics to be a sub-field of moral and political economy.[92]

Equally problematic is the way economics has become ahistorical. Yet history is fundamental to understanding the workings of markets and the wider economy. That applies in spades to the global financial crisis and subsequent Great Recession. Many have been tempted to attribute the crisis to what the author Nassim Nicholas Taleb calls black swans, or high-impact, hard-to-predict events that are beyond the realm of normal expectations. Yet anyone who knew anything about the financial crises of 1907, which prompted the creation of the US Federal Reserve, and of 1929, which led to the 1930s depression, would have been well equipped to see the risks in the property bubble that preceded the latest crisis. Indeed, financial crises have been normal, regular events since the invention of modern banking. And Nassim Nicholas Taleb was himself immensely prescient about the crisis. Those black swans, if the reader will excuse a solecism, were a canard. With financial crises the problem of prediction, as we saw earlier, is about timing and scale rather than the probability of them happening.

A much better rationale for the crisis is to be found in the work of the economist Hyman Minsky, who had an acute sense of history. He recognised that the modern economy is fundamentally unstable and that one of the lessons of economic history is that there have always been big discontinuities in economic performance and policymaking. Minsky argued in the 1980s in his book *Stabilising an Unstable Economy* that long periods of stability and prosperity breed complacency and encourage risk taking, which is precisely what the so-called Great Moderation was all about.[93] The moderation was, in fact, thoroughly immoderate.

More specifically, he described how individuals, companies and banks borrow too much and overstretch their balance sheets; also how regulators are lulled into a false sense of security by the conviction that the economy is working differently than in the past – that beguiling belief that 'this time is different'. An accumulation of risk in the system, Minsky argued, leads ultimately to a financial crisis and to morally hazardous bailouts, which can be so expensive as to call into question the solvency of governments. In short, this economist, sadly unfashionable in the first decade of the new millennium, provided a remarkably accurate route map to the credit bubble and subsequent crisis.

The ahistorical economist, busily building models on crazy assumptions, has become a much less user-friendly support for policymakers than the likes of John Maynard Keynes, who warned of the risk of sacrificing realism to mathematics. The approach of his generation of economists, infused by historical understanding, was usefully empirical. Meantime, another aspect of economists' work – forecasting – is often absurdly over-precise and devoid of utility. Denis Healey, Labour Chancellor of the Exchequer in Britain in the 1970s, wrote eloquently in his memoirs of the difficulties this posed for policymaking:

> Economics has acquired a spurious respectability through the use of numbers, which appear to many people ... much more meaningful than mere adjectives or adverbs, because they appear to be precise and unambiguous. Unfortunately I soon discovered that the most important numbers were nearly always wrong. This applied not only to the economic forecasts, which usually admitted a sizeable range of error; that is why an economist is often defined as a man who, when you ask him for a telephone number, gives you an estimate. It applied also to the statistics about what was actually happening in the economy at the time. It even applied to what had happened in the previous twelve months. As Defence Secretary I had found it possible to get fairly accurate figures for the Russian armed forces, or for the range and payload of a Soviet missile, which the Kremlin tried its best to keep secret. As Chancellor I found it impossible to get accurate figures of our national output the previous year, or of our imports and exports; yet all the data appeared to be readily available.[94]

The usefulness of modern economists is thus seriously in question. It is hard to disagree with John Kay's assertion that they fail to engage with the issues that confront real businesses and households. Their forecasting abilities are not a great advertisement for the economics profession. And their modelling activity is rooted in a form of deductive reasoning reminiscent of the medieval schoolmen. The underlying assumptions

belong to the world of fantasy. Yet these Walter Mitty economic models are central to the macro-economic analysis used
in finance ministries and central banks, which have been slow
to respond to the shortcomings revealed by the financial crisis.
The risk in all this is that economists end up discrediting the
workings of the market in the eyes of ordinary people. To address that concern, the fundamentalist streak in capitalism
so closely associated with Chicago University badly needs to
acquire a greater real-world connection. It is a curious irony
that so many economists who believe passionately in the
market process are surprisingly myopic in their understanding
of markets.

CHAPTER SIX

TRADE AND THE
FATAL EMBRACE

China's extraordinary transformation since 1978 into the world's second largest economy – quite possibly the first within the next ten years – poses a direct challenge to the hegemonic power of the United States. Yet the Communist regime in Beijing makes that challenge from a position of extreme economic interdependence. Between 2010 and 2012, the World Trade Organization estimates that trade accounted for 53.6 per cent of gross domestic product, which compares with just 29.5 per cent for the US, while the aspiring superpower's official foreign exchange reserves amounted to $4 trillion in 2013.[95] China does not publish detailed figures for its reserves, but around 70 per cent of that sum is reckoned to be in US Treasury bonds and other dollar-denominated securities. That means that the US is currently relying on a strategic rival to finance its budget deficits and, indirectly, its military interventions overseas. At the same time, nearly a fifth of US imports come from China – more than from any other country – while China is the third largest export market for the US after Canada and Mexico. It follows that China, which has become increasingly nationalistic and assertive in its relations with its neighbours, will serve as a litmus test for one of the longer-standing arguments about the nature of market capitalism, which I first encountered in a paper by a colleague in the British Foreign Office in the early 1980s. This quoted the eighteenth-century French political theorist Montesquieu, who asserted that international trade and, implicitly, financial interdependence were conducive to peace and stability.

The belief in trade as a benign influence on relations between states is a fine example of the kind of thinking eschewed by modern economists, as explained in Chapter Five, since it is unsupported by any economic model and is rooted in analysis of human motivation. It is no less interesting for that. In fact, the idea is a relative parvenu in intellectual history. For centuries, trade was regarded as a necessary evil or worse. Aristotle in his *Politics* roundly declared: 'In the state which is best governed and possesses men who are just absolutely, and not merely relatively to the principle of the constitution, the citizens must not lead the life of mechanics or tradesmen, for such a life is ignoble, and inimical to virtue.'[96]

The thought was admittedly aspirational, since Athens depended for much of its food supply on foreign imports. Yet it reflected an underlying fear that the individualistic nature of a mercantile economy potentially threatened the sense of common purpose and willingness to make sacrifices for the public good that were essential to the survival of the city state in a hostile world. Hence the refusal to give rights of citizenship to Athenian merchants and money lenders. Plato was of a similar mind, arguing in his *Laws* that a great export trade and a great return of gold and silver would have 'most fatal results on a State whose aim is the attainment of just and noble sentiments'.[97]

The Christian tradition was equally hostile, if not more so, heavily emphasising the moral dangers of trade. The English politician and economist Charles Davenant, son of William Davenant, the poet and playwright, made the arguments zestfully in 1699 in his *Essay Upon the Probable Methods of Making a People Gainers in the Balance of Trade*:

> Trade, without doubt, is in its nature a pernicious thing; it brings in that wealth which introduces luxury; it gives rise to fraud and avarice, and extinguishes virtue and simplicity of manners; it depraves a people, and makes way for that corruption which never fails to end in slavery, foreign or domestic. Lycurgus [the Spartan lawgiver], in the most perfect model of government that was ever framed, did banish it from his commonwealth.[98]

Underlying both what might be called the civic republican view and the Christian view is the notion, expounded in Chapter One, that trade is a zero-sum game. In a pre-capitalist world where there was virtually no growth in per capita incomes, it was natural to assume that if one party to a transaction gained, the other party must necessarily lose. The morality of trade was thus questionable. The only real source of economic wealth was perceived to be land, while revenues that did not derive from the land or from physical effort tended to be regarded as suspect – a stricture that applied especially to lending at interest, which, as we saw in Chapter Three, Aristotle dubbed the most unnatural of all the modes of getting wealth. Vestiges of that belief still survive in the modern world and have understandably strengthened in the aftermath of the 2007–08 financial crisis.

Davenant was typical of his time in thinking that international trade was a form of economic warfare. Colbert, finance minister of Louis XIV, referred to it as 'perpetual combat'.[99] The mercantilists, of whom Davenant and Colbert were notable exemplars, believed that the purpose of trade was to accumulate precious metals such as gold and silver and to rack up surpluses on the balance of payments. The aim was to impoverish competing nations while strengthening the nation's military capability. To that end, the mercantilists argued for protectionist measures such as tariffs on imports, which generated revenue for the Exchequer. Landowners and merchants who stood to benefit from reduced competition naturally enough lobbied monarchs and lawmakers in support of protection.

This negative view of trade was not universal. As far back as the twelfth century, Hugh of Saint Victor, a canon at the Abbey of Saint Victor in Paris and a leading philosopher and theologian in the Augustinian tradition, had taken a distinctly non-Aristotelian view of trade in his *Didascalicon*, a guide to Christian learning, philosophy and the arts:

> Commerce penetrates the secret places of the world, approaches shores unseen, explores fearful wildernesses, and in tongues unknown and with barbaric peoples carries on the trade of mankind. The pursuit of commerce reconciles nations, calms wars, strengthens peace, and commutes the private good of individuals into the common benefit of all.[100]

Not only is this a remarkably vivid and imaginative piece of writing; it is an astonishingly advanced economic sentiment for the period, prefiguring Adam Smith's notion that the pursuit of self-interest has benign unintended consequences for society. It also anticipates Montesquieu's thinking on trade as being conducive to peace. Yet it failed to roll back the Aristotelian tide, proving less influential over time than the views of Thomas Aquinas in the thirteenth century, who in his treatise *De regimine principum* followed Aristotle almost to the letter in declaring contact with foreigners an undesirable, corrupting influence and seeing trade as an inducement to anti-social vice.

Not until the seventeenth century was there a marked retreat from this negative view of commerce, and the timing was significant. The change in intellectual climate came partly as a reaction to the terrible human toll inflicted in religious wars since the Reformation. Philosophers such as Grotius, Spinoza, Hobbes and Locke attacked both the militaristic values that had prevailed through the Middle Ages and the anti-materialism of the Christian tradition. Their aim was to divert people away from military heroics and a preoccupation with eternal salvation in the afterlife to prosperity in the here and now, with a view to securing social stability and peace. At the same time, writers such as Cervantes lampooned the heroic values of the medieval aristocracy; La Rochefoucauld in his *Maximes* emphasised human hypocrisy, self-interest, vanity and greed rather than chivalric virtue; and Blaise Pascal in his *Pensées* described man as a *roseau pensant* – a decidedly unheroic thinking reed. This assault on centuries-old values intensified in the early eighteenth century, when the conventional wisdom to which Davenant subscribed still held that material prosperity, or 'luxury', was incompatible with moral virtue. It was also thought to be conducive to effeminacy and national decline, while being potentially subversive of social hierarchy if the lower orders gained access to luxury goods.

At the forefront in promoting the materialist cause was Bernard Mandeville, author of *The Fable of the Bees*, encountered in Chapter One. With a wicked wit, Mandeville accepted part of the Christian argument by declaring that the wellspring of trade lay in vices such as vanity, pride and luxury. Yet he then inverted the argument spectacularly by invoking the law of unintended consequences: pernicious human motivation, he suggested, was directly responsible for contributing to the prosperity of the nation. In the poem, the economy of the bees collapses when they abandon self-interest in favour of self-denying behaviour. They then triumphantly rediscover the secret of prosperity:

> *Thus Vice nurs'd Ingenuity,*
> *Which joined with Time and Industry,*
> *Had carry'd Life's conveniencies,*
> *Its real Pleasures, Comforts, Ease,*
> *To such a Height, the very Poor*
> *Liv'd better than the Rich before.*

Adam Smith in Britain and Voltaire in France put the case for material values rather differently. For Voltaire, the great merit of commerce was that the pursuit of self-interest was less dangerous than the pursuit of other goals such as military expansion or religious salvation. He also believed that the self-interested pursuit of profit through commerce had a socialising influence, not least because it helped reduce religious differences. For his part, Adam Smith in *The Wealth of Nations* argued that consumption was socially benign and that the market economy was the best means for achieving what he called 'universal opulence'. He also took up the cudgels against the mercantilists, ridiculing their arguments with a brilliantly effective illustration:

> By means of glasses, hotbeds, and hotwalls, very good grapes can be raised in Scotland, and very good wine too can be made of them at about thirty times the expense for which at least equally good can be brought from foreign countries. Would it be a reasonable law to prohibit the importation of all foreign wines, merely to encourage the making of claret and burgundy in Scotland? ... As long as the one country has those advantages, and the other wants [lacks] them, it will always be more advantageous for the latter, rather to buy of the former than to make.[101]

Smith pointed out that the mercantilists were confusing money with wealth, arguing that 'the wealth of a country consists, not in its gold and silver only, but in its lands, houses, and consumable goods of all different kinds'. He also made the more subtle point that while protectionist measures such as import tariffs might promote the growth of companies in a given industry, it would simultaneously divert resources from other industries where investment might be more productive. An important part of his argument was that such governmental influence on investment through fiscal policy was both counterproductive and unnecessary because the self-interested individual investor had an instinctive home bias anyway:

> He generally, indeed, neither intends to promote the public interest, nor knows how much he is promoting it. By

preferring the support of domestic to that of foreign industry, he intends only his own security, and by directing that
industry in such a manner as its produce may be of the greatest value, he intends only his own gain, and he is in this, as
in many other cases, led by an invisible hand to promote an
end which was no part of his intention. Nor is it always the
worse for the society that it was not part of it. By pursuing
his own interest he frequently promotes that of the society
more effectually than when he really intends to promote it.

That reference to the invisible hand is perhaps the most celebrated positive example of the law of unintended consequences. While the expression is original, the thought is not.
Similar ideas had been articulated not only by Hugh of St
Victor but by Pascal in the mid-seventeenth century and by the
Italian political philosopher Gianbattista Vico in his *Scienza
Nuova* of 1725. Yet Smith went further than this. As well as
suggesting that a commercial society was conducive to greater
individual liberty, he thought that trade contributed to more
peaceful relations among nations.

In this, which leads directly to the central theme of the current chapter, he was far from alone. Earlier in the century, in a
famous essay on London's Royal Exchange, Joseph Addison,
co-founder of *The Spectator* with Richard Steele, celebrated
the global nature of business, arguing that commercial exchange and economic interdependence turned men into frater-
nal citizens of the world:

There is no Place in the Town which I so much love to frequent
as the *Royal-Exchange*. It gives me a secret Satisfaction, and,

in some measure, gratifies my Vanity, as I am an *Englishman*, to see so rich an Assembly of Country-men and Foreigners consulting together upon the private Business of Mankind, and making this Metropolis a kind of *Emporium* for the whole Earth. I must confess I look upon High-Change to be a great Council, in which all considerable Nations have their Representatives. Factors in the Trading World are what Ambassadors are in the Politick World; they negotiate Affairs, conclude Treaties, and maintain a good Correspondence between those wealthy Societies of Men that are divided from one another by Seas and Oceans, or live on the different Extremities of a Continent. I have often been pleased to hear Disputes adjusted between an Inhabitant of *Japan* and an Alderman of *London*, or to see a Subject of the *Great Mogul* entering into a League with one of the *Czar of Muscovy*. I am infinitely delighted in mixing with these several Ministers of Commerce, as they are distinguished by their different Walks and different Languages: Sometimes I am justled among a Body of *Armenians*: Sometimes I am lost in a crowd of *Jews*, and sometimes make one in a Groupe of *Dutch-men*. I am a *Dane*, *Swede*, or *French-Man* at different times, or rather fancy myself like the old philosopher, who upon being asked what Country-man he was, replied, That he was a Citizen of the World.

This grand Scene of Business gives me an infinite Variety of solid and substantial Entertainments. As I am a great Lover of Mankind, my Heart naturally overflows with Pleasure at the sight of a prosperous and happy Multitude, insomuch that at many publick Solemnities I cannot forbear expressing my Joy with Tears that have stolen down my Cheeks. For this reason I am wonderfully delighted to see such a Body of Men thriving in their own private Fortunes, and at the same time promoting the Publick Stock; or in other Words, raising Estates for their own Families, by bringing into their Country whatever is wanting, and carrying out of it whatever is superfluous.

Nature seems to have taken a particular Care to disseminate her Blessings among the different Regions of the World, with an Eye to this mutual Intercourse and Traffick among Mankind, that the Natives of the several Parts of the Globe might have a kind of Dependance upon one another, and be united together by their common Interest. Almost every *Degree* produces something peculiar to it. The Food often grows in one Country, and the Sauce in another. The Fruits of *Portugal* are corrected by the Products of *Barbadoes*: The Infusion of a *China* Plant sweetned [sic] with the Pith of an *Indian* Cane: The *Philippick* Islands give a Flavour to our *European* Bowls. The Single Dress of a Woman of Quality is often the Product of an hundred Climates. The Muff and the Fan come together from the different Ends of the Earth. The Scarf is sent from the Torrid Zone, and the Tippet from beneath the Pole. The Brocade Petticoat rises out of the Mines of *Peru*, and the Diamond Necklace out of the Bowels of *Indostan*. Nor is it the least part of this our happiness, that whilst we enjoy the remotest Products of the North and South, we are free from those Extremities of Weather which give them Birth; That our Eyes are refreshed with the green Fields of *Britain*, at the same time that our Palates are feasted with Fruits that rise between the Tropicks.

For these Reasons there are not more useful Members in a Commonwealth than Merchants. They knit Mankind together in a mutual Intercourse of good Offices, distribute the Gifts of Nature, find Work for the Poor, add Wealth to the Rich, and Magnificence to the Great.

This lyrical outpouring must surely be the most romantic tract on business in all literature. At a time of growing awareness of the benefits of foreign trade to the English economy, Addison's feelings were widely shared and even penetrated the world of the novel. Much of Daniel Defoe's *Robinson Crusoe*, for example, can be interpreted as a homily on the benign effects of trade, though Karl Marx preferred to use it to illustrate his labour theory of value. Economists have written at length on how Crusoe, cast away alone on his island, seeks ways of maximising his utility in the absence of trade, money and markets by striking an efficient balance between production – searching for food – and leisure. The arrival of Man Friday then provides a practical illustration of the potential gains from trade. A conspicuous theme of Defoe's *Moll Flanders*, meantime, is the morally redemptive power of commerce. It is trade that provides Moll with an escape route from criminality to a legitimate existence and prosperity. *Roxana*, whose heroine is an acquisitive capitalist with a genius for monetising her sexual attractions, trumpets the values of the commercial world and, like Moll, is deeply preoccupied with the minutiae of money. Defoe puts his own economic views in the mouth of a sympathetically portrayed merchant, Sir Robert Clayton, in a dialogue with Roxana:

> Sir *Robert* said, and I found it to be true, that a true-bred Merchant is the best Gentleman in the Nation; that in Knowledge, in Manners, in Judgement of things, the Merchant out-did many of the Nobility; that having once master'd the World, and being above the Demand of Business, tho' no real Estate, they were then superior to most Gentlemen, even in Estate; that a Merchant in flush Business, and a capital Stock, is able to spend more Money than a Gentleman of 5000 *l.* a Year Estate; that while a Merchant spent, he only spent what he got, and not that; and that he laid up great Sums every Year.
>
> That an Estate is a pond; but that a Trade was a Spring; that if the first is once mortgag'd, it seldom gets clear, but embarrass'd the Person for ever; but the Merchant had his Estate continually flowing; and upon this, he nam'd me Merchants who liv'd in more real Splendor, and spent more Money than most of the Noblemen in *England* cou'd singly expend, and that they still grew immensely rich.[102]

Note, in passing, that the morality of Defoe's heroines incorporates a solid capitalist principle akin to the economist's life-cycle theory whereby people borrow when young, save in middle age and spend in retirement. These women sin and accumulate capital while they retain their bloom and repent while enjoying their nest egg as their looks fade.

On the relationship between trade and peace, a more dispassionate and forceful version of Addison's argument was provided by Charles-Louis de Secondat, Baron de Montesquieu, the man best known for the doctrine of the separation of powers adopted by the American Founding Fathers in the US Constitution. His idea of constitutional checks and balances grew naturally from his belief that dangerous passions were innate in humanity and needed to be restrained by something stronger than mere reason, namely countervailing powers or material interests such as the desire for financial gain. And just as the passion for power was insatiable, the passion for gain was equally prone to excess.

In his *De L'Esprit des Lois*, Montesquieu, following Addison, says: 'It is almost a general rule that wherever the ways of man are gentle there is commerce; and wherever there is commerce, there the ways of men are gentle.'[103] He then becomes, if anything, more extreme than Addison, declaring: 'The spirit of commerce brings with it the spirit of frugality, of economy, of moderation, of work, of wisdom, of tranquillity, of order, and of regularity. In this manner, as long as this prevails, the riches it creates do not have any bad effect.'

The economist Albert O. Hirschman, in 'The Passions and the Interests', a fine essay written in 1997 on the political arguments for capitalism, suggests that it is almost tempting to dismiss this praise of commerce because it is so extravagant. Yet, as he points out, it is followed by a more detailed and closely reasoned argument on the favourable political effects of commerce. This leads on to the famous exposition of what we would now call liberal internationalism in the quote that I first encountered in the British Foreign Office, referred to earlier: 'The natural effect of commerce is to lead to peace. Two nations that trade together become mutually dependent: if one has an interest in buying, the other has one in selling; and all unions are based on mutual needs.'

Montesquieu then extends the argument by showing how trade can act as a constraint on the arbitrary exercise of sovereign power. Discussing how the Jews had suffered violence and constant extortion at the hands of nobles and kings, while having to work within the constraints of usury laws, he points out that they reacted by developing the bill of exchange, a clever trade financing device that helped detach the Jews' wealth from the physical properties inherent in investment in land or goods. This leads to a thought that carries an implicit echo of Defoe's comparison of trade with a spring:

> ... and through this means commerce could elude violence, and maintain itself everywhere; for the richest trader had only invisible wealth which could be sent everywhere without leaving any trace ... In this manner we owe ... to the avarice of rulers the establishment of a contrivance which somehow lifts commerce right out of their grip.
>
> Since that time, the rulers have been compelled to govern with greater wisdom than they themselves might have intended; for, owing to these events, the great and sudden arbitrary actions of the sovereign (*les grands coups d'autorité*) have been proven to be ineffective and ... only good government brings prosperity [to the prince].

Montesquieu illustrates his point by referring to rulers' frequent resort in history to debasing the coinage. This, he says, would be counterproductive in modern (i.e., mid-eighteenth-century) times because it would be nullified by bankers' foreign exchange operations and arbitrage – that is, bankers had learned to compare and assess a currency against competing currencies from around the world and could use bills of exchange rather than currency to finance trade. It is an excitingly modern thought in that Montesquieu anticipates twentieth-century public choice theory's emphasis on the benefits of market constraints on self-serving politicians' and bureaucrats' freedom of action. It also looks forward to the activities of so-called bond market vigilantes, modern institutional investors such as pension funds, insurance companies and hedge funds that shun government debt markets and so force up interest rates when they fear policymakers will resort to inflation by printing money and monetising debt. Yet the underlying idea is still very much of its time in the conclusion Montesquieu draws from it relating to the workings of human passions and interests: 'And it is fortunate for men to be in a situation in which, though their passions may prompt them to be wicked [*méchants*], they have nevertheless an interest in not being so.'

The high tide of such liberal internationalism came in the mid-nineteenth century with the textile manufacturer and politician Richard Cobden, who, with John Bright, led the free trade campaign for the repeal of the Corn Laws, the system of tariffs that protected English landowners from foreign grain imports. Cobden was a pacifist and anti-imperialist. In his most idealistic and visionary speech on the case for free trade, he made it clear that securing peace through international trade was far more important to him than any economic consideration, although many of his supporters in the business community were probably more interested in the capacity of free trade to cheapen labour:

I have been accused of looking too much to material interests. Nevertheless I can say that I have taken as large and great a view of the effects of this mighty principle as ever did any man who dreamt over it in his own study. I believe that the physical gain will be the smallest gain to humanity from the success of this principle. I look farther; I see in the Free-trade principle that which shall act on the moral world as the principle of gravitation in the universe,—drawing men together, thrusting aside the antagonism of race, and creed, and language, and uniting us in the bonds of eternal peace. I have looked even farther. I have speculated, and probably dreamt, in the dim future—ay, a thousand years hence—I have speculated on what the effect of the triumph of this principle may be. I believe that the effect will be to change the face of the world, so as to introduce a system of government entirely distinct from that which now prevails. I believe that the desire and the motive for large and mighty empires; for gigantic armies and great navies—for those materials which are used for the destruction of life and the desolation of the rewards of labour—will die away; I believe that such things will cease to be necessary, or to be used, when man becomes one family, and freely exchanges the fruits of his labour with his brother man. I believe that, if we could be allowed to reappear on this sublunary scene, we should see, at a far distant period, the governing system of this world revert to something like the municipal system; and I believe that the speculative philosopher of a thousand years hence will date the greatest revolution that ever happened in the world's history from the triumph of the principle which we have met here to advocate.[104]

This radical idealism, which harks back to the internationalism of Immanuel Kant, found a profound echo in literature. In
Tennyson's poem of unrequited love, 'Locksley Hall', the nar-
rator has an extraordinary prophetic vision of aerial warfare
which is then succeeded by a peace in which an enlightened
global parliament rules:

> *For I dipt into the future, far as human eye could see,*
> *Saw the vision of the world, and all the wonder that would be;*
> *Saw the heavens fill with commerce, argosies of magic sails,*
> *Pilots of the purple twilight dropping down with costly bales;*
> *Heard the heavens fill with shouting, and there rain'd a ghastly dew*
> *From the nations' airy navies grappling in the central blue;*
> *Far along the world-wide whisper of the south-wind rushing warm,*
> *With standards of the peoples plunging thro' the thunder-storm;*
> *Till the war-drum throbb'd no longer, and the battle-flags were furl'd*
> *In the Parliament of man, the Federation of the world.*
> *There the common sense of most shall hold a fretful realm in awe,*
> *And the kindly earth shall slumber, lapt in universal law.*[105]

The immediate consequence of Cobden's victory in the campaign against the Corn Laws was an acceleration in British
trade and economic growth. For Britain, at least, the rest of
the century was relatively peaceful domestically. By the start of
the twentieth century, meantime, Cobden's idealism had been
developed by the British journalist and politician Norman
Angell into a more general theory about the futility of war in
conditions of economic interdependence. In a book called *The
Great Illusion*, which appeared in 1910 during the first period
of globalisation in the world economy, he argued that the costs

of victory always outweighed the gains; and not just because of the loss of life and destruction of wealth. The illusion in question was that

> a nation's financial and industrial stability, its security in commercial activity – in short, its prosperity and wellbeing, depend upon its being able to defend itself against the aggression of other nations, who will, if they are able, be tempted to commit such aggression because in so doing they will increase their power and consequently *their* prosperity and wellbeing, at the cost of the weaker and vanquished.[106]

It was foolish, Angell thought, to assume that war could ever be economically advantageous. He illustrated his point by referring to Alsace and Lorraine, whose acquisition by Germany in the Franco-Prussian war of 1870–71 did not lead to the German people taking possession of French coal and steel assets. Germans had to go on buying goods from the former French territories as they had done before the war. Much the same applied after the British conquest of South Africa. There, the gold and diamond mines continued to be run by their original proprietors. The notion that war was economically wasteful was further reinforced by Angell's comparison of living standards in small countries such as Switzerland and Norway with those of the Great Powers. He showed that by dint of trading in open markets these countries were more prosperous in terms of per capita income and wealth without colonies or wars of acquisition than were imperialist countries. War, then, was a negative-sum game in which the winning side was simply a lesser loser than the losing side.

The 1914–18 war dealt a near fatal blow to this strand of liberal internationalism and to Norman Angell's reputation as an international relations theorist, although he had never argued that economic interdependence made war impossible. Clearly, the attempt to put capitalism and self-interest to work in the interests of peace had over-reached itself, not least because industrial capitalism facilitated mass destruction of human life on an unprecedented scale. But what precisely was it about the liberal argument that was flawed?

For Wickham Steed, editor of *The Times*, Angell's theories were flawed because

if the war taught us one lesson above all others it was that the calculations of economists, bankers, and financial statesmen who preached the impossibility of war because it would not pay were perilous nonsense ... Germany went to war because she made it pay in 1870–71, and believed she could make it pay again.[107]

On that basis, war might simply be the result of politicians and rulers making bad judgements about the national interest or making the wrong calculus of the costs and benefits of military action. Keynes, like Angell, put much emphasis on economic motivation in decisions to go to war, but drew the opposite conclusion. He declared that free trade combined with international mobility of capital was more likely to provoke war than constrain warmongers because at times of stress the ownership of national assets by foreigners was likely to 'set up strains and enmities' that were potentially conducive to war. In 1933, in a lecture in Dublin on national self-sufficiency, he put a powerful case for protectionism and argued that finance in particular should be primarily national.[108] Given the scope that financial interconnectedness opens up for contagion in a financial crisis, this point still resonates. Keynes rightly perceived that if trade and capital flows bind economies more closely together, the process can spread negative as well as positive developments from one country to another at times of economic and financial stress.

A more fundamental criticism of the liberal internationalist economic view is that it shares, rather incongruously, the Marxist conviction that the world is governed by material interest rather than ideas or non-material values. In reality, many conflicts in the modern world are essentially tribal in nature, and nationalism is often a more powerful force than the desire to maximise economic gain or minimise economic costs, especially when reinforced by a sense of extreme insecurity. As the British diplomat Robert Cooper has put it, statesmen represent not simply states, but communities with identities based on non-rational values; and in the conduct of foreign policy, 'identity beats interest'.[109] In that context, it should not be forgotten that the proximate cause of the First World War was the murder of Archduke Franz Ferdinand of Austria in Sarajevo by an obscure Yugoslav nationalist, Gavrilo Princip, who was a Bosnian Serb. His aim was to secure a unified Yugoslavia while bringing down the Austro-Hungarian Empire. Looked at from Princip's point of view, his action was brilliantly successful on both scores and his personal cost–benefit calculus was, of course, devoid of any economic consideration.

Amartya Sen, winner of the Nobel Prize in economics, offers a telling caricature of what, in the end, is an over-simplistic train of thought, by making a Hollywood-style analogy. Consider a situation, he says, in which you are being chased by murderous bigots who passionately dislike something about you – the colour of your skin, the look of your nose, the nature of your faith, or whatever. As they zero in on you, you throw some money around as you flee, and each of them gets down to the serious business of collecting the notes. Could anyone really believe that this stratagem would have worked in the recent murderous circumstances of Bosnia, Rwanda or Burundi?[110]

For all that, the notion that economic interdependence is conducive to peace has proved remarkably resilient. After the Second World War, French foreign minister Robert Schuman's proposal for a Franco-German coal and steel community, which later metamorphosed into the European Union, had the explicit objective of binding France and Germany so close together that, in Schuman's phrase, it would make war 'not only unthinkable but materially impossible'. Against a background of renewed globalisation and increased threats from nuclear proliferation and climate change, the World Trade Organization, the official body that sets the global rules for trade between nations, continues to make the connection between trade and peace in its official pronouncements. International relations academics and academic economists have conducted detailed statistical research on the likelihood of countries going to war if they are democracies, members of international organisations and economically or financially interdependent. They have tended to find that economic and financial interdependence through cross-border direct investment is a particularly good predictor of a low incidence of military conflict between states.

Such findings seem intuitively sensible given that interdependence raises the cost of conflict. A popular form of this hypothesis is the argument that no country into which McDonald's has inserted a fast-food restaurant chain has ever subsequently fought a war. While the evidence for the McDonald's theory of conflict resolution is questionable, the underlying notion does draw strength from the fact that international companies' supply chains are now organised in such a way that most products are assembled with inputs from several countries. Indeed, most trade now takes place within multinationals and their suppliers, with interesting consequences for the long-standing debate for and against protectionism. According to the World Trade Organization, the import content of exports in 1990 was 20 per cent; in 2010 it had risen to 40 per cent; and it is expected to be around 60 per cent by 2030. Against that background, the idea that a country's strength depends on it being able to export more than it imports loses its potency. It has also renewed interest in the idea of trade as a restraining influence on international conflict.[111] It certainly restrains the readiness to use economic sanctions. The European Union's willingness to offer a robust response to Russia's annexation of Crimea in 2014 was severely impaired by its dependence on Russia for its gas supplies.

Perhaps the most powerful modern advocate in the tradition of Montesquieu is the Yale economist Robert Shiller, who advances a very strong version of the thesis:

> Financial interconnectedness may help prevent war for deeper reasons than those associated with the perceived risk to capital movements. Financial interconnectedness

> provides another outlet for aggressions, a civilized stage for
> the playing out of aggressive impulses and an environment
> in which exposure to risk is carefully chosen by each player,
> not determined arbitrarily by a military commander ... Thus
> financial development may lead to a kinder and gentler – if
> not altogether kind and gentle – society.[112]

The difficulty with this kind of argument is exposed when we
return to where we began, with the case of China. China now oc-
cupies a large environment in which, in Shiller's phrase, its 'con-
flictual tendencies have space to roam' in a way that should, on
his thinking, mitigate aggression. It is far from clear that this has
led to a kinder and gentler society in China. The modest extent
to which the country has become more liberal since 1978 does, it
is true, owe something to interconnectedness. But the connection
comes more from the internet, which the Communist authorities
have been unable fully to control, than from trade.

As far as trade and investment are concerned, China for more
than three decades adopted a model of capitalism that amounted
to a modern version of mercantilism. The ultimate objective was
not to increase consumption but to reassert Chinese power and
influence in the world and keep the ruling Communist Party
free from challenge. The addition to household incomes that
resulted from economic growth was essentially a convenient
by-product for the Beijing authorities of their push for power.
In pursuit of export-led growth, the Chinese government in
recent years subsidised industrial producers either directly or by
managing the exchange rate to improve their competitiveness.
It also maintained, until recently, strict controls on the capital
account of the balance of payments. The accumulation of the

country's vast official foreign exchange reserves, and thus its extraordinary financial interdependence with the US, was a consequence of the mercantilist policy of holding down the value of the currency and of a vast surplus of domestic savings over investment. In 2013, by which time China was trying to shift from investment- and export-led growth to a more consumer-orientated economic model, the country's $4 trillion reserves were equivalent to more than 40 per cent of gross domestic product. The People's Bank of China had become the largest foreign holder of US Treasury securities, holding over 32 per cent of the total stock of Treasuries in 2011.

Why had the Americans allowed themselves to become so dependent on Chinese money? The answer was that they had been borrowing from the Chinese at incredibly low rates of interest to buy extremely cheap foreign goods, albeit at the cost of lost jobs in mature, smokestack industries, which had been hit by Chinese competition. An unfortunate consequence was that there had been a build-up of private sector debt while Americans absorbed China's excess savings as they consumed more than they spent. Public sector debt had also ballooned as US government deficits increased. So the Chinese, who were still among the world's poorest people, were subsidising consumption in one of the developed world's richest economies. The question is how the political and economic dynamic of this extraordinary interdependence works.

There are some in China who would like to use financial leverage to influence US policy. Ding Gang, a senior editor at *People's Daily*, argued in an editorial in August 2011 that China should use its financial weapon to teach the US a lesson in response to its arms sales to Taiwan. Yet China cannot do that without running the risk of causing the dollar to plunge and US interest rates to rise, which would wreck the value of its dollar investments. There is anyway nowhere else to put the money. Even Europe does not have markets that are big enough to absorb these phenomenal sums. Since a cheaper dollar would make Chinese goods more expensive for Americans, Chinese exports to the US would also be hit.

For its part, the US has to fear that there might be circumstances in which China would be prepared to incur large economic costs in pursuit of broader strategic ambitions. If the Chinese chose to disinvest suddenly, it would equally be exposed to the risk that US interest rates would rise and the dollar would plunge amid panic in the markets. Recession might ensue. The US also risks damage if the long-forecast slowdown in the Chinese economy proves to be sharp and disorderly. There is, then, a financial balance of terror, which the former Federal Reserve chairman Paul Volcker has called 'the fatal embrace'. Yet the US Defense Department appears unruffled by all this. In a report in 2012 it said:

> Attempting to use US Treasury securities as a coercive tool would have limited effect and likely would do more harm to China than to the United States. As the threat is not credible and the effect would be limited even if carried out, it does not offer China deterrence options, whether in the diplomatic, military or economic realms and this would remain true both in peacetime and in scenarios of crisis or war.[113]

Perhaps there is something in this, because the pool of domestic and global savings available to provide alternative sources of finance for the US budget deficit is huge. Yet it could nonetheless prove complacent, since the potential for financial leverage will fluctuate according to how much the US needs to borrow. The economist Charles Dumas, of Lombard Street Research, describes the risks:

> This Sino-US synergy is not a formal arrangement and certainly not marriage ... It is not even agreed cohabitation. It is as if China has simply moved into the basement and taken over as servant. The danger of such arrangements was illustrated by *The Servant* (a Harold Pinter play made into a film by Joseph Losey in 1963), in which the master continued to go out into society as the man of the world, while in the home a role reversal took place: his increasing dependence on the servant transferred true power to the latter.[114]

In practice, the striking thing about the relationship is how many unintended consequences have resulted from these two countries pursuing economic policies that are driven primarily by their own domestic concerns. The excess savings of China, together with the savings of other developing countries and of northern Europeans, contributed to the credit bubble that preceded the great financial crisis. This was because it facilitated cheap finance for housing and property booms in countries such as the US, UK, Spain, Ireland and Australia. At the same time, the policies that have been adopted to address the financial crisis, such as the Federal Reserve's loosening of monetary policy through its multi-billion purchases of US Treasuries, have caused the dollar to fall relative to the Chinese renminbi. This has been a source of anguish to the Chinese. As so often in the past, the US has tended to regard any weakness in the dollar as everyone else's problem. Yet, ironically, congressmen continued to attack China for manipulating its exchange rate without grasping, during the period of dollar weakness, that China had started to import inflation from the US. This caused China's real exchange rate, which reflects the purchasing power of the currency after adjusting for inflation, to appreciate, making its exports less competitive.

In effect, the US wreaked revenge on China for its mercantilist policies, even if this outcome was a by-product of policies pursued primarily for domestic purposes. The Chinese were further scared in 2014–15 by the readiness of Republican politicians to risk driving the US government into default in the interests of humbling President Obama and dismantling his health-care legislation. Chinese concern was palpable when Standard & Poor's, the rating agency, removed its triple-A rating from US government debt. The result of this complex economic interaction, then, has been a dialogue of the deaf in which the Americans accused the Chinese of fuelling the housing bubble that led to the financial crisis while the Chinese attacked American profligacy, its fiscal and monetary irresponsibility. The dialogue continues and it carries the potential for considerable friction of the kind envisaged by Keynes.

Frictions with China's other trading partners take a rather different form. The country has enjoyed substantial inward investment from Japan, whose businesses have played an important part in China's industrialisation. Yet, in the row that broke in 2013 over the disputed Senkaku Islands, known as the Diaoyu Islands in China, both sides have shown signs of putting fierce nationalist instinct before economic calculation. Many Japanese businesses in China have been vandalised by angry mobs that have been encouraged to run riot by government officials. In these circumstances, the security guarantee that the US extends to Japan may be a greater restraining influence on China than trade dependence, although it is conceivable that China's imposition of an air defence identification zone over the islands was a way of testing the robustness of the US security guarantee.

The trade and peace conjunction also runs into the problem that unelected Chinese politicians may put the interests of the Communist Party elite before those of the nation. Their legitimacy, after all, rests chiefly on the continuation of high rates of economic growth. If they fail to deliver, their survival in an economic crisis may depend on whipping up nationalist popular feeling against Japan, Taiwan or other Asian neighbours, intensive trade relations notwithstanding. As for China's financial interconnectedness with the US through its dollar-denominated official reserves, it is an irrelevance. China will not go to war with the US because Beijing knows that it could not possibly win.

So, much as I sympathise with the instincts of the liberal internationalists, I suspect that statistical research by academics on the propensity to go to war or refrain from war will not have much explanatory power in this, the most fraught case of trade and financial interdependence. Future events in the Pacific region may also give the lie to those who think the greatest security threats now come from terrorism, not states. The dynamic there looks dangerously akin to the flawed balance-of-power system that destabilised Europe in the twentieth century. In extreme circumstances, it is possible that, as before the First World War, nationalism will trump economic interest.

There may nonetheless be room for a less strong version of the liberal internationalist thesis. It appears, for example, to make good sense in the context of relations between states in the developed world. Many believe that the founding fathers of the European Union were right in thinking that strong trade links would help reduce the risk of war. It certainly now seems inconceivable that a German army will ever again sweep into the Netherlands, Belgium or France. Nor does the US seem remotely likely to use force against another developed country.

That said, it is hard to know the relative contribution of the complex political ecosystem of the EU in maintaining the peace as against that of economic linkages. Moreover, the Cold War provided France and Germany with a common enemy and a dangerous nuclear context that was well designed to bring about a psychological shift away from militarism and nationalism. In addition, post-war Europe unloaded much of the responsibility and cost of its external security onto the US, thereby reducing internal threats, with the US obtaining a quid pro quo through its substantial direct investments in Europe. Perhaps most importantly of all, Germany, having suffered the appalling consequences of defeat in two world wars, has little appetite for a third self-inflicted catastrophe.

Even so, it is not unthinkable that democratic, advanced countries will engage in future wars of plunder. Oil is widely believed to have been an important factor, for example, in the decision of George W. Bush's administration to invade Iraq, and is known to have loomed large in the thinking of the Vice-President Dick Cheney, a former chairman and chief executive of the oilfield services company Halliburton.

Another more modest version of the liberal internationalist

hypothesis on interdependence is offered by the Singaporean academic and former diplomat Kishore Mahbubani. He is one of many who have argued that a consequence of globalisation is that we are all crammed into this boat together and that interdependence increasingly forces states to look for cooperative solutions to geo-political problems, whether successfully or otherwise.[115] Looked at from another perspective, there are also good grounds for thinking that trade protectionism – a retreat from open trade – can increase the risk of war. This is an important lesson of 1929–32, when a collapse of trade acted as a spur to German and Japanese imperialism, which was directed, among other things, at improved access to food and raw materials.

The verdict on the kind of thinking exemplified by Montesquieu and other liberal-minded intellectuals must nonetheless be that while it was an interesting attempt to legitimise what we now call market capitalism and to make the profit motive respectable, its claims to be able to restrain human passions were overstated. The astonishing thing is that this essentially romantic idea has such enduring appeal despite its manifest failure to prevent a world war at a time in the early twentieth century when international trade links had never been more intense.

CHAPTER SEVEN

SPECULATION – THE MISSING SHAME GENE

'You have brought this country to the greatest financial panic in history.'

'We brought this country, sir, to its standing in the world through speculation.'

That exchange in 1932 between Smith Brookhart, of the US Senate banking and currency committee, and Richard Whitney, head of the New York Stock Exchange, about who was to blame for the 1929 crash, is a reminder that speculation is as divisive a subject as money itself. It also has a special place, as we shall see, in the nagging debate on the moral character of capitalism.[116] Yet in one quite literal sense, Whitney was right. The American frontier was, after all, driven by land speculation. And that in turn reminds us that there is a deal of hypocrisy about the subject – a notable case in point being the seventh President of the United States of America. Andrew Jackson, famous general and virulent scourge of speculators, had, in fact, been a land speculator himself. But the prize for hypocrisy surely goes to Karl Marx. In his biography of the author of *Das Kapital*, Francis Wheen reveals that this rabid opponent of capitalism confessed to a friend that he had been speculating

> partly in American funds, but more especially in English stocks, which are springing up like mushrooms this year (in furtherance of every imaginable and unimaginable joint stock enterprise), are forced up to quite an unreasonable level and then, for the most part, collapse. In this way I have made over £400 and, now that the complexity of the political situation affords greater scope, I shall begin all over again. It's a type of operation that makes small demands on one's time, and it's worthwhile running some risk in order to relieve the enemy of his money.[117]

In short, Marx was what would now be called a day trader. He otherwise depended for his living on handouts, most notably from Friedrich Engels, the fox-hunting, factory-owning capitalist who co-authored *The Communist Manifesto*. The ironies abound.

Discussing the rights and wrongs of speculation calls for the making of important and often difficult distinctions. When, in 1867, the British Prime Minister William Gladstone pressed the case with Queen Victoria for the grant of a peerage to the banker Lionel Rothschild, the response from Buckingham Palace was as follows:

> The Queen really cannot make up her mind to do it. It is not only the feeling of which she cannot divest herself, against making a person of the Jewish religion, a Peer; but she cannot think that one who owes his great wealth to contracts with

Foreign Govts for Loans, or to successful speculation on the Stock Exchange can fairly claim a British peerage.

However high Sir L. Rothschild may stand personally in Public Estimation, this seems to her not the less a species of gambling, because it is on a gigantic scale – and far removed from the legitimate trading which she *delights* to *honour*, in which men have raised themselves by patient industry and unswerving probity to positions of wealth and influence.[118]

In due course, royal anti-Semitism waned and the Rothschilds found their way into the House of Lords. Yet many people today would entirely sympathise with Queen Victoria's preference for what she called legitimate trading and patient industry, feeling instinctively that dealing with tangible goods is somehow more virtuous than intangible finance – a theme already explored in Chapter Four.

Other distinctions are less easy to draw. Sir Ernest Cassel, banker to Queen Victoria's son Edward VII and thus jocularly known as 'Windsor' Cassel, said: 'When I was young, people called me a gambler. As the scale of my operations increased I became known as a speculator. Now I am called a banker. But I have been doing the same thing all the time.' In his fine book *Devil Take the Hindmost: A History of Financial Speculation*, Edward Chancellor writes:

The line separating speculation from investment is so thin that it has been said both that speculation is the name given to a failed investment and that investment is the name given to a successful speculation. Fred Schwed, a Wall Street wit, declared that clarifying the difference between investment and speculation was 'like explaining to a troubled adolescent that Love and Passion are two different things. He perceives that they are different, but they don't seem quite different enough to clear up his problem.' Schwed concluded that the two could be separated on the grounds that the first aim of investment was the preservation of capital while the primary aim of speculation was the enhancement of fortune. As he put it: 'Speculation is an effort, probably unsuccessful, to turn a little money into a lot. Investment is an effort, which should be successful, to prevent a lot of money becoming a little.'

Similar problems of definition are encountered in distinguishing speculation from gambling. While a bad investment may be a speculation, a poorly executed speculation is often described as a gamble. The American financier Bernard Baruch was once dismissed from the presence of Pierpont Morgan for uttering the word 'gamble' in relation to a business proposition. Later, Baruch recalled that 'there is no investment which doesn't involve some risk and is not something of a gamble'. The psychologies of speculation and gambling are almost indistinguishable: both are dangerously addictive habits which involve an appeal to fortune, are often accompanied by delusional behaviour and are dependent for success on the control of emotions.[119]

Perhaps the simplest way to think of the difference between speculation and investment is to distinguish between people who try to profit from changes in the prices of assets, usually over a relatively short time horizon, and those who wish to secure an income by participating in the earning power of an asset over a longer period. The former are speculators; the latter investors. As for assets, some are almost by definition speculative because they generate no income. Gold and other commodities fall into this category. Works of art are even more speculative, because their value is entirely dependent on taste and fashion. (As we shall see in a later chapter, that did not prevent the pension fund of the nationalised British Rail in the UK from building up a portfolio of artworks in the great inflationary panic of the 1970s, or Japanese insurance companies from buying Van Goghs in the Japanese bubble of the 1980s.) Now commodities increasingly find their way into institutional investors' portfolios. Some financial instruments are, so to speak, dual-use: options, swaps and credit derivatives can be used either to hedge, or to speculate, while investing with borrowed money – investing on margin – always counts as speculative. So, too, does short selling, where people borrow shares in order to sell them in the hope of being able to buy them back more cheaply at a later date and make a profit on the return of the shares to the lender.[120]

Such activities are by nature short-termist, especially where investment judgements are divorced from underlying economic fundamentals. John Maynard Keynes in his *General Theory* famously described how long-term investment came to be superseded by speculation. The aim of most skilled investment, he said, was, in the American phrase, 'to beat the gun'. And he compared it to newspaper competitions where competitors had to pick out the six prettiest faces from a hundred photographs, the prize going to the competitor whose choice most nearly corresponded to the average preferences of the competitors as a whole. To be successful, the competitor had to pick not what he judged to be the prettiest faces, but those he thought most likely to appeal to other competitors, all of whom were looking at the problem from the same point of view:

> It is not a case of choosing those which, to the best of one's judgement, are really the prettiest, nor even those which average opinion genuinely thinks the prettiest. We have reached the third degree where we devote our intelligences to anticipating what average opinion expects the average opinion to be. And there are some, I believe, who practise the fourth, fifth and higher degrees.[121]

From a historical perspective, the most impassioned debate over the pros and cons of speculation took place between two of the American Founding Fathers, Alexander Hamilton and Thomas Jefferson. Hamilton, the US Treasury Secretary, wanted the federal government to have centralised power to tax and create credit for the new republic. Hence his proposal for a central bank modelled on the Bank of England. Yet for Jefferson, banks, and especially central banks, were anathema, while the cities of the eastern seaboard, where Big Money ruled, were sinks of iniquity. So was London, home of banks to which Jefferson himself owed money. Like so many people before and since, he preferred business to produce real things – ideally agricultural produce – rather than make money out of money, which he – like Aristotle – thought was a nonsense.

What irked Jefferson as much as Hamilton's plan for the First Bank of the United States was his proposal to issue new federal debt in exchange for the IOUs with which soldiers had been paid in the Revolutionary War. After the war, both the federal and state governments were overloaded with debt. Some states were simply not creditworthy. Hamilton wanted to consolidate all this debt at federal level to boost the credit standing of the country. Yet Jefferson's reservations were not ill founded. New York speculators, acting on inside information about Hamilton's plans, bought up great quantities of these IOUs at depressed prices. This left Hamilton with a dilemma. Should the soldiers be compensated for their losses, or should the speculators be allowed their profits? In the interests of establishing the creditworthiness of the new country, he decided that the government should honour contracts and stand behind the transferability of the bonds. Hamilton's biographer Ron Chernow remarks:

> Hamilton stole the moral high ground from opponents and established the legal and moral basis for securities trading in America: the notion that securities are freely transferable and that buyers assume all rights to profits and losses in transactions. The knowledge that government could not interfere retroactively with a financial transaction was so vital … as to outweigh any short-term expediency. To establish the concept of the 'security transfer' Hamilton was willing, if necessary, to reward mercenary scoundrels and penalise patriotic citizens.[122]

And that is precisely what he did. It was clearly unjust, but also a symbolic moment for the fledgling United States. With hindsight we can see that Hamilton succeeded in conveying a message to moneybags around the world that they could invest in the US in the knowledge that property rights were strong and that debt contracts were sacrosanct. There followed a wave of capital inflows that were immensely beneficial for the developing economy. That was another profound sense in which Richard Whitney's assertion to Smith Brookhart about the value of speculation to the United States was correct. Yet this controversial decision left an aftertaste down the ages. As historian Simon Schama has remarked:

> From the time around 1790, when Thomas Jefferson, that lyricist of the agrarian life (as long as the slaves did the heavy lifting) attempted to persuade President George Washington that Andrew Hamilton's plan for a central bank was a threat to American liberties, the tripwire of suspicion about banks, especially central banks, has seldom stopped humming.[123]

The irony here is that the rural community idealised by Jefferson has benefited hugely from one of the more controversial financial innovations. Commodity futures, so often regarded as highly speculative, have allowed farmers to sell crops in advance at prices that enable them to lock in a safe profit before the outcome of the harvest is known. Risk is thereby mitigated. Indeed, much of the economic case for speculation rests on the fact that speculators take on the risks that other people do not want. Without them, conventional investors would not be able to hedge or to sell so quickly, so they make markets work more efficiently.

The Harvard economist Jeff Frankel has illustrated the classic moral dilemma inherent in speculation by citing the film version of John Steinbeck's *East of Eden*, in which the charismatic James Dean plays the character Cal.[124] Like Cain in Genesis,

Cal competes with his brother for the love of his father, a mor-
alising patriarch. He takes a long position in the market for
beans, expecting an increase in demand if the United States
enters the First World War. When the price of beans duly rock-
ets, he makes a fortune and offers it to his father to make up
money he had lost in another venture. Unfortunately for Cal,
the father is morally offended because he does not want to
profit from the misfortunes of others and urges him to 'give the
money back' – a singularly difficult proposition, incidentally,
in large, diverse financial markets.

Frankel's point is that a 'bearer of bad tidings' like Cal per-
forms an important social function in the capitalist system by
delivering the news that increased demand is likely to drive
prices upwards in future. His actions send the price signal that
is needed to bring real resources more closely into line with
the future balance between supply and demand. Without the
speculator, the subsequent price rise would be even greater because there would be less supply.

Short sellers can likewise have an important social function.
Consider the case of a financially stressed company that wants
to raise capital. Many investors will be willing to buy its IOUs
on the basis that they will hedge the risk of holding the debt by
taking an offsetting short position in the company's shares. If
the company runs into trouble, the profit on the short-selling
transaction will offset the losses on the debt. That would strike
many people as morally acceptable. And most short selling,
incidentally, consists of arbitrage trades like this rather than
straight bets on companies performing badly. Yet it arouses
passionate (and selective) criticism. The same people who
are delighted if short sellers in the oil market bring down the

price of oil will criticise those who go short of shares in an oil company. Chairmen and chief executives are among the more virulent because they hate the negative verdict on their own performance and fear that a sharp fall in the share price may undermine their job security.

Such controversy goes back at least as far as the early seventeenth century, when the Dutch East India Company filed complaints against the Amsterdam Stock Exchange over the large profits made by short sellers in 1609. This led to regulations being imposed on short selling the following year – a pattern that would be repeated time and again after market collapses including the Wall Street Crash of 1929, which prompted a witch hunt against short sellers when scapegoats were urgently needed.[125] The usual impact of these regulations is that market liquidity – the ability to trade in large amounts without causing volatile price movements – becomes thin, and capital raising is consequently more difficult. In more recent times, Kenneth Lay, chairman of the failed energy group Enron, attributed the company's downfall to malevolent short sellers, while Dick Fuld of Lehman Brothers notoriously declared: 'When I find a short seller, I want to tear his heart out and eat it before his eyes while he's still alive.' Yet the short sellers were the ones who were right. They identified the weaknesses of Enron and Lehman, and the resulting slide in their share prices was an accurate reflection of economic reality as these sorely mismanaged outfits approached collapse. That fundamental point has, incidentally, been well understood by great novelists. The dramatic dénouement of Zola's late nineteenth-century work *L'Argent* consists of a short-selling operation in which a brilliant financier realises that a rival's bank is fraudulent, and brings about its demise. While Zola was anxious to convey the financial sleaze and corruption of the French Second Empire and to emphasise the terrible effects of speculation on ordinary people, he nonetheless showed how short selling could uncover the unpalatable truth.

Milton Friedman, economist and great propagandist for free market capitalism, argued that speculation was a stabilising influence in markets generally. And there is widespread acceptance among economists that stabilising speculation can dampen volatility in markets because speculators are prepared to take a contrary view. Yet Friedman went further. People who think speculation destabilising fail to realise, he said, that this is the equivalent of saying that speculators lose money, since speculation can only be generally destabilising if speculators on average sell when prices are low and buy when prices are high. In other words, they can only destabilise market if, on average, they fail to take a contrary view. Yet here he was on shakier ground. The economic historian Charles Kindleberger countered that speculators in a bubble were not a homogeneous group. There was invariably a small group of permanent insiders who bought shares, or promoted companies, when prices were low, and sold shares when they were high, so precipitating a collapse. A much larger group of gullible outsiders – the legendary waiters and bootblacks of the 1929 crash, for example – came in late to buy, lost money and returned to waiting and boot blacking after the market collapsed.

Dickens understood this better than many ideological free market economists – witness in *Nicholas Nickleby*, already referred to in Chapter Five, the flotation of the portentously named United Metropolitan Improved Hot Muffin and

Crumpet Baking and Punctual Delivery Company.[126] The promoters, who included Nicholas Nickleby's uncle Ralph, one of
Dickens's many money-lending ogres, were floating a company
that had no existing business and which was most unlikely to
extract from Parliament the monopoly on which those future
riches depended. Such crooked behaviour is a characteristic
bubble phenomenon. Based on data from the second half of
the twentieth century, economists have established that companies coming to the stock market without any record of
making profits underperform on average and have a higher
failure rate than others. The insider nature of such scams is
revealed by a promoter and colleague of Ralph Nickleby, Mr
Bonney, described as a man in a violent hurry:

'My dear Nickleby,' said the gentleman, taking off a white
hat which was so full of papers that it would scarcely stick
upon his head, 'there's not a moment to lose; I have a cab
at the door. Sir Matthew Pupker takes the chair, and three
Members of Parliament are positively coming. I have seen
two of them safely out of bed; and the third, who was at
Crockford's all night, has just gone home to put a clean shirt
on, and take a bottle or two of soda-water, and will certainly
be with us in time to address the meeting. He is a little excited by last night, but never mind that; he always speaks the
stronger for it.'

'It seems to promise pretty well,' said Mr Ralph Nickleby,
whose deliberate manner was strongly opposed to the vivac-
ity of the other man of business.

'Pretty well!' echoed Mr Bonney; 'It's the finest idea that
was ever started. 'United Metropolitan Improved Hot Muffin

and Crumpet Baking and Punctual Delivery Company. Capital, five millions, in five hundred thousand shares of ten pounds each.' Why the very name will get the shares up to a premium in ten days.'

'And when they *are* at a premium,' said Mr Ralph Nickleby, smiling.

'When they are, you know what to do with them as well as any man alive, and how to back quietly out at the right time,' said Mr Bonney, slapping the capitalist familiarly on the shoulder.[127]

Many of the greatest speculators are also on Kindleberger's side of the argument because their experience tells them that prices can remain out of line with fundamentals for considerable periods. Indeed, George Soros, the hedge fund manager and philanthropist who made billions betting against sterling when it fell out of Europe's exchange rate mechanism in 1992, says the belief that markets are self-correcting is a form of economic fundamentalism – a point already explored in Chapter Five. In his view, an innate feature of capitalism is that markets are inherently unstable. He has made fortunes by analysing and profiting precisely from these market aberrations. From an economic perspective, then, there is good speculation and bad speculation. The good sort, based on sharp analysis of economic fundamentals, makes markets work more efficiently. The bad sort results from a bandwagon effect where speculators simply follow a trend. By adding to momentum in the market they can contribute to a bubble in which prices part company with economic reality. When the bubble bursts, it can precipitate severe recession or even slump.

If making the case for the economic and social benefits of speculation is difficult, it is partly because, as in *East of Eden*, speculators such as short sellers are making profits from others' misfortunes: the collapse of the housing market, a shortage of grain or the decline of a company. One consequence is that they make highly attractive scapegoats. The former Wall Street trader Fred Schwed, quoted earlier, understood this perfectly:

> An injured party cannot get his hands on unsound credit infla-tion or the law of gravitation. It is much more satisfactory, for instance, to get Mr J. P. Morgan, the perfect personification of Wealth, down to Washington to be asked, by men of moder-ate means, a lot of questions he can't satisfactorily answer.
>
> However, Mr Morgan and the great bankers are not quite the perfect scapegoats: after all, it requires some mental strain to connect up their unwise or allegedly criminal ac-tivities with our own plight. They may have played ducks and drakes with the national credit (and everybody knows what that is, even if he can't quite explain it) or maybe it was something else they did which was even worse and even harder to understand.
>
> Our own personal plight, however, is crystal clear. We are long, on margin, several hundred shares of Radio, and the margin is disappearing. We originally got the tip from our brother-in-law, and he got it from a Very Big Man whom he met at a clambake. That Man, big as he was, was not nearly so big as Mr Morgan and had not ever met him or any other 'robber baron' either.
>
> But how about those short-selling fellows? Now we are getting close to home. At the very moment when we were

buying that stock, hopefully and constructively, looking forward and upward toward better things, those fellows, men
without bowels, were *selling* it, and they didn't even have it
to sell![128]

Schwed, who believed that short sellers' influence on markets
was 'a little more than a drop in the bucket and something
less than a hill of beans', was writing in the late 1930s, but
his caricature applied with equal force in the post-war period.
When Britain was forced to devalue in 1967, the Labour Prime
Minister Harold Wilson blamed the 'gnomes of Zurich' for the
run on sterling. More recently, when food prices were soaring
in 2011, President Sarkozy of France declared that speculation
in agricultural commodities was nothing more than extortion
and pillage. And it is true that the rise in food prices across the
world at that time was a very serious problem which gave rise
to widespread rioting in developing countries. It also played a
part in starting the Arab Spring. Yet research by the International Monetary Fund, the Organisation for Economic Cooperation and Development, the US Federal Reserve and other
worthy bodies threw up no conclusive evidence of causality
between market speculation and commodity prices in this
case. Easy money, the growing demand for food in emerging
markets such as China and India, instability in oil-producing
countries in the Middle East, extreme weather conditions and
subsidies for ethanol may have been more powerful influences
on prices than speculation when President Sarkozy was sound-
ing off. That said, there is a growing body of evidence that
financial speculation is causing extreme price movements as
investment banks and pension funds treat commodities as a

specific asset class that supposedly offers the benefits of diversification. These movements may also be exacerbated by the activities of high-frequency traders, who use computerised algorithms to analyse market data and trade frenetically in milliseconds or even microseconds. There is also an arguable case against short selling in banking when confidence is fragile, because a collapsing share price may encourage a run on the deposits of a solvent bank, thereby precipitating its collapse.

Another reason that speculation has always evoked mixed reactions is that the stock and commodity exchanges where so much of it takes place have until recently been pretty unsavoury places, and the speculators themselves have been pretty unsavoury folk. A flavour of what market life was like in the early days of stock exchanges can be gleaned from the title of the tract from 1719 by Daniel Defoe already mentioned in Chapter Five:

> The anatomy of exchange alley, or A system of stock-jobbing: proving that scandalous trade, as it is now carry'd on to be knavish in its private practice and treason in its publick … to which is added some characters of the most eminent persons concern'd now, and for some years past, in carrying on this pernicious trade, by a jobber.

In fact Defoe was himself a jobber and one of the more notable speculators of the day. In the City at that time, insider dealing was rife. Speculators tried to corner stocks to create artificial scarcity and were adept at other forms of share manipulation, short selling and, with the help of corrupt journalists, false rumour mongering. It was not until the twentieth century that such practices were vigorously, but by no means completely, reined in by regulation. Much of the regulation was introduced in response to the 1929 crash. And it is worth noting, in passing, that Richard Whitney, the great defender of speculation, ultimately went to jail for embezzlement.

As with capitalism itself, speculation has made progress towards a degree of respectability. This started, predictably enough, in the US, where the epitome of the respectable speculator was Bernard Baruch, who made a fortune in the sugar market around the start of the twentieth century. Baruch's view on speculation and short selling, expressed before the Committee on Rules of the US House of Representatives in 1917, was that 'to enjoy the advantages of a free market, one must have both buyers and sellers, both bulls and bears. A market without bears would be like a nation without a free press. There would be no one to criticise and restrain the false optimism that always leads to disaster.'[129]

The fact that Baruch was a well-known speculator did not prevent him from becoming an adviser to President Woodrow Wilson on defence in the First World War. He also made an important contribution to stepping up wartime industrial production. Then he became an adviser to President Franklin Roosevelt, and in the period after 1945 made important recommendations for the control and elimination of nuclear weapons. Yet Baruch's fame is as much down to his reputation for having predicted the 1929 crash as for his public service. This is paradoxical. The financial commentator and historian James Grant has shown, through meticulous research, that Baruch lost a great deal of money in the crash, although he still managed to hold on to a very large fortune. As a multi-purpose

sage and political courtier, he was inevitably open to the charge
that his influence owed more to his fortune than his wisdom.
That suspicion is evident in Grant's quotation from the celebrated wit Dorothy Parker, who once said that two things
confused her: the theory of the zipper and the exact function
of Bernard Baruch.

Other speculators had respectability thrust upon them,
the most conspicuous being Joseph Kennedy, father of Jack,
Robert and Edward, who made a fortune from short selling
during the 1929 crash. He was the first head of the Securities
and Exchange Commission, which was charged with cleaning
up the US stock market after a welter of manipulative and
fraudulent schemes was exposed in the market downturn.
Kennedy proved to be one of history's most effective poachers
turned gamekeepers in a period when the Hamilton–Jefferson
debate on the morality of speculation resurfaced against a
background of widespread bank failures and virulent Main
Street antipathy for Wall Street. Today's speculators more
often than not operate under the guise of hedge fund managers. Huge killings were made, for example, from the collapse
in the value of asset-backed securities and the subsequent collapse in equities in 2007–09 by such red-in-tooth-and-claw
hedge fund men as John Paulson.

Yet to say that speculation has finally achieved respectability would be pushing the case too far. In Western culture, the
Christian legacy means that many people still feel uncomfortable about profiting from the misfortunes of others and making
money out of money – something that does not trouble, say, the
Chinese, who are more at ease with speculation. Yet there are
some categories of people who seem to have a greater ability

to overcome the inhibition than others. Clearly stockbrokers have fewer worries about it than most. Yet this also applies to many economists, perhaps because their discipline encourages them to think entirely objectively about market behaviour.

In the UK, some of the greatest speculators have, in fact, been economists. David Ricardo, best known for developing the law of comparative advantage, one of the most powerful ideas in economics, made a killing (as did Nathan Rothschild) by betting against a French victory at Waterloo. He amassed a considerable fortune in his stockbroking business, which allowed him to retire early to write and become a Member of Parliament. Keynes was also a great speculator, despite his reservations about speculation and about capitalism more generally. This brought him close to bankruptcy when, after the First World War, he discovered that playing the currency markets on the basis of long-term economic judgements was a recipe for disaster. He lost everything and had outstanding debts with his broker, Buckmaster & Moore, of nearly £5,000. Fortunately for him, Sir Ernest Cassel, a family friend, came to his rescue and lent him the money to stay in the game and recoup his position. Yet the great economist lost almost all his money again in 1929. He rebuilt his net worth to more than £500,000 in 1936, equivalent to £25 million in 2008 money, but then suffered another setback in 1937–38.

Keynes was willing to take some hair-raising plunges. On one occasion in 1936, he was required, as a consequence of taking a speculative position in the commodity markets, to take delivery of a month's supply of wheat from Argentina when the market was plunging. He wanted to store the wheat in King's College Chapel, which happened to be one of the finest examples of perpendicular gothic architecture in England. When he discovered it was too small to house all the grain, he decided to object to the grain's quality. By the time it had been cleaned, the wheat price had recovered sufficiently for him to close the trade without incurring a loss or taking delivery. In the end, he emerged on top. On his death in 1946 he was worth more than £12 million in today's money.

Despite his statement in the *General Theory* that investment based on long-term expectations was so difficult as to be scarcely practicable, it is worth mentioning in passing that Keynes also invested with exceptional success over long periods of time. From 1924 to his death, he was responsible for managing a fund at King's College called the Chest. Here he brought together his understanding of market psychology and economic fundamentals, analysing company accounts for much of his life on a daily basis. Robert Skidelsky, from whose much-admired biography of Keynes this information largely comes, says that the Chest's capital increased sevenfold from 1920 to 1936, which is a remarkable performance against the depressed market background. It also substantially outperformed the stock market indices over the period.

Others are driven to speculation by desperation. Claude-Henri de Rouvroy, Comte de Saint-Simon, the social reformer and economist whose ideas pre-figured those of Keynes, was ruined by the French Revolution and tried to make good his losses by speculating in *biens nationaux*, the land confiscated by the revolution from the Church and the king. He made a fortune, promptly lost it and then decided to devote himself to the worthier causes for which he is better known. That once again underlines the point of how dangerous speculation can be. Even the most experienced market operators can go wrong. Jesse Livermore, one of the most celebrated speculators of all time, made fortunes first of $3 million, then of $100 million through short selling in the crashes of 1907 and 1929. Yet he also had a genius for losing money, and squandered these sums by failing to follow his own disciplined rules for playing the market. His greatest misfortune was to suffer from a manic depressive temperament. When his luck ran out in 1940, he shot himself in the washroom of New York's Sherry Netherland Hotel.

Desperation may also play a part in the speculative activity of rogue traders, who fall into a category all their own. The essence of rogue trading is that it takes place within a large organisation where internal controls are deficient. Rogue traders play with other people's money and in most cases do not profit personally. This is because their speculative activity is more often than not about trying to trade their way out of loss-making positions incurred on behalf of their employer. They do this by taking further big, risky bets, a practice sometimes referred to as gambling for redemption.

In times gone by there was a modicum of honour among thieving traders. When Lazard Brothers, the London arm of the Lazard banking empire, was brought to its knees by a rogue trader in its Brussels office in 1931, the miscreant made a confession and shot himself. Nick Leeson, a trader who provided a fine example on the trading floor in Singapore of the delusional behaviour mentioned earlier by Edward Chancellor, brought down Barings, another great British investment bank. Yet he and other recent rogue traders such as Jérôme Kerviel at Société Générale appear to have no shame gene. Nowadays it is only a mild exaggeration to say that European rogue traders serve relatively short jail sentences before taking to the lecture circuit to tell the world that the damage they wrought was largely the fault of their arrogant and stupid bosses. Their counterparts in the US face much tougher jail sentences and tend to show more humility, or reveal new-found religious belief, when they come out.[130]

Today, much of the financial speculation that goes on has become institutionalised in the banking system. From the early 1980s, big banks moved from being deposit takers and lenders to holding conglomerate status with substantial trading operations. These mega-banks started to sell most of the loans they initiated in packaged form to investors and to run large proprietary trading departments to take bets in the markets for their own account. Andrew Haldane of the Bank of England has estimated that the share of the major global banks' assets held in their trading books doubled between 2000 and 2007 from 20 per cent to 40 per cent. The growth especially of trading in derivative instruments and structured products such as collateralised debt obligations and credit default swaps has been spectacular. In the first decade of the new millennium, much of this dealing in what the investor Warren Buffett calls 'financial weapons of mass destruction' took place not on organised exchanges, but in opaque over-the-counter markets where transactions take place on computer screens and over the telephone between individual banks and companies. By the end of 2008, the gross market value of such over-the-counter derivative instruments had topped $32 trillion, according to the Bank for International Settlements. The result was that the biggest banks in the world became more like hedge funds than conventional banks, except that they backed all this activity with far less capital, which underlines the speculative nature of the whole operation. George Soros, a real hedge fund manager, has questioned the social utility of much of this frenetic hedge fund-type activity, as has Adair Turner, the British peer who headed the UK Financial Services Authority after the financial crisis.

When all this trading came to grief as the financial world came crashing down in 2007–09 and the biggest banks had to be bailed out by the taxpayer, the Jeffersonian antipathy for finance naturally enjoyed a vigorous new lease of life, leading to the greatest re-regulatory effort since the 1930s, an effort that included attempts to curb the banks' proprietary trading. Yet the battle between the politicians and the banks is uneven, because Big Money in the US pays for politicians' campaign finance. No sooner was the reforming Dodd–Frank Act placed on the statute book than an army of politicians, with wads of money from Wall Street in their back pockets, worked strenuously to dismantle it.

Of course, there will always be those who feel, like the late-nineteenth-century stockbroker quoted in David Kynaston's history of the London broker Cazenove, that 'a stock exchange restricted to investment business would be as useful and as popular as a public house licensed only for ginger beer'. For every one of those, there will be many more who share Henry Ford's view, not far removed from Queen Victoria's, that 'speculation is only a word covering the making of money out of the manipulation of prices, instead of supplying goods and services'.

Yet perhaps the real problem with speculation, as with so much in the workings of capitalism, is the in-built tendency towards excess. In the great debate on speculation, Keynes is closer to Hamilton than Jefferson. Yet he also understood the shortcomings of the Hamiltonian argument in one of his most famous quotes:

> Speculators may do no harm as bubbles on a steady stream of enterprise. But the position is serious when enterprise becomes the bubble on a whirlpool of speculation. When the capital development of a country becomes a by-product of the activities of a casino, the job is likely to be ill-done.[131]

It is, in the end, a question of balance. If speculation becomes excessive, the economic costs, as we learned in 2007–09, can be horrendous. We will be living with a hugely increased debt burden as a result, as will our children. In the light of that, another of Jefferson's aphorisms has a profound echo today: 'Every bank in America is an enormous tax upon the people for the profit of individuals.'

CHAPTER EIGHT

THE DYNAMICS OF DEBT

Deeply embedded in the human psyche is a profound am-bivalence about debt. We love our credit cards, those vital props of the modern capitalist economy, yet many find the pleasure in the spending spree is tinged with guilt. Somehow, saving seems more virtuous than debt-financed spending. This matters in the current context because in the debate on ethics and capitalism, the relationship between creditors and debtors looms uncomfortably large. Indeed, after the First World War, in *The Economic Consequences of the Peace*, John Maynard Keynes referred to relations between debtors and creditors as the ultimate foundation of the capitalist system. And the ambivalence about debt has been reinforced throughout the ages by a heavy legal and cultural bias in favour of creditors against debtors – a bias that Keynes was seeking to attack in his polemical post-war tract.

It is a bias that goes back a long way. The code of the an-cient Babylonian king Hammurabi, the first recorded legal code, from around 1790 BC, sets out gruesomely the terms on which a defaulter should sell himself, his wife, children, concu-bines or slaves to a creditor, or give his family away for forced labour to discharge unfulfilled debt obligations.[132] The code also set maximum rates of interest, amounting to 33 per cent per annum for loans of grain, repayable in kind, and 20 per cent per annum for loans of a given weight of silver.

That reminds us that conflicts between creditors and debtors are an age-old reflection of the unending struggle between rich and poor. So, too, does the remark by the classical historian Moses Finley that the perennial revolutionary programme of antiquity was a call to cancel debts and redistribute land.[133] And, as the journalist Philip Coggan writes in a compelling recent book on money and debt, one can see all of economic history through this prism – a battle between those who lend money and those who borrow it. He aptly quotes an early-nineteenth-century American thinker, John Taylor, who remarked that the banking industry 'divides the nations into two groups, creditors and debtors, and fills them each with malignity towards the other'.[134] The history is a good starting point because it helps explain how, in the modern world, debt also has the capacity to destabilise economies if households, companies or governments are allowed by creditors to take borrowing to excess. Excessive debt, like fragile banking, can pose a serious threat to the workings of capitalism.

Note, first, that the savage regulation of the relationship between debtor and creditor initiated by Hammurabi was tempered in the ancient world by one outstanding outbreak of liberalism. Around 600 BC, the Athenian constitutional reformer Solon responded to an economic crisis for which excessive debt was partly responsible by introducing laws that scrapped all limits on the rate of interest, reducing or cancelling many debts and forbidding personal slavery for debt. Despite this example, the Romans, when confronting a similar economic crisis 150 years later, chose instead to go the way of Hammurabi, introducing limits on loan interest and permitting debt slavery.

Since then, the relative power of creditors and debtors has constantly shifted back and forth, although extreme punishments such as debt slavery are long gone. In more recent times, creditors nonetheless continued to enjoy extraordinary legal powers to throw defaulting borrowers into jail. Debtors' prisons such as the Marshalsea, which plays a prominent part in Dickens's *Little Dorrit*, are a notably inhumane (and now happily defunct) illustration of this pro-creditor bias.

Even language tends to reinforce disapproval of indebtedness. The word for debt in Aramaic, the language spoken by Christ, doubles as the word for sin, while there is an etymological link between debt and guilt in the German word *schuld*, which may be a factor, albeit one of many, in the extreme financial conservatism displayed by Germans both in managing their domestic economy and in international monetary relations. Yet the morality of debt is less straightforward than this good housekeeping view might suggest – a view, moreover, which sits uncomfortably with modern capitalism, being a classic example of how what appears to be common sense can be bad economics. As for Polonius's advice to Laertes in Shakespeare's *Hamlet* –

> *Neither a borrower nor a lender be:*
> *For a loan oft loses both itself and friend;*
> *And borrowing dulls the edge of husbandry.*[135]

– it is psychologically acute, but a sure recipe for economic stagnation.

Few would disagree with the proposition that the relationship between debtor and creditor is fraught with difficulty. For a start, a transaction that involves the exchange of money today for a promise to return more money in future is inevitably hostage to economic fortune because all debt-financed investment is subject to risk. Even honest borrowers are not always able to pay up. Antonio, Shylock's debtor in Shakespeare's *The Merchant of Venice*, exemplifies the point. And, indeed, until relatively recently the extension of credit was perceived as an act of friendship and trust. There was a moral and social dimension to it and financial obligations could be repaid in different ways. In the eyes of Shakespeare's contemporaries, Shylock could only take a narrowly legalistic and financial view of his loan to Antonio because, as a Jew, he was outside the bonds of kinship and friendship that were at the heart of a Christian society.

While the terms of Shylock's loan, with a pound of flesh as the penalty for default, were unique, the discharge of debt was frequently not in financial form. The father of the poet John Milton was a scrivener who made loans at interest. The young poet's first wife, Mary Powell, was the daughter of a man who was in default on a £300 loan to Milton's father. The daughter was offered in marriage in lieu of collateral.[136] Something similar occurs in Mozart's *The Marriage of Figaro*, based on the play by Beaumarchais, where the penalty for default on a loan granted to Figaro by an ageing housekeeper, Marcellina, is to marry her. He escapes enforcement when it turns out that he is Marcellina's illegitimate son. Note, too, that while the plots of countless nineteenth-century novels turn on the non-payment of debt, this is a plot line that is largely in abeyance today. That no doubt reflects in part the declining moral and social dimension of debt relationships as the capitalist financial system has become more sophisticated and impersonal. At the same time, liberal legislation has tempered the ruthlessness of creditors and diminished the scope for debt to reduce people to dishonour, beggary, prostitution and suicide, as occurs in the works of Balzac, Zola, Dickens and Dostoyevsky.

The relationship between debtors and creditors is, then, a subtle one. And while there has always been an innate bias in favour of the creditor, that bias erodes as the size of the debt increases. As Keynes is said to have remarked: 'If you owe your bank a hundred pounds, you have a problem. But if you owe a million, it has.' This creates an interesting dynamic when the debtor is on the brink. A revealing case in point was the UK property company British Land in the financial crisis of the mid-1970s. In 1977, under the leadership of John Ritblat, the company suffered a severe cash crunch. The company history records:

Every day there were meetings with bankers. In the boom days before the credit crisis, not all loan documents had been as precise or as extensive as the banks would have liked, so there were marathon sessions with lawyers, all of which had to be paid by the borrower. The consequence was that, the more onerous the new conditions, the harder it became for the borrower to restore stability in its business ... At one stage a senior banker to the company insisted on addressing the board to expound at considerable length on his bank's view of British Land's financial condition at the time. Very gloomy he was, and he ended by asking whether the board agreed with his assessment and his grasp of the fine detail.

'Oh no,' said John Ritblat. 'It's very much worse than that.'

He went on to explain where and why – to the great embarrassment of the banker and his team who had missed so much.[137]

Recognising how big a hole they had dug for themselves, the banks wisely concluded that they needed John Ritblat to help them escape from the consequences of their earlier imprudent lending.

Much the same logic applies to sovereign debtors, whose defaults have been the single biggest cause of bank failures throughout history. The Bardi and Peruzzi banking families of Florence who helped finance the English in the Hundred Years War were bankrupted when Edward III defaulted in 1348. Florence suffered again in 1521 when François I of France seized Florentine property in Paris, Bordeaux and Lyons in an act of revenge against the bankers who betrayed his war preparations against the Spanish in Flanders. He defaulted a second time in 1529 after paying a huge ransom for his sons after the Treaty of Cambrai, which left him short of money to pay his debts. Louis XIV was similarly cavalier, bankrupting Samuel Bernard in 1709 when the Lyons banker refused to increase his lending to finance the War of the Spanish Succession, while Frederick the Great of Prussia, who never did anything by halves, destroyed more than fifty banks in Amsterdam in 1763 when he was in financial straits after the Seven Years War. These are just a handful of the sovereign defaults that have punctuated financial history, demonstrating that where monarchs were concerned, morality was neither here nor there when it came to paying up. The sovereign debtor–creditor relationship was a Darwinian struggle for supremacy in which bankers charged very high interest rates to compensate for the risk of default.

Perhaps the most extreme example of the vulnerability of bankers to determined sovereign borrowers is that of the Knights Templar. The medieval military order had an important sideline acting as banker and trustee to crusaders. Its castles around the Mediterranean doubled, in effect, as a branch banking network. This operation became what was then the world's biggest international banking institution. Yet it was not proof against a financially stretched Philippe IV of France when he had run through the usual expedients of debasing the currency and seizing the property of Jews and Lombards. In 1307, he started a vilification campaign aimed at robbing the Templars of their moral standing as a preliminary to looting their assets. He then arrested Templar leaders, who were accused of heresy, devil worship, sexual perversion and much else besides, to which they confessed under torture. They subsequently recanted, but many were nonetheless burned to death. Observing that the Templars' financial empire was up for grabs, Pope Clement V joined in the looting spree and abolished the order in 1312. That is the ultimate lesson in the Darwinian realpolitik of banking and it remains a profoundly shocking episode in the history of finance and the Catholic Church.

Ordinary individuals do not, of course, enjoy such power in dealing with their banks and have long suffered from the bias in favour of creditors, except in rare circumstances such as the French Revolution, where the mob sent bankers to the guillotine. This bias has huge economic disadvantages, as Daniel

Defoe, twice a bankrupt, pointed out in comments on English bankruptcy law in his first work, *An Essay upon Projects*:

> If I may be allowed so much liberty with our laws, which are generally good, and above all things are tempered with mercy, lenity, and freedom, this has something in it of barbarity; it gives a loose to the malice and revenge of the creditor, as well as a power to right himself, while it leaves the debtor no way to show himself honest. It contrives all the ways possible to drive the debtor to despair, and encourages no new industry, for it makes him perfectly incapable of anything but starving. This law, especially as it is now frequently executed, tends wholly to the destruction of the debtor, and yet very little to the advantage of the creditor.[138]

That view, from around 1697, was subsequently echoed by Dr Johnson, who, like the author of *Robinson Crusoe*, had first-hand experience of being arrested for debt. In *The Idler*, which contains two powerful essays inveighing against debtors' prisons and the ability of creditors to have hapless defaulters imprisoned, Johnson wrote:

> As I was passing lately under one of the gates of this city, I was struck with horror by a rueful cry, which summoned me to remember the poor debtors
>
> The wisdom and justice of the English laws are, by Englishmen at least, loudly celebrated: but scarcely the most zealous admirers of our institutions can think that law wise, which, when men are capable of work, obliges them to beg; or just, which exposes the liberty of one to the passions of another.

The prosperity of a people is proportionate to the number of hands and minds usefully employed. To the community, sedition is a fever, corruption is a gangrene, and idleness an atrophy. Whatever body, and whatever society, wastes more than it acquires, must gradually decay; and every being that continues to be fed, and ceases to labour, takes away something from the publick stock.

The confinement, therefore, of any man in the sloth and darkness of a prison, is a loss to the nation, and no gain to the creditor. For of the multitudes who are pining in those cells of misery, a very small part is suspected of any fraudulent act by which they retain what belongs to others. The rest are imprisoned by the wantonness of pride, the malignity of revenge, or the acrimony of disappointed expectation.[139]

In fact, Johnson may have exaggerated the awfulness of imprisonment to make his point. When his friend the poet Richard Savage was thrown into Bristol's Newgate Prison for debt, the jail keeper, the intriguingly named Abel Dagge, accompanied him on country walks outside the jail and drank with him in a Gloucestershire pub.[140] This probably owed more than a little to Savage's fabled charm. But it is also true that the inmates of many debtors' prisons, including those portrayed by Dickens in *Little Dorrit*, enjoyed greater freedoms than criminals in modern penal institutions. Since his own father had been imprisoned for debt when Dickens was in his teens, he knew whereof he spoke.

There is, of course, a fundamental tension between the ethical notion that people should take responsibility for their actions and the economic and social case for giving people a fresh start.

That reflects the conflict between notions of morality common to the Abrahamic religions and the utilitarianism that provides the ethical basis, such as it is, of capitalism. Conventional ideas of honesty require that debts be repaid in full. The imperative of economic growth, which we rely on to raise living standards, may mean that it is sensible to relieve the debtor of the full obligation. The question is how to strike a balance between these two positions. In the event, modern society increasingly embraced the logic implicit in the Biblical notion of the jubilee, a year in which slaves and prisoners were freed and debts were forgiven. English ministers under Queen Anne responded to the case made by Defoe, Johnson and others with a new bankruptcy law in 1706, which introduced the concept of legal discharge from debt on partial repayment. The legislation, which came at a time when debtors accounted for a majority of the prison population, was prompted by the economic disruption caused by the jailing of much of the English merchant class. This was a result not of improvidence but of the combined impact of bubonic plague, a storm that wrecked the country's merchant fleet, and war with France. The initiative was, in fact, a precursor of modern macro-economic management. Nobody in the seventeenth century thought to manipulate interest rates and budget deficits to smooth out economic cycles as governments and central banks do today, but debt forgiveness was another form of manipulation that could prevent the economy going into freefall when hit by adverse conditions.

The new legislation struck a more humane and economically productive balance between borrowers and lenders. As well as offering creditors a mechanism to retrieve their money, this and other more liberal laws that followed in England and elsewhere relieved debtors of debt burdens that had become oppressive and unmanageable. The underlying idea is precisely that if borrowers are hopelessly overloaded with debt, they will see no point in working like slaves merely to repay creditors. So there is mutual advantage for both parties in a legally sanctioned element of forgiveness – the concept of discharge – to permit a fresh start. Debtors then have more reason to work hard in the hope of keeping their business afloat, thereby ensuring that creditors will be repaid more. Equally important, if a would-be entrepreneur knows that he or she will not end up in jail if the business fails and loans cannot be repaid, the climate for risk taking, and thus for economic growth, will be more favourable.

In nineteenth-century Britain, liberal attitudes to debt were further extended as a result of the introduction of limited liability, which meant that creditors could no longer seek redress against shareholders if a company defaulted on its debts. This was a clear retreat from punitive attitudes to non-payment of debt. Yet such liberalism co-existed with a continuing view of debt as sinful. The historian Henry Roseveare has written of the opposition to indebtedness in the UK at that time:

> An ethic transmuted into a cult, this ideal of economical and therefore virtuous government passed from the hands of prigs like Pitt into those of high priests like Gladstone. It became a religion of financial orthodoxy whose Trinity was Free Trade, Balanced Budgets and the Gold Standard, whose Original Sin was the National Debt. It seems no accident that 'Conversion' and 'Redemption' should be the operations most closely associated with the Debt's reduction.[141]

The retreat from moralistic attitudes to debt nonetheless continued in the twentieth century, not least because of the greatly enlarged role credit plays in a modern capitalist economy driven by a more pronounced business cycle. The underlying point is that it is difficult to secure a genuinely robust economy if an obsession with a narrow conception of justice is allowed to trump economic logic. The majoritarian principle of the greatest happiness of the greatest number – the utilitarian ethic – has to prevail over the injunctions of the Abrahamic religions for capitalism to do its work in raising living standards and reducing poverty.

It is no coincidence that a country like the US, whose bankruptcy laws are famously liberal, has an exceptionally vibrant venture capital sector and a very entrepreneurial culture. As a fledgling nation it borrowed heavily from England, so the protection of debtors was naturally perceived to be in the national interest. Nor is it entirely coincidental that three American presidents, Abraham Lincoln, Ulysses S. Grant and William McKinley, experienced bankruptcy personally, as did a number of great entrepreneurs, including William C. Durant (founder of General Motors), Henry Ford, Milton Hershey, H. J. Heinz and Walt Disney. British attitudes to bankruptcy have also been relatively sympathetic to debtors: witness the fact that six of the Bank of England's nine governors between 1828 and 1847 went through personal bankruptcy during their careers. One even went bankrupt while in office. In contrast, many continental European countries have made it difficult for bankrupts to obtain a discharge from their debts, holding to the old view that an inability to pay must be the result of recklessness and immorality. Few European governments, central banks or great European corporations, as far as I am aware, have been headed by former bankrupts.

If Johnson's chief economic worry about penalising debtors was to do with the waste of resources involved, the economist Joseph Schumpeter took the argument forward by highlighting the role of debt in economic development and in fostering a more meritocratic society: 'That the structure of modern industry could not have been erected without it [finance], that it makes the individual to a certain extent independent of inherited possessions, that talent in economic life "rides to success on its debts", even the most conservative orthodoxy of the theorists cannot well deny.'[142]

Indeed, Schumpeter saw credit creation and the contracting of debt obligations as being at the very centre of modern capitalism's process of creative destruction. The entrepreneur, he argued, could

> only become an entrepreneur by previously becoming a debtor. He becomes a debtor in consequence of the logic of the process of development ... What he first wants is credit. Before he requires any goods whatever, he requires purchasing power. He is the typical debtor in capitalist society.[143]

While bankers may be objects of hatred to the public in the wake of the great financial crisis that struck in 2007, most academic specialists now accept that finance lubricates wealth creation. The economists Luigi Zingales and Raghuram Rajan have rightly remarked that every revolution that sends bankers to the guillotine soon finds the need to resurrect them as the wheels of commerce grind to a halt.[144]

Nor is it just the business community that benefits from access to finance. A central function of any financial system is to recycle the savings of those with no immediate use for them to those who can put them to good use. As a result, to take an obvious example, young people with a lifetime's earning power ahead of them, but no significant savings, can borrow for house purchase through the good offices of banks from people in their fifties and sixties who are saving for retirement. The banking system brings the two groups together in the process known as financial intermediation. Yet this is more common in the English-speaking countries than elsewhere. In much of continental Europe, regulations hinder borrowing for house purchase by requiring the borrower to save a significant amount as a pre-condition of the loan or by imposing tough loan-to-value ratios and short repayment periods. This is one of the reasons why over 80 per cent of Italian men between eighteen and thirty live at home with their parents. Note, in passing, that when a conservative view of debt prevails over libertarian values, it tends to create a very favourable climate for loan sharking. Japan is an interesting case in point. Experience here suggests that conservatism can be as much part of the debtor's psychology as an imposition by the creditor. Japan's *sarakin* banks, short-term consumer lenders, have frequently used *yakuza* gangsters to enforce repayment, often in very public ways designed to humiliate the debtor. The loss of face involved for the debtor has been an important contributor to the high rate of suicide in Japan.

Where private individuals are concerned, the historic trend has been for intolerance towards defaulting debtors to wane over time, as modern bankruptcy laws attest. No doubt this reflects the extension of the franchise, which ensures that the political clout of debtors, who enjoy a numerical advantage in voting power over creditors such as bankers, has been used to good effect. The growth and profitability of retail banking, which serves the mass consumer market, has also encouraged bankers to take a more liberal view. Modern banks even assume a specific level of defaults on their loan portfolio and price credit to reflect that assumption. In the US the tax system even sanctifies the debtor by making interest payments tax allowable. Tax breaks for mortgage interest fuelled the property bubble in the US and in other countries such as Spain. And in most countries, interest is deductible for tax purposes against corporate profits so that debt is privileged relative to equity. This fiscal bias encourages excessive risk taking, not least in the banking system. One of the reasons banks ran down their capital before the financial crisis was that they were seeking to save tax by making their balance sheets more 'efficient'. The bias in favour of debt interest and against equity dividends is a case of the pendulum swinging too far in favour of the debtor. It has contributed to the excessive accumulation of debt in many economies of the developed world. But the political obstacles to removing such tax breaks are formidable.

That said, the exceptional lobbying power of American banks has led to some erosion of pro-debtor bias in recent bankruptcy legislation. A proposal by the White House in 2009 to allow judges to reduce the principal on home mortgages to help mitigate the economic crisis was rejected by Congress after a ferocious campaign by bank lobbyists. The same industry pressure also ensures that student debts arising from college loans in the US follow a borrower to the grave.

Broadly speaking, though, the liberal ethos towards private individuals' indebtedness in the English-speaking world remains
in place. Liberalism can nonetheless be taken too far in bankruptcy law, as in taxation. This is almost certainly the case in
the US where companies are concerned. Under the American
Chapter 11 bankruptcy procedure, executives can walk away
from the company's obligations by asking the courts to sanc-
tion the write-off of old debts. A doctrine known as debtor-in-
possession allows the managers who reduced the company to
bankruptcy to remain in control. This means that in industries
with surplus capacity that badly need to shrink, mismanaged
companies stay in business. More companies then go into
Chapter 11 bankruptcy and the sector risks becoming peren-
nially unprofitable. The American airline industry, where US
Airways has gone in and out of Chapter 11 bankruptcy twice,
is a good example of this syndrome.

With public debts of monarchs and sovereign governments, the trend has been in the opposite direction. The
high-handedness of these grandiose debtors started to be seriously curbed by parliaments in the seventeenth century, most
notably in England where the rise of the landed gentry after
Henry VIII's dissolution of the monasteries fundamentally al-
tered the balance of power. The failure of the monarchy to
understand this did, of course, lead to the Civil War and the
execution of Charles I. On the restoration of the monarchy,
the free-spending instincts of his son Charles II confronted
the countervailing power of the elected parliament. The new
financial relationship was beautifully captured in an exchange
between the king and the great preacher Edward Stillingfleet,
who asked Charles why he always read out his speeches in the

House of Commons rather than addressing parliamentarians directly. The king responded: 'Why truly, doctor, your question is a very pertinent one, and so will be my answer. I have asked them so often, and for so much money, that I am ashamed to look them in the face.'[145]

That did not prevent Charles II from doing considerable damage to his creditors. His Stop of the Exchequer in 1672, which involved repudiating debts for a year, was disastrous for London's goldsmiths and seriously damaged London's financial markets.

Small wonder, then, that Enlightenment thinkers such as Adam Smith and David Hume worried about the potential for the continuing abuse of debt by monarchs and politicians. In 'Of Public Credit' in the *Political Discourses*, Hume argued:

> It is very tempting to a minister to employ such an expedient, as enables him to make a great figure during his administration, without overburthening the people with taxes, or exciting any immediate clamours against himself. The practice, therefore, of contracting debt will almost infallibly be abused, in every government. It would scarcely be more imprudent to give a prodigal son a credit in every banker's shop in London, than to impower a statesman to draw bills, in this manner, upon posterity.[146]

That is a perennial anxiety that continues to be reflected in modern economists' tendency to distinguish 'virtuous' debt, contracted to finance productive investment in infrastructure and social welfare, from 'bad' debt that finances current consumption.

To return to the issue of sovereign default in the seventeenth century, only after the Glorious Revolution of 1688 and the founding of the Bank of England in 1694 did England acquire a reputation for honouring its national debts. And only in the eighteenth century did the growth of sovereign debt markets – markets in government IOUs – start to act as a wider restraining influence on monarchs and governments. A sovereign borrower cannot bankrupt a bond market, which nowadays consists of a loose confederation of bankers, money managers, university foundations, mutual funds, insurance companies, pension funds and individual investors. But by defaulting on obligations to these investors, the borrower may forfeit access to bond funds in future. A strike by bond market investors is a powerful thing. Hence the celebrated statement by James Carville, when an adviser to President Bill Clinton in the early 1990s: 'I used to think if there was reincarnation, I wanted to come back as the President or the Pope or a .400 baseball hitter. But now I want to come back as the bond market. You can intimidate everybody.'

That said, bond investors are always vulnerable to governments and central banks that let inflation rip, which is now a more common form of default than failure to pay interest or repay the outstanding debt. In effect, inflation provides an adjustment mechanism when the political process has proved unable to reconcile the interests of debtors and creditors. And there can also be very special circumstances in which the power of the bond market is neutered and the sovereign borrower enjoys a kind of *laissez-passer* from creditors – circumstances, moreover, in which saving, regarded by so many as an innately virtuous activity, turns into an economic and social blight. This is because if we all individually cut our spending to increase our savings, then our collective savings will paradoxically fall because one person's spending is another's income. If no one else in the economy wants to use all the increased savings for investment, we are up against the phenomenon known as the paradox of thrift. This arises in circumstances where a debt-induced financial crisis robs interest rates of their ability to stimulate increased consumption, investment and economic recovery – in other words, where cutting interest rates no longer has much impact.

This concept is usually attributed to Keynes, who undoubtedly did a great deal to make debt respectable in the Great Depression, but it goes back at least as far as Bernard Mandeville, whose *Fable of the Bees* we encountered in Chapter One. Mandeville wrote:

> As this prudent Oeconomy, which some People call *Saving*, is in Private Families the most certain Method to encrease an Estate, so some imagine that, whether a Country be barren or fruitful, the same Method if generally pursued (which they think practicable) will have the same effect upon a whole Nation, and that, for Example, the *English* might be much richer than they are, if they would be as frugal as some of their Neighbours. This, I think, is an Error…[147]

The problem of excessive saving and deficient demand is a recipe for deflation and slump in a single economy.[148] This is what happened to the US in the 1930s, and the Great Depression was made worse by the moralistic, anti-debt financial conservatism exemplified by US Treasury Secretary Andrew Mellon, who notoriously declared:

Liquidate labour, liquidate stocks, liquidate farmers, liquidate real estate ... it will purge the rottenness out of the system. High costs of living and high living will come down. People will work harder, live a more moral life. Values will be adjusted, and enterprising people will pick up from less competent people.[149]

Today, the globalisation of capital flows means that excess savings in one country can be offset by the borrowing and spending of other countries. This was the story of the global economy in the first decade of the new millennium. Japan, China and Germany ran up large trade surpluses with the rest of the world. Since a surplus on the balance of payments equals the difference between saving and investment in the domestic economy, these countries were racking up a surplus of savings over investment. Together with the surpluses of the petro-economies that were inflated by a rising oil price, these surpluses were broadly matched by deficits in the US, the UK and the other English-speaking economies, plus others such as Spain.

The trouble with this aspect of globalisation is that it is not sustainable. A country simply cannot go on accumulating debts year in, year out, without giving rise to doubts about its creditworthiness. This was well understood by another Enlightenment thinker, Montesquieu, who, in discussing public finance in *De L'Esprit des Lois*, said: 'It is necessary that there should be a proportion between the state as creditor and the state as debtor. The state may be a creditor to infinity, but it can only be a debtor to a certain degree, and when it surpasses that degree the title of creditor vanishes.'[150]

In the event, the financial crisis of 2007–09 exposed just such flaws in the debtor–creditor relationship between states. With hindsight, it appears that the developed world's capacity for innovation and productivity growth had waned since the 1970s. It could only maintain strong growth by encouraging households to borrow and spend. And many governmental promises for public spending on such things as health care, education and pensions were based on assumptions about economic growth that now look over-optimistic.

A further important flaw exposed by the financial crisis was a problem of excessive interdependence: as we saw in Chapter Six, the creditor and debtor countries are locked into what former Federal Reserve chairman Paul Volcker called a fatal embrace. With a majority of its $4 trillion of official reserves invested in dollar securities, China cannot now pull out except at the risk of precipitating a dollar crash that might wreck the value of this humungous nest egg. So the world's biggest creditor country has not imposed discipline via the bond market on the world's biggest debtor and would probably only do so in extreme political circumstances.

Worse, Americans whose real incomes were declining for years enjoyed the illusion of rising living standards on the basis of a credit bubble that allowed them to treat their constantly re-mortgaged homes as automated teller machines. Then the residential property market collapsed. Meantime, the US cannot lightly alienate China because a Chinese financial exodus would, as suggested earlier, run the risk of precipitating a currency and financial crisis that would cause the government's borrowing costs to rocket. Yet the US can legitimately complain that China's trillions of reserves operated, until recently, as a gigantic export subsidy resulting from undervaluation of the Chinese currency brought about by capital outflows, and that China's export-led model of growth is no longer in China's own interest or that of the rest of the world. By 2010, this fatal embrace had created intense pressure in the US for protectionism and had driven countries around the world to respond by boosting exports through competitive devaluations reminiscent of the *sauve qui peut* psychology behind the currency wars that exacerbated the 1930s Great Depression.

A regional variant of the fatal embrace took place in Europe, where trade and financial imbalances created similar frictions. This was because Germany and other northern European countries ran up large trade surpluses with southern Europe in the first decade of the new millennium. The counterpart trade deficits in southern Europe were financed largely by northern European banks. Thanks to the rules of the European Monetary Union and its single currency, the illusion was created that countries such as Greece were as creditworthy as Germany, which meant that the banks went on lending despite deteriorating government budgets and widening trade deficits. They were encouraged in this by the regulatory regime. The rules on bank capital, set by international agreement in Basel, granted privileged status to sovereign debt, so that banks were not required to back their investment in government IOUs with a cushion of capital. When the European sovereign debt crisis exploded in 2009, northern European governments and the European Central Bank had little option but to come to the rescue because the solvency of banks that had lent so heavily to southern Europe during the earlier boom was in question. Yet the Germans were reluctant to support a new political and fiscal framework capable of making economic and monetary union work, because of the high potential cost to German tax-payers. They also had a moralistic urge to impose austerity on indebted members of the eurozone, regardless of the economic consequences – shades, once again, of Andrew Mellon.[151] This was despite the fact that countries such as Spain and Ireland had not been profligate. Their governments were not running big deficits before the crisis and their public sector indebtedness was less than that of Germany. Their problem was, rather, that the one-size-fits-all interest rate set by the European Central Bank was far too low in relation to their domestic economic circumstances and they had to accommodate big capital inflows from return-hungry savers in northern Europe. This caused construction and property bubbles in their private sectors, with disastrous results for their respective banking systems. Public sector indebtedness then arose because the governments had to bail out the banks. The result of German-inspired austerity in the more heavily indebted countries of the eurozone is that the debtors are being forced to save an ever higher share of income to pay down debt whose real value keeps rising.

The demoralising consequences of these punitive policies were movingly expressed by Archbishop Hieronymous of Athens in a letter to Greek prime minister Lucas Papademos in 2012 setting out the concerns of the church in the face of an economic disaster on the scale of the US Depression of the 1930s. It was translated from the website of the Archdiocese of Athens by staff at the Bank of England:

Our hearts are shattered and our minds are blurred by recent events in our country. Decent people are losing their jobs, even their homes, from one day to the next. Homelessness and hunger – phenomena last seen in times of foreign occupation – are reaching nightmare proportions. The unemployed are growing by the thousands every day... Young people – the best minds of our country – are migrating abroad... Those making decisions are ignoring the voices of those in despair, the voices of the Greeks. Unfortunately, we cannot find a response – neither to explain what has happened, nor to the demands made by foreigners. Indeed, foreigners' insistence on failed recipes is suspect at best. And their claims against our national sovereignty are provocative. The exhaustion of the people cannot be ignored.

The curious thing about this entrenched presumption of guilt against the debtor is that Germany has been one of the greatest historic beneficiaries of debt forgiveness. Having made the foolish error of inflicting excessive reparations on the Germans in the 1920s, the Allies changed tack when confronted with the problem for a second time. The economic commentator Robert Kuttner points out that the occupying powers after the Second World War wrote off 93 per cent of the Nazi-era debt and postponed collection of other debts for nearly half a century. So Germany, whose debt to GDP ratio in 1939 was an astonishing 675 per cent, had a debt burden of about 12 per cent of GDP in the early 1950s after the so-called London debt agreement – far less than that of the victorious Allies. This debt amnesty, as Kuttner rightly remarks, was an extraordinarily magnanimous act. It allowed the West Germans to embark on their economic miracle on the basis of a clean balance sheet. Yet while most Germans can cite the

Marshall Plan as an act of post-war American generosity, this larger act of macro-economic mercy on the part of the Allies has disappeared from the political consciousness of Germany's current austerity police.[152] Few Germans are aware that theirs is the only major European country in modern times to have enjoyed the benefit of debt restructuring and debt relief, whereby creditors reduce the rate of interest on the debt and stretch out the payments over a longer period. Few seem seriously concerned that austerity is fostering the rise of extremist, xenophobic parties all across Europe, as a result of appallingly high rates of unemployment. What makes this doubly strange is that modern Germans have been so admirable in their willingness to acknowledge the heinous nature of the atrocities perpetrated under the Third Reich, unlike the Austrians and the Japanese who have never confronted their history in the same direct way.

To return from the specific to the general, Dr Johnson recognised that there can be no feckless debtor without a reckless creditor. He saw a need for balance in the debtor–creditor relationship. That view is as relevant today as it was two and a half centuries ago; and while he was talking about private individuals, the logic applies equally to countries:

Those who made the laws have apparently supposed, that every deficiency of payment is the crime of the debtor. But the truth is, that the creditor always shares the act, and often more than shares the guilt, of improper trust. It seldom happens that any man imprisons another but for debts which he suffered to be contracted in hope of advantage to himself, and for bargains in which he proportioned his profit to his own opinion of the hazard; and there is no reason why one should punish the other for a contract in which both concurred.[153]

Yet realpolitik stands in the way of balance in international discussions. At the Bretton Woods Conference in 1944, where the Allies laid the ground plan for the post-war international monetary order, Keynes tried to persuade US officials that there should be penalties for running persistent current account surpluses as well as for current account deficits. Since the US was then the world's largest creditor country and likely to remain so for quite some time, it no longer saw a pro-debtor bias as being in the national interest. The great British economist lost the argument with Harry Dexter White, who led the US Treasury delegates and whose agenda, as Benn Steil has shown in a recent book, was to eliminate Britain as a rival political and economic force in the post-war world.[154]

Moreover, the financial crisis has shown that there is one respect in which the balance between creditor and debtor in the modern capitalist economy has become hopelessly confused. For, while banks used to act as lenders to the state, the state has now become the chief financier of the banks. This is because governments have to stand behind central banks when they are forced to act as lenders of last resort if credit markets seize up or systemically important banks collapse. Never has the bill been greater than after the colossal last-resort lending operation that took place in the US and Europe from 2007 onwards. Intervention to support US, UK and eurozone financial institutions in the crisis amounted to more than $14 trillion, which is almost a quarter of global gross domestic product.

And that does not include the much bigger bill arising from lost economic output.

Andrew Haldane and Piergiorgio Alessandri of the Bank of England explain the turning of the tables like this:

> As in the Middle Ages, perceived risks from lending to the state are larger than in some corporations. The price of default insurance is higher for some G7 governments than for McDonald's or the Campbell Soup Company. Yet there is one key difference between the situation today and that in the Middle Ages. Then, the biggest risk to the banks was from the sovereign. Today, perhaps the biggest risk to the sovereign comes from the banks. Causality has been reversed.[155]

So the bankers have had their revenge on sovereign debtors. Yet today it is not the sovereign that stumps up, but the hapless taxpayer. As the economist Brian Reading of Lombard Street Research puts it:

> Losses circulate and snowball until they reach the pockets of those who can bear them. Ultimately that means the taxpayers. Or, in the case of the eurozone, foreign taxpayers, because losses on the sovereign debt of Greece, Cyprus, Spain, Italy or whoever can no longer be confined to the home country. The idea that the Germans can avoid footing the bill is idiotic.

Of the many injustices in the workings of modern capitalism, this is surely one of the most painful – especially in the US, where the bankers have seriously complicated what the historian Paul Kennedy has called 'the age-old task of relating national means to national ends'.[156] Since there is a significant long-run correlation between productive and revenue-raising capacity and military strength, the question now is whether the high level of government indebtedness after the financial crisis and Great Recession is a potential harbinger of national decline in the world's great superpower.

The truth is that while debt may be economically and socially desirable, the debtor–creditor relationship turns into a Faustian compact if debtors, whether people, corporations or countries, fail to exercise self-restraint. For, when creditors, most notably the banks, accommodate improvident debtors while dropping their lending standards and weakening their balance sheets, the consequences scarcely bear thinking about, since big banks have it in their power to wreck the capitalist economy if they throw prudence to the winds. As we have already seen in Chapter Three, that horrendous outcome cannot be completely ruled out.

CHAPTER NINE

GOLD: THE 6,000-YEAR-LONG BUBBLE

Seen through the lens of Richard Wagner's nineteenth-century music drama *The Ring of the Nibelung*, gold is the ultimate object of capitalist accumulation. Its grip on the human psyche is enduring. But why? As the great American investor Warren Buffett once remarked in a characteristically pithy boutade against the precious metal: 'Gold gets dug out of the ground in Africa, or someplace. Then we melt it down, dig another hole, bury it again and pay people to stand around guarding it. It has no utility. Anyone watching from Mars would be scratching their head.'[157]

Buffett was right. Unlike silver, gold no longer has much remaining worth as a producer good because there are now better or equivalent alternatives for its industrial uses, an obvious case in point being the disappearance of gold in Western dentistry. It has some value as a consumer good, though many people who use it as jewellery regard it as a store of value. The social value of gold is also non-existent or negative. The cost and waste involved in extracting gold from the ground and then holding it idle in underground bank vaults is considerable. As for the process of mining and refining the metal, it is environmentally degrading, especially where the operation is open cast. The extraction process requires the use of toxic chemicals such as cyanide, which do great damage to the environment when they spill.

In fact, Buffett is in a long line of sceptics about the yellow metal. The inhabitants of Thomas More's *Utopia*, to give another notable example, had no time for it:

> They eat and drink from earthen ware or glass, which make an agreeable appearance though they be of little value; while their chamber-pots and close-stools are made of gold and silver; and this not only in their public halls, but in their private houses. Of the same metals they also make chains and fetters for their slaves; on some of whom, as a badge of infamy, they hang an ear-ring of gold, and make others wear a chain or a coronet of the same metal. And thus they take care, by all possible means, to render gold and silver of no esteem. Hence it is, that while other countries part with these metals as though one tore-out their bowels, the Utopians would look upon giving-in all they had of them, when occasion required, as parting only with a trifle, or as we should esteem the loss of a penny.[158]

Lenin was on the same side of the argument, wanting gold to be used for building public lavatories. So it is extraordinary that this chemical element has for so long had the capacity to mesmerise alchemists, kings, misers, investors, capitalist entrepreneurs and even some economists. To understand why, it is necessary to go back, first, to the ancient world.

Maurice Bowra, the Oxford scholar and polymath, had this to say about the Greeks' enthusiasm for gold:

If wealth was necessary to the good life, it had also an imaginative appeal for a people which had long delighted in making delicate golden objects and began to use gold coins in the seventh century. In its beauty and brightness and permanence, gold is indissolubly associated with the gods, whose palaces, thrones, chariots, lyres, arrows and armour are made of it. They themselves, and even their horses, are 'golden' because of the divine light which shines from them. The legendary time when men came closest to the life of the gods was called the Golden Age. Because gold recalls the radiance of the gods, it is regarded as in some sense divine. Pindar not only calls it 'child of Zeus', because neither moth nor weevil devours it, but gives to Theia, the august daughter of Heaven and Earth, who sheds grace on many human actions, credit for the honour in which it is held:

Mother of the Sun, many-named Theia,

Because of you men think that gold

In strength and power surpasses all other things.

Because of its divine associations, gold had a symbolic value, and when Pindar wishes to stress the splendour of something, he calls it golden, whether it is the victor's crown of wild olive or the opening of a song. Gold stood for wealth in it most magical and least prosaic form, for the radiance with which it invests the art of living and for the graces which it makes possible.[159]

This reverence for the yellow metal was reflected in all spheres of human activity. Aristotle's philosophical concept of moderation was called the Golden Mean. The mathematical proportion known as the Golden Ratio has been regarded by architects, painters and musicians up to the present day as having a uniquely pleasing aesthetic quality. In ethics, the Golden Rule remains forever relevant – the injunction 'do unto others as you would have done unto yourself' – though some question whether this categorical imperative can work in a business context.

For all their respect for gold, the Greeks believed that it should not be allowed to become an end in itself. That view is embodied in the myth of Midas, King of Phrygia, whose wish that all he touched should turn into gold was granted by Dionysus, to disastrous effect. Gold is, it seems, a material that constantly blinds people to the merits of the moderate path enjoined by the Golden Mean. Among the blindest were the alchemists – most famously personified in the German legend of Faust – who searched fruitlessly for the Philosophers' Stone in the attempt to turn base metal into gold. The dottiness of their enterprise consisted, to my mind, not only in the physical challenge but the nonsensical economics. Since a successful alchemist would have been no more able to keep his formula secret than the first claimant in a gold rush, the prospect of infinite supply would have turned gold into a commodity about as valuable as sand. Yet even Sir Isaac Newton, father of modern physical science, devoted much of his career to alchemical research.

Few were more immoderate in their blindness than sixteenth-century European adventurers, whom John Maynard Keynes regarded as the originators of capitalism. We owe the Europeans' discovery of the Americas to gold, for gold was the probable motive that drove Christopher Columbus westward: his diary of a voyage that lasted less than a hundred days mentions gold sixty-five times. The Spanish *conquistadores* who followed – Cortés, Pizarro and their men – were not only brutal and rapacious in their imperialist incursions into Mexico and Peru; by bringing European diseases to the Americas, they also inadvertently wiped out much of the population of the areas they colonised.

The resulting inflow of precious metals into Europe bore striking witness to the profound truth in the Midas myth, albeit that silver played a much greater part than gold. The mere existence of this treasure trove discouraged the pursuit of agriculture, commerce and industry, while contributing to existing inflationary pressures across the continent. At the same time, it provided the wherewithal for Ferdinand and Isabella, and later Spanish monarchs, to dissipate wealth in warfare. They managed to rack up huge debts despite the windfall.

This is a recurring historical pattern and is sometimes referred to as the natural resource curse. In the modern world, it is noteworthy that countries that have enjoyed huge oil or mineral endowments have often ended up worse off than before – consider Nigeria, which has squandered the equivalent of a Marshall Plan since the discovery of oil – while many of the economies that have prospered mightily, such as South Korea, Taiwan or Singapore, have no natural resources to speak of and relied initially on their competitive advantage in the global labour market to opt successfully into industrial market capitalism. The trouble with such windfalls is that the proceeds tend to be monopolised by corrupt governments rather than going to support enterprise in the private sector. Government budgetary processes are overwhelmed. Exchange rates appreciate, reflecting the newfound wealth, making existing and potential export industries uncompetitive while imports soar.

After the excesses of the sixteenth century, the gold rushes of the nineteenth century look far less brutal. They were, in fact, a form of spontaneous, individualistic, working-class capitalism. In the US, they helped define the culture of the American frontier. Yet, like the process of industrialisation, from whose drudgery many prospectors were escaping, the rampage after gold was still very disruptive. Contemporary accounts of the Californian gold rush that began in 1848 talk of mills in the area of the initial find lying idle, fields of wheat open to cattle and horses, houses vacant and farms going to waste. John Sutter, owner of Sutter's Mill, where the first finds were made, saw his business ruined, while his property rights proved not to be robust against the legal challenge of settlers. Native Americans, previously the main occupants of the territory, were displaced amid considerable environmental damage.

In literature, the power of the Midas myth is reflected in a rich haul of misers whose relationship with gold was obsessive. Shakespeare's Shylock, Ben Jonson's Volpone, Molière's Harpagon, Balzac's Gobseck and Félix Grandet, and of course Dickens's Ebenezer Scrooge, among countless others, are well known. Less familiar is a particular favourite of mine, Malbecco in Spenser's *Faerie Queene*. Malbecco perfectly exemplifies the destructive power of the love of lucre as he jealously guards a young and beautiful wife, Hellenore, in his castle:

> *Therein a cancred crabbed Carle [old man] does dwell,*
> *That has no skill of Court nor courtesie,*
> *Ne Cares, what men say of him, ill or well;*
> *For all his dayes he drownes in privitie,*
> *Yet has full large to live, and spend at libertie.*

> *But all his mind is set on mucky pelfe,*
> *To hoord up heapes of evill gotten masse,*
> *For which he others wrongs, and wreckes himselfe;*
> *Yet he is lincked to a lovely lasse,*
> *Whose beauty doth her bounty far surpasse,*
> *The which to him both far unequall years,*
> *And also far unlike conditions has;*
> *For she does joy to play emongst her peares,*
> *And to be free from hard restraint and gealous feares.*
> *But he is old, and withered like hay,*
> *Unfit faire Ladies service to supply;*
> *The privie guilt whereof makes him always*
> *Suspect her truth, and keepe continuall spy*
> *Upon her with his other blincked eye...*[160]

Paridell, a knight, makes off with Hellenore. But he is an un-principled opportunist who abandons her to the company of satyrs. Malbecco, having failed to persuade her to return to him, is robbed of his treasure and spends the rest of his life consumed by jealousy.

The German philosopher Schopenhauer has an interesting take on the miser's syndrome. 'Money', he said, 'is human happiness in the abstract; and so the man who is no longer capable of enjoying such happiness in the concrete sets his whole heart on money.' In similar vein, Marx thought that money was commoditised labour, a means whereby the surplus from the hapless workers' honest toil could be turned into capitalist accumulation. Yet the richest description of the paradoxical qualities of gold comes from Shakespeare's *Timon of Athens*. Ruined and ostracised by the community, Timon, before his cave in the woods, delivers this magnificent denunciation of the omnipotence and malevolent potential of the metal:

> *Gold? Yellow, glittering, precious gold?*
> *No, gods,*
> *I am no idle votarist...*
> *Thus much of this will make black white, foul fair,*
> *Wrong right, base noble, old young, coward valiant.*
> *Ha, you gods! Why this? What, this, you gods? Why, this*
> *Will lug your priests and servants from your sides,*
> *Pluck stout men's pillows from below their heads –*
> *This yellow slave*
> *Will knit and break religions, bless the'accurs'd,*
> *Make the hoar leprosy ador'd, place thieves*
> *And give them title, knee, and approbation,*
> *That makes the wappen'd widow wed again –*
> *She whom the spital-house and ulcerous sores*
> *Would cast the gorge at this embalms and spices*
> *To th'April day again. Come, damn'd earth,*
> *Thou common whore of mankind, that puts odds*
> *Among the rout of nations...*

A recurring theme in the story of gold, well understood by Shakespeare, concerns the role of the precious metal as a means of acquiring power. The supreme example arises in Wagner's *Ring Cycle*, quoted at the start of this chapter, which many have interpreted as a romantic critique of industrial capitalism. The message the Rhine maidens give to the dwarf Alberich at the outset is that the ring will bring immeasurable power and wealth to the owner if he is prepared to forswear love. The wretched dwarf steals the ring and turns his fellow Nibelungs into miserable toilers in a huge gold factory where the working conditions are worse than those in the most hellish Victorian mill.

Yet the ring is stolen from Alberich by the gods, prompting him to place a curse on it – that curse again:

> *Since its gold gave me measureless might,*
> *now may its magic bring death to whoever wears it!*
> *It shall gladden no happy man;*
> *its bright gleam shall light on no one lucky!*
> *Whoever possesses it shall be consumed with care,*
> *and whoever has it not be gnawed with envy!*
> *Each shall itch to possess it,*
> *but none in it shall find pleasure!*
> *Its owner shall guard it profitlessly,*
> *for through it he shall meet his executioner!*[161]

The curse is fulfilled when Siegfried is murdered and his Valkyrie lover Brünnhilde wisely hurls the ring back into the Rhine before throwing herself onto a funeral pyre as the god's home Valhalla is destroyed in a blazing inferno. Yet if Wagner did intend *The Ring* to contain an allegorical reference to capitalism, its prophetic qualities were flawed: the capitalist system has proved more durable than Valhalla, as has the human fascination with gold.

After so much negative comment on the yellow metal, it is time to acknowledge that it has served mankind pretty well throughout history as money, being a means of exchange and a store of value. It comes into its own in times of war or during financial crises. A classic example of this function of gold is to be found in Samuel Pepys's diary. When a hostile Dutch fleet came up the Thames in 1667 and broke the navy's defensive chain at Gillingham, Pepys, a senior official at the Admiralty, knew what he had to do:

> So home, where all our hearts do now ake; for the newes is true that the Dutch have broken the chaine and burned our ships, and particularly 'The Royal Charles': other particulars I know not, but most sad to be sure. And the truth is I do fear so much that the whole kingdom is undone that I do this night resolve to study with my father and wife what to do with the little that I have in money by me, for I give all the rest that I have in the King's hands for Tangier, for lost ... I presently resolved of my father's and wife's going into the country; and at two hours' warning they did go by the coach this day, with about £1,300 in gold in their night-bag. Pray God give them good passage, and good care to hide it when they come home! But my heart is full of fear ... I have also made a girdle by which with some trouble I do carry about me £300 in gold about my body, that I may not be without something in case I should be surprised: for I think in any nation but our's people that appear (for we are not indeed so) so faulty as we, would have their throats cut.[162]

For all its merits in such circumstances, gold was clearly a great deal more cumbersome than a modern deposit in a Swiss bank. When Pepys went into the country to dig up the gold his father and wife had buried, it took a long time to find. There was a constant fear, in transporting the treasure back to

London by coach, that someone might detect the nature of the mission. Small wonder that around this time the use of paper money became more widespread.

In due course, gold was also taken down a peg in terms of intellectual respectability. In economics, Pepys's contemporaries were mercantilists. They believed, as outlined in Chapter Six, that the purpose of international trade was to acquire gold and other forms of bullion in order to increase national wealth. Trade surpluses were thought of as good because they brought about an inflow of gold, while deficits were bad because they drained bullion overseas. Thanks to David Hume and Adam Smith, we now know that this equation of gold imports with an increase in national wealth was wrong. These great Scottish intellectuals argued that the source of a nation's wealth was not the amount of gold that its citizens hoarded, but the production of goods and services.

Note, though, that for nearly two centuries from 1717, gold provided stable monetary underpinning for the economy after the introduction of the gold standard. This was at the suggestion of Sir Isaac Newton, who persuaded the parliament to fix the price of gold at £3.17s. 10½p an ounce. John Maynard Keynes argued that the success of the gold standard in the nineteenth century was accidental. The supply of gold did not increase in line with economic growth, which was a potential curb on the money supply and thus on economic activity. Yet this restraint was offset by better financial technology. So Keynes favoured an officially managed currency because it was too much 'to expect a succession of accidents to keep the metal steady'. He famously dubbed the gold standard (though not gold itself) a 'barbarous relic'.

Keynes nonetheless allowed himself to be duped by the investment lure of gold. After the 1929 crash, he became a member of the Macmillan Committee, which was asked to establish whether the financial system was a help or hindrance to British trade and industry. (This has been a recurring idée fixe in British economic policy and still exercises people today.) The editor of Keynes's complete works discovered in his private papers long after his death that there was an unexpected consequence of this role, which brought him into contact with the chairman of the Midland Bank, Reginald McKenna, a former Home Secretary in the British government. At committee meetings, McKenna, according to Keynes, would often produce from his pocket a small bar of gold and ask the great economist how much gold would be needed to solve the world's monetary problems. On 9 April 1930, McKenna took Keynes aside and swore him to secrecy, telling him that a German chemist called Charles Gladitz had discovered a method of producing unlimited quantities of gold at the cost of one shilling per ounce. Gladitz claimed to be able to extract gold from volcanic lava. A syndicate had been established to exploit this new extraction process, in which McKenna had taken a large personal stake.

Disposing secretly of the large volumes of bullion that the syndicate expected to generate was clearly going to be a problem. Once the secret was out, competitors would learn about the process, and the price of gold would collapse, taking the gold standard with it. Because he regarded the gold standard as a barbarous relic, Keynes was attracted to the idea. German reparations, against which he had railed after the Treaty of Versailles, were denominated in gold, as were all Britain's foreign borrowings. They stood to be wiped out, whereas the foreign loans that Britain had advanced were in sterling and would thus hold their value. But then, Keynes wrote:

> on second thoughts all this seemed superficial. At any rate it would not suit those who wanted to make money (very much money) out of the invention. Besides would it really be prac-tically or morally possible to enforce contracts expressed in gold, once the gold standard had collapsed? Obviously the maximum individual and national advantage, probably the greatest international advantage also, could be won by using the invention to control and regulate the gold situation.

Equally to the point, McKenna had given Keynes 500 shares for advice and assistance, which would become hugely valu-able if the process worked and the secret remained intact.

The two men recognised that the only way to protect the secret was to let the Chancellor of the Exchequer and the Gov-ernor of the Bank of England in on it, so they decided to offer to sell the invention, though not the gold, to the Chancellor for £150 million, which would be worth several billion in today's money. Their idea was that the government should pay by in-stalments against gold deliveries. The Bank of England would then be in a position to manipulate the world gold market in its own interest and pay off the war debts owed to the United States. If the Chancellor said no, they planned to blackmail him by threatening to sell the invention to the Americans. Brian Reading of Lombard Street Research, who alerted me to this little-known episode, rightly calls this 'real James Bond stuff'.

Keynes was well aware that the new gold extraction process could be a hoax. But he was so excited by the prospect of a huge capital gain that he kept an open mind about it. In the end, nothing came of it. Gladitz was charged with fraud on another matter in 1935 and died before appearing in court. So the whole thing was probably a hoax and the backers understandably kept quiet. All of which provides a remarkable insight into the ethical – or rather, unethical – standards of two leading figures of the day. In Keynes's case, the behaviour was very much at odds with his damning comments on capital accumulation. But in this, as in so much else, he was a bundle of contradictions. The postscript to the story is that Britain went off the gold standard in 1931, the US followed in 1933 and the gold standard collapsed completely in 1936.[163]

Another sceptic on the virtues of a gold standard was Frank Baum, author of *The Wonderful Wizard of Oz*. Most people think of it as a children's story. Yet it is also a political and monetary allegory that encapsulates the 1890s debate in the US on bimetallism, a monetary standard based on both gold and silver. Baum's heroine, Dorothy, goes down a yellow brick road, representing the gold standard, shod in magic silver slippers, which recall the bimetallic system. This was the platform of the pro-inflation US populist movement in the Great Depression of the late nineteenth century. On her travels, Dorothy kills the Wicked Witch of the East, who stands for the repressive East Coast bankers – bogeymen for much of America since Thomas Jefferson's great battles with Alexander Hamilton. She encounters a tin man who has gone to rust and doesn't have a heart. He represents the factory-line proletariat, afflicted by something that looks like Marxist alienation. A scarecrow does service for farm workers pauperised in the depression.

Then comes the Cowardly Lion, the presidential candidate William Jennings Bryan, who argued for bimetallism but lost the election to William McKinley. Bryan favoured silver in the interests of loosening the money supply and was firmly on the Jeffersonian side of the Jefferson–Hamilton argument. He may have lost the election, but through charismatic oratory succeeded in transforming the Democratic Party into the party of the common man, famously telling the Midases of the Republican Party: 'We will answer their demand for a gold standard by saying to them, "You shall not press down upon the brow of labour this crown of thorns, you shall not crucify mankind upon a cross of gold."'

Finally, there was the Wizard in Emerald City, or Washington DC, who turned out to be incapable of solving any of their problems. He was McKinley or, alternatively, some believe, Grover Cleveland, the earlier Democratic President who supported the gold standard. And Oz is, no doubt, a reference to an ounce of gold. Needless to say, Hollywood traduced the allegory by putting Judy Garland into red shoes on the Yellow Brick Road.

The trouble with abandoning the barbarous relic, in Keynes's famous phrase, was that it led to inflation or, in the case of Weimar Germany or modern Zimbabwe, to hyperinflation. This was a lesson first learned by the Chinese, who introduced the first paper currency in the world under the Song dynasty in the eleventh century. Paper was first used by private money changers. This was because base metal currency, the chief money in China at the time, was inconvenient to use and especially to remit funds over long distances, so paper tokens were used instead. As Song officials struggled to produce enough bronze coin to satisfy the needs of a growing economy, they took over this privately issued paper and used it, in effect, as an instrument of monetary policy. Like so many subsequent governments, they then discovered the advantages of issuing paper when confronting a fiscal crisis. After the Song, the Jin, Yuan and Ming states took the same dangerous path to the point where paper money became so unpopular that it went out of use. From 1430 to the early twentieth century, China operated on a silver standard. Only in 1935, under the Republic of China, did the country adopt a unified system of paper money.

There, in a nutshell, is the explanation for investors' enthusiasm for the yellow metal. Gold may be intrinsically worthless, but it has important advantages over fiat money. That is, money such as paper currency – or cowrie shells on Pacific islands – that has no intrinsic value, is not backed by any valuable commodity and derives its worth from the conviction of enough people that it has a value. While the cost of producing gold is very high, the marginal cost of producing more paper money is very low. And the outstanding stock of physical gold of around 160,000 tonnes is huge relative to the amount of new gold that can be mined and refined in a given year. So while fiat currency and gold both suffer from the disadvantage that they are always potentially worthless, fiat currencies are invariably more likely to become worthless than gold because central bankers can churn out fiat paper at the turn of a tap, while the supply of gold is heavily restricted. It follows that when countries are fiscally profligate and their governments rack up Godzilla-like quantities of public sector debt, the risk that politicians and central bankers resort to inflation via the printing press increases dramatically. Inflation becomes the politically acceptable way to avoid explicit default and reconcile the conflicting demands of different groups in society. Gold then becomes an attractive store of value relative to paper currency because it is inherently scarce compared with paper. Equally to the point, no one has ever defaulted on gold.

The gold standard, then, may have been flawed, but it could not rival the worst excesses of managed paper currency regimes. And in a hyperinflation those excesses are almost beyond comprehension. In mid-November 2008, for example, the monthly inflation rate in Zimbabwe reached 79,600,000,000 per cent, while the comparable figure in the Weimar Republic in 1923 was 29,500 per cent. The amount of time it took for prices to double at such rates was, respectively, 24.7 hours and 3.7 days.[164] Even without hyperinflation, the experience with fiat money has been dismal. In 2012, the world's pre-eminent currency, the dollar, could buy the equivalent of about 4 per cent of what it bought in 1913 when President Woodrow Wilson signed the Federal Reserve Act, the legislation that gave birth to the American central bank. Over the same period, the record of other central banks as guardians of the currency has been as bad or worse.

Lenin is reputed to have said that the best way to destroy the capitalist system was to debauch the currency, which may be part of the reason he wanted gold to be devalued and, echoing Thomas More's Utopians, put to practical use in building public lavatories. The only source for this view is Keynes, who quoted Lenin with approval. He is generally assumed to have picked it up through conversations with Russians at the Paris Peace Conference after the First World War. Whether the idea makes sense is moot. Even in the 1920s and 1930s, when it appeared that communism offered a plausible alternative to capitalism, extreme monetary dislocation in the developed world merely resulted in a change in the emphasis of capitalism. In the US as a result of the New Deal, in Germany under the Nazis, in Italy under Mussolini, in the UK after the devaluation of sterling urged by Keynes, the state intervened, in varying degrees, in the economy to address market failure. Yet it did not go all the way to socialism or communism. Today, after the financial crisis, the same logic applies. In the US, the state acquired large chunks of the financial sector and the motor industry. In the UK, the government acquired large chunks of the Royal Bank of Scotland and the Lloyds Banking Group. While the emphasis of the capitalist model changed temporarily, there was no fundamental challenge to the capitalist system of the kind predicted by Lenin.

That is not to say that inflation is not a potential threat in the aftermath of the financial crisis, as central banks have tried to keep economies ticking over by pumping vast sums of money into the system. The fear is that they may end up monetising government debt – that is, financing the debt directly by printing paper money or, its modern equivalent, creating electronic money in the banking system. Yet gold itself has not been a good investment for much of the past millennium. In real terms, the price of gold in 2012 was similar to the prevailing price in 1265. Over much of that time, though, the yellow metal failed to live up to its reputation as a solid store of value. Market strategist Dylan Grice, while at Société Générale, wrote:

> A fifteenth-century gold bug who'd stored all his wealth in
> bullion, bequeathed it to his children and required them to

do the same would be more than a little miffed when gazing down from his celestial place of rest to see the real wealth of his lineage decline by nearly 90 per cent over the next 500 years.

In our own time, gold has been equally capricious. Anyone who bought gold at the peak of the 1971–81 bull market in the metal would have seen a loss in real terms on their investment of 80 per cent over the next twenty years. And there, of course, is the rub. Gold is not an investment. Because it yields no dividends or interest it is a speculation. That is not to say that its price will at some point go to zero. The economist Willem Buiter points out that it has had a positive value for nigh-on 6,000 years, making it the longest-lasting bubble in human history. Maybe it will be good for another 6,000 years.

Like Warren Buffett, I am a sceptic about gold, but, unlike him, I do not think it is completely irrational to hold it. Forgoing income on this precious metal is the equivalent of paying an insurance premium against future inflation or deflation. The snag is that because gold is purely speculative and unsupported by an underlying income stream, the price is inevitably volatile and tends to overshoot both upwards and downwards, sometimes over very long periods. Yet the lesson of the past 6,000 years is that, however uncertain the payout on the insurance policy, it will be a better bet than holding government IOUs in a period of monetary dislocation. Governments can, after all, default even on their index-linked debt.

The people who are instrumental in creating inflation are the central bankers. Since 2010, their official reserve managers have been heavy buyers of gold. That revealing fact, together with the historic failure of central bankers to fulfil their remit to maintain the stability of the currency, is a compelling argument for taking out insurance against extreme fluctuations in the price level. The only question is whether the price at any given moment is right.

CHAPTER TEN

HIGH-MINDED ABOUT ART

Like gold, art is a purely speculative investment. Its price is driven more by fashion than financial calculation. And it constitutes a more sanctified object of capital accumulation than gold in that the art market marries high aesthetic values to base financial instinct. Yet for some, it should never be a financial asset at all. 'Where any view of money exists,' wrote the impoverished literary and artistic genius William Blake, 'art cannot be carried on…' In the twenty-first century, that notion sounds wildly ideal- istic. It was nonetheless shared by no less a man than John May- nard Keynes, the economist of genius who, among other things, founded the Arts Council of Great Britain, the state-funded patron of the arts which came into being in 1946. Keynes did not accept that the ethical basis of capitalism was purely utilitarian. Heavily influenced by the Cambridge moral philosopher G. E. Moore and the values of his friends in the Bloomsbury group, he saw capitalism as instrumental, providing the means for people to enjoy non-material things, most notably the arts and culti- vated friendship, once their material needs were looked after. In this, incidentally, he differed markedly from capitalism's greatest critic, Karl Marx, who, in one throwaway thought, talked of the ultimate objective of economic activity in oddly philistine terms:

> In communist society, where nobody has one exclusive
> sphere of activity but each can become accomplished in any
> branch he wishes, society regulates the general production
> and thus makes it possible for me to do one thing today and
> another tomorrow, to hunt in the morning, fish in the after-
> noon, rear cattle in the evening, criticise after dinner, just
> as I have a mind, without ever becoming hunter, fisherman,
> herdsman or critic.[165]

Above all, Keynes had serious reservations about speculation
in works of art, believing that it was potentially destructive of
artistic values.[166] He hated the notion that art could be a focus
of capitalist accumulation and felt that capitalism had nullified
the aesthetic sensibilities of the bourgeoisie, of which more
in Chapter Twelve. That high-minded view of art is shared
by many artists and art lovers today who are convinced that
money corrodes the creative imagination and are appalled at
the values placed by the market on contemporary works of
art. Similar thinking lies behind the modernist critique of capitalist consumerism.

Yet this idealistic position sits very oddly with historical reality. Artists, composers and literary people have always dirt-
ied their hands and often made a great deal of money. Latterly,
some have even boasted about their commercial motivation. In
a no doubt intentionally shocking formulation, Andy Warhol,
taking the opposite view from Blake, said:

> Business art is the step that comes after Art ... Being good
> in business is the most fascinating kind of art. During the
> hippie era people put down the idea of business – they'd say

'Money is bad,' and 'Working is bad,' but making money is
art and working is art and good business is the best art.[167]

To name but a few of those who have combined business with
the arts: Chaucer was an accountant in the Customs office;
Cervantes was a tax collector; Alexander Pope made a fortune from his verse translations of Homer; Daniel Defoe was a
stockjobber and merchant; Gauguin spent ten years of his life
as a stockbroker before becoming a full-time painter; Anthony
Trollope never resigned from his job at the Post Office despite
his phenomenally successful career as a novelist; the German
Romantic poet Novalis was a mining engineer; Robert Burns
combined poetry with a job in the excise, collecting taxes;
T. S. Eliot wrote some of his best poetry while working for
Lloyds Bank in London and was a director of the publishing house Faber & Faber; Franz Kafka worked in insurance
(which may explain his obsession with surreal, nightmarish
bureaucracy); Charles Ives, the American composer, chaired
one insurance company, while the poet Wallace Stevens was
vice-president of another.

Stevens, who was a corporate lawyer as well as an expert on
surety bonds (whatever they may be), is noted for his remark
that 'money is a kind of poetry'. Frustratingly, he never elaborated what he meant; nor did he allow his daily monetary pre-
occupations to infiltrate his verse. Yet the British novelist John
Lanchester offers an interpretation of Stevens's gnomic phrase
that I find almost convinces:

Money is like poetry because both involve learning to com-
municate in a compressed language that packs a lot of

meaning and consequence into the minimum semantic space. It's also like poetry because there is a kind of beauty in the way money works, at least in the mathematical abstract: an absence of hypocrisy or redundancy, or floweriness, or of anything that is there purely for its own sake.[168]

Among many painters who made serious money – and the visual arts have always been a more lucrative pursuit than music or literature – was Sir Joshua Reynolds, one of William Blake's especial hates and a founder of the Royal Academy, where Blake studied. Blake could well have had Reynolds in mind when he made the remark with which this chapter began. His notes in the margins of his copy of Reynolds's *Discourses* are steeped in vitriol, suggesting that money was a serious concern even if he wanted it to exert no influence over art:

> Having spent the Vigour of my Youth & Genius under the Oppression of Sr Joshua & his Gang of Cunning Hired Knaves Without Employment & as much as could possibly be without Bread, The Reader must Expect to read in all my remarks on these Books Nothing but Indignation & Resentment. While Sr Joshua was rolling in riches ... [he] & Gainsborough Blotted & Blurred one against the other & Divided all the English World between them.[169]

It is true that Reynolds and his fellow founders of the Royal Academy were impressed by the business models and financial success of such continental artists as Rubens. Yet Reynolds, who was much loved by the British aristocracy, had laudably public-spirited ideals. He saw the Royal Academy as a means for British artists and architects to escape craft status and achieve professional standing. He also wanted to bring art to a wider public by providing a venue for exhibitions and establishing a school for artists.

Indeed, much of the history of the relationship between art and money is about the attempt by artists to escape from dependence on patronage. For, while patronage offered the advantage of financial security, it often came at the cost of low status and constraints on artistic freedom. For anyone acutely conscious of their own artistic worth and originality, this was a form of hell. Few felt it more acutely than Wolfgang Amadeus Mozart. When his employer, the autocratic prince-archbishop Colloredo of Salzburg, summoned the composer to Vienna while he was attending the celebrations for the accession of Emperor Joseph II, Mozart had to stay in the archbishop's entourage. Having just returned from a triumphant trip to Munich where he conversed with nobles on equal terms, he found himself positioned at table below the valets but above the cooks. The archbishop also prevented him from earning money by playing at concerts. Mozart was understandably desperate to forge an independent career.

Patronage could also be extraordinarily capricious, as Samuel Johnson found when he looked for financial backers for his project to compile a dictionary of the English language. An approach to Lord Chesterfield produced the less than princely sum of £10. Yet after seven years at work on this single-handed project he was taken aback when Lord Chesterfield wrote two anonymous essays praising his work. Johnson's response was contained in one of the most brilliantly acerbic letters ever penned, which conveys the frustration felt by so many creative people at the servile nature of their position:

To The Right Honourable The Earl of Chesterfield
7th February, 1755.

My Lord, I have been lately informed, by the proprietor of The World, that two papers, in which my Dictionary is recommended to the public, were written by your lordship. To be so distinguished is an honour which, being very little accustomed to favours from the great, I know not well how to receive, or in what terms to acknowledge.

When, upon some slight encouragement, I first visited your lordship, I was overpowered, like the rest of mankind, by the enchantment of your address, and could not forbear to wish that I might boast myself *Le vainqueur du vainqueur de la terre;* —that I might obtain that regard for which I saw the world contending; but I found my attendance so little encouraged, that neither pride nor modesty would suffer me to continue it. When I had once addressed your Lordship in public, I had exhausted all the art of pleasing which a retired and uncourtly scholar can possess. I had done all that I could; and no man is well pleased to have his all neglected, be it ever so little.

Seven years, my lord, have now passed, since I waited in your outward rooms, or was repulsed from your door; during which time I have been pushing on my work through difficulties, of which it is useless to complain, and have brought it, at last, to the verge of publication, without one act of assistance, one word of encouragement, or one smile of favour. Such treatment I did not expect, for I never had a patron before.

The shepherd in Virgil grew at last acquainted with Love, and found him a native of the rocks.

Is not a patron my lord, one who looks with unconcern on a man struggling for life in the water, and, when he has reached ground, encumbers him with help? The notice which you have been pleased to take of my labours, had it been early, had been kind; but it has been delayed till I am indifferent, and cannot enjoy it: till I am solitary, and cannot impart it; till I am known, and do not want it. I hope it is no very cynical asperity not to confess obligations where no benefit has been received, or to be unwilling that the public should consider me as owing that to a patron, which providence has enabled me to do for myself.

Having carried on my work thus far with so little obligation to any favourer of learning, I shall not be disappointed though I should conclude it, if less be possible, with less; for I have been long wakened from that dream of hope, in which I once boasted myself with so much exultation, My Lord,

Your lordship's most humble, most obedient servant,
Sam. Johnson.[170]

Not that capriciousness was all on the side of the patrons. Michelangelo flounced out of Rome in a huff when Pope Julius II changed his mind about a commission to design a marble tomb. The Pope held the artist in such high regard that he then went to extraordinary lengths to persuade Michelangelo to return to Rome from his native Florence. If he succeeded, it was only because the Florentine Signoria – the government of Florence – did not want to go to war with the Pope over Michelangelo. To protect the artist, it nonetheless wrote to Pope Julius saying that if he harmed Michelangelo, he would be regarded as directly harming the Signoria.

For others, patronage worked. The composer Joseph Haydn spent more than thirty relatively happy years in the household of the Princes of Esterházy, feeling that the discipline of being a Kapellmeister in an isolated provincial environment encouraged originality. A biography written by Georg August Griesinger shortly after Haydn's death records him saying:

My prince was content with all my works. I received approval. I could, as head of an orchestra, make experiments, observe what created an impression, and what weakened it, thus improving, adding to, cutting away, and running risks. I was set apart from the world, there was nobody in my vicinity to confuse and annoy me in my course, and so I had to become original.[171]

Haydn, though, was fortunate in his chief patron Prince Nikolaus Esterházy. Admittedly, the composer was obliged to remedy the shortage of pieces for the prince's favourite instrument, the baryton, a curious relative of the viola d'amore which has never been popular. This resulted in 125 or more trios for baryton, violin and cello, which took up time that could no doubt have been better employed on other things and which have not given much pleasure to posterity. Yet this kind of minor irritation was a small price to pay for the relative freedom and comfort Haydn otherwise enjoyed. He was even more fortunate when Prince Nikolaus died, since his successor, Prince Anton, was less interested in music and chose to dismiss his orchestra. Yet he retained Haydn as titular Kapellmeister on a full salary with no obligations at all. The composer was thus able to move to Vienna and to embark on his two highly lucrative trips to London, where he wrote some of his finest symphonies while being fêted by London society.

Other composers of the seventeenth and eighteenth centuries received income from multiple sources, such as teaching, performing, the sale of music to publishers and financing public performances of their own works, as well as from patronage. Some became rich. George Frideric Handel enjoyed royal and aristocratic patronage in Rome, Hanover, London and elsewhere. But he was also an impresario who put on operas and oratorios at his own risk. In this he lost a great deal of money, though in the end he made much more than he lost. In fact, Handel was rich enough to speculate in the markets. He invested in South Sea stock as the South Sea Bubble was inflating but appears to have made his exit before the bubble burst. Records in the Bank of England archives show that he was back speculating in South Sea annuities in 1723, three years after the market collapse.[172] On his death in 1759 he left £20,000, which in today's money would be more than £2.5 million. Given the very generous charitable donations he made throughout his life both in cash and through benefit concerts, that suggests he made a considerable fortune over the course of his career.

For those who tried to do without patronage, life was not easy. When Mozart left Archbishop Colloredo's employ, after being delivered a kick in the arse (Mozart's words) at the archbishop's order, his attempt to carve out an independent career was never attended by much financial security despite the enormous success of his operas and other works. Antonio Vivaldi had earlier suffered a similar fate, dying in penury despite his considerable reputation across all Europe as a composer and violin virtuoso.

Freedom from patronage was more readily achieved in the visual arts. Looking back over time, medieval artists were paid, like manual workers, at fixed daily rates. That changed during the Renaissance as artists sought to liberate themselves from craft guilds. Many adopted a view of their work that came close to that of Blake. Leon Battista Alberti, author of the treatise *On Painting*, written in 1436, declared that 'greed is the enemy of artistic eminence'.[173] Yet great artists, who were increasingly scholarly figures, demanded high fees from their patrons to reflect their skill and the quality of their work. By the sixteenth century, the best of them could name their price. This progression from journeyman status to creative intellectual was, incidentally, an exact repetition of what had happened previously in ancient Greece. Before the classical period, the Greeks regarded art as the product of manual labour, which was mainly executed by slaves. So while musicians and poets were admired, artists were lowly folk, never mentioned in the literature of the period. Only by around the fourth century BC did art become a status symbol of the educated.

In Renaissance Europe, the arrival of the printing press also provided artists with an opportunity to mass-produce copies of their work and to develop a broad European art market. Initially, prints were used by artists as a marketing tool for promoting their painted work. But in the late fifteenth century,

Albrecht Dürer devoted himself increasingly to selling copies of the woodcuts and engravings printed at his Nuremberg workshop. It was far more lucrative than painting and Dürer was an astute businessman – one who always signed his work with the distinctive monogram 'AD'. This was, in effect, a trademark. There was a problem, in that others could make unauthorised copies of an artist's work. Yet this could be dealt with, up to a point, by a precursor of copyright developed in Italy known as *cum privilegio*, which was a means of protecting the artist's investment. In both Nuremberg and Venice, Dürer successfully turned to the courts to defend his sole use of his trademark. Other artists chose to collaborate with printmakers and publishers to reach out to a wider audience. Titian, for example, gained a *privilegio* from the courts in Venice to give an exclusive right to the Flemish engraver Cornelis Cort to reproduce his paintings. The growing status of printmakers was further enhanced when, in the 1550 edition of *Lives of the Painters, Sculptors and Architects*, Vasari added a chapter on printmaking.

By this time, top artists in Italy and in the Low Countries were often celebrities, pulling in fees commensurate with their star status. While many regarded their work as a high calling rather than a trade, some were conspicuously materialistic. Titian, for example, was notoriously preoccupied with money-making. So, too, was Raphael, who resisted the recommendations for marriage provided by his uncle, Simone Ciarla, for purely materialist reasons. In 1514 he wrote to Ciarla:

> With regard to marrying I reply that I am very glad indeed and forever grateful to God that I neither accepted the one

> you first wanted to give me nor any other, and in this respect
> I was wiser than you who suggested them. I am sure that
> you will now agree that I would never have got where I am,
> having 3,000 gold ducats put aside in Rome.[174]

Raphael's amorous instincts were directed exclusively at his mistresses. Both he and Titian were immensely rich by the standards of the day and enjoyed princely lifestyles.

Perhaps the greatest of all the stars of the pre-modern period was Peter Paul Rubens, a protean figure of the baroque era who combined his roles as an artist, diplomat and scholar with an extraordinary business flair. Rubens developed a factory approach to painting whereby he produced ideas, embodied in initial sketches that were then transposed onto canvas by a team of talented assistants and pupils. He also had what would now be called an international marketing and distribution network, which made good use of licences forbidding the distribution of unauthorised reproductions. Rubens amassed a substantial fortune that included a large art collection in the house he built in Antwerp. If anyone demonstrates that the values of art are not incompatible with those of business it is surely Rubens, who was the embodiment of the versatile, cultured artist-cum-man of the world.

One of history's lessons, then, is that freedom turns artists into entrepreneurs. As with more conventional business entrepreneurs, the motivation of the artist-entrepreneur has always varied across a spectrum that runs from idealism to commercialism. At one extreme are those like Leonardo or Michelangelo, for whom making money was incidental to the calling – or, at a less exalted level, Banksy, the street artist, who is completely unmotivated by financial concerns but whose works sell for a fortune in the market. At the other is Andy Warhol, who was nakedly materialistic. Recalling how he looked to friends for ideas in the 1960s, he famously said that 'finally one lady friend of mine asked me the right question: "Well, what do you love most?" That's how I started painting money.'[175] That statement is a serendipitous (and, I suspect, unconscious) endorsement of the view of the German-Jewish intellectual Walter Benjamin that capitalism is a religion without dogma or theology, an unceasing celebration of money.[176] The art critic Harold Rosenberg neatly characterised the radical nature of Warhol's view of the artist as the producer of just another commodity:

> It was in creating the creator of his works that Warhol proved genuinely creative, and penetrating to the point of subversion. The archetype of the modern artist has been the Dandy, Baudelaire's detached and intellectually tormented 'hero of modern life'. This figure survived in a variety of versions to the threshold of the sixties ... Warhol buried the Dandy under an avalanche of soup cans.[177]

Even before Warhol trumpeted his commercialism, plenty of artists were equally obsessive about money, even if they were less vocal about it. While Joshua Reynolds was dedicated to raising the status of artists for the best of reasons, he also dealt actively in works of art, sometimes with naked dishonesty. In 1785, for example, he colluded with a Rome-based agent to deceive the Roman authorities by substituting copies after Nicolas Poussin in the Palazzo Boccapaduli, for which export licences would probably not have been granted, in order to spirit off the originals to England. Reynolds immediately sold one off to the Duke of Rutland for £2,000, which would be equivalent to millions in today's art market.[178] Picasso has not been accused of comparable dishonesty. The accusation is rather one of hypocrisy. In his early days in Paris he busily advanced his career by cultivating the artistic intelligentsia and painting numerous portraits of the leading dealers – despite claiming to regard them as enemies. The Catalan painter Joan Miró, who admired Picasso, nonetheless disliked his values, saying: 'Everything is done for his dealer, for the money. A visit to Picasso is like visiting a ballerina with a number of lovers.'[179]

What exactly is the nature of this market which puts a price both on works of genius and artistic dross? From the Middle Ages until the nineteenth century, artworks were not traded to the extent they are today, although artists themselves were often active speculators in the art market. Leaving aside the sale of prints, artists were paid mainly by the Church, aristocrats or rich merchants for their work. The main focus of the market was thus chiefly for new works – a primary market, in the economic jargon – and relatively opaque. It was not until the nineteenth century that a really competitive, transparent art market finally emerged, most notably in France, in which a great volume of second-hand works were traded.

This more sophisticated market was helped, first, by the emergence of the state as a patron, both directly and through museums, and the interest of a growing middle class in art; then by the Impressionists' exhibition of their works in unofficial salons, which broke the monopoly of the government-sponsored official Salon as the sole channel for the display of new art to the public. With the backing of dealers, who were often prepared to take a long-term view of an artist's potential saleability and to try to influence taste, the Impressionists ultimately saw their work validated by escalating prices in the market, despite the ridicule that had been heaped on them by the public. For the artist, the dealer also provided a convenient way of outsourcing contact with lucre in a world where artists were still inclined to think that their high calling precluded being interested in money – or at least giving the appearance of being interested.

While it took centuries for this really active market in works of art to develop, money and art were always intertwined because the rich commissioned artworks as a form of consumer luxury. Art provided a visible demonstration of their high status. In Italy, the transition from a feudal system in which the ruling class was rich in land but less rich in cash to a proto-capitalist one dominated by cash-rich merchants and bankers had a dramatic consequence: a huge expansion in the production of beautiful artworks and artefacts, as patronage provided a link between art and the real economy. These mercantile princes not only wished to flaunt their wealth; paying for chapels, altarpieces, frescoes and devotional paintings, in which the donor and his wife often featured, was a way of assuaging the guilt that came from making fortunes from usury. While they managed to avoid lending at interest directly, which was prohibited by the Church, they did so by backdoor means, using instruments such as bills of exchange, as explained in Chapter One. This legal sleight of hand left them feeling spiritually uncomfortable, so pouring money into devotional art – the equivalent of doing penance – made them feel better about themselves. It also guaranteed them immortality. A member of the Salviati banking family quoted Cosimo the Elder, the greatest of the Renaissance art patrons, on his motivation thus: 'All these things have given me the greatest satisfaction and contentment, because they are not only for the honour of God but are likewise for my own remembrance.'[180]

The motivation of the nineteenth-century American robber barons who bought art from impoverished European aristocrats through dealers such as Joseph (later Lord) Duveen, was little different, if more secular. Duveen's phenomenal business success was built on selling the idea that art could confer social status on upstart entrepreneurs such as John D. Rockefeller, Henry Clay Frick and Andrew Mellon. No doubt the same logic applies to today's hedge fund managers, who pay vast sums for the work of Jeff Koons, Damien Hirst or, in the case of Steven Cohen of SAC Capital, an astonishing $155 million for Picasso's painting of his mistress, *Le Rêve*. In a caustic but perceptive jibe, the Norwegian-born economist Thorstein Veblen, best known for his critique of conspicuous consumption, remarked that 'beauty is commonly a gratification of our sense of costliness masquerading under the name of beauty'. Hence, the coinage in economics of the term 'Veblen goods', which refers to commodities of which people will buy more when the price goes up because this confers increased status, whereas higher prices more normally choke off demand. Or, in the language of the thought-provoking British economist Fred Hirsch, many works of art such as Old Masters are 'positional' goods. These are goods that are inherently scarce, so acquiring them can only benefit one person at the expense of others. They are thus a way of demonstrating high status and superiority over others. Typically, Andy Warhol had an instinctive understanding of this and rejoiced in it, saying: 'I don't think everybody should have money. It shouldn't be for everybody – you wouldn't know who was important.'[181]

Only recently has art come to be seen as an investment. The art critic Robert Hughes saw the origins of this financialisation of art in events in the mid-1960s, highlighting the invention of the Times-Sotheby art index as an important factor in the change. These statistics on price movements across the art market were dreamed up by a public relations man who was hired to give the well-known but stuffy auction house a more exciting image. They attracted huge interest, partly because they conveyed the impression that prices always went up. And certainly, over a long period, that was true. Hughes attributed this to the dawn of the museum age in the nineteenth century. With its civilising mission and reverential view of art, it fundamentally changed the supply-and-demand dynamic of the market by introducing a people's form of collective capitalist accumulation. Before then, the Victorians paid higher prices for new Pre-Raphaelite paintings than for Old Masters, whose prices were, with occasional exceptions, low because supply exceeded demand:

From the attics of ducal homes in Kent to the crypts of churches in Umbria, Europe was crammed with unrecorded, uncleaned, unrestored, unstudied works of art, the raw material for another century of intensive dealing. The number of collectors then, as against today, was tiny … Our great grandfathers could not have foreseen what the growth of the museum age would do. And as the major works entered museums, there was more competition for the minor ones; and then the task of revival and re-evaluation of schools and artists for whom our Victorian forbears had no time at all began in earnest. In due course there would be no schools or artists left to rescue from oblivion. There is no oblivion. Today, virtually everything that was made in the past is equally revived: there will be no more argument about its meaning and its relative merits, but the universal resurrection of the formerly dead is pretty well an accomplished fact.[182]

Hughes pointed out that the disinterested motives of the scholar went hand in hand with the intentions of the art market because to resurrect something, to study and to endow it with a pedigree, was to make it saleable.

I believe that Hughes was right about the change in the balance of supply and demand in the nineteenth century, but wrong in his dating of financialisation. Since he wrote on this, economists have established that from 1830 to 2007 there was a strong positive relation between the movements of the equity market and the art market. In other words, capital gains drive art prices up as investors cash in their profits to buy art and status, while losses in declining equity markets reduce the urge to spend on art and lead to forced sales of artworks as investors are required to put up more collateral by their creditors or pay down bank borrowings. They have also found that the price level in the art market is heavily influenced by top incomes, identifying powerful evidence of a relation between inequality and art prices over the period from 1908 to 2005. And it is very striking that over the past three decades, when art prices have achieved particularly dizzy levels, the rich in Britain and

America have collected most of the gains in income growth while ordinary people's incomes have stagnated.[183]

What this all tells us is that contemporary artists increasingly deliver, in effect, what hedge fund managers want, while the public increasingly sees the kind of contemporary art that hedge fund managers buy, since museums often follow the trends set by the richest private buyers. That, to my mind, highlights the importance of maintaining pluralism in the sources of funding that are available to living artists.

There is another sense in which monetary conditions and investment fashions influence the art market. At times of monetary dislocation, art becomes more attractive as a store of value. This was certainly the case in the great inflation of the 1970s. As both equities and government bond markets collapsed across much of the developed world, institutional investors such as pension funds and insurance companies sought desperately for 'real' assets that would hold their value in the face of inexorably rising prices. They plunged into real estate, gold, copper, forestry and, in the case of the British Rail pension fund, art. With advice from Sotheby's, this nationalised industry retirement scheme accumulated a large and varied collection, embracing Tiepolos, Paninis, Renoirs and Picassos, French and Chinese porcelain, antique furniture, silver-gilt cutlery and numerous other kinds of *objets d'art*.[184]

The paradox here is that art has poor investment characteristics. It yields no income and bears no relation to the labour that goes into its production. The value of works of art is, in fact, dictated by fashion rather than any rational calculus, as indicated earlier. The investment is thus purely speculative. That explains why most institutional investors eschew putting money into art. Pension fund trustees do not, after all, derive personal benefit from buying positional goods – this is a peculiarly detached form of capital accumulation – and there are better ways of discharging their obligations to pensioners. Yet in a great inflation, artworks can appear more promising as a store of value than more conventional investments or cash. This logic also holds in the aftermath of the great financial crisis of 2007–08. With central banks in the developed world abandoning their mission to curb inflation in order to prop up debt-laden economies, the fear of monetary chaos has induced renewed interest in real assets. So despite the beginnings of a retreat from income inequality and a reduction in the level of bankers' bonuses, the fact that art prices still looked frothy five years after the crisis may partly be the result of twitchy investors searching for insurance against runaway inflation.

Inequality is also a fundamental feature of the artistic labour market. Going back to the Renaissance it appears to have been marked by a very unequal income distribution where a small number of artists hog a high proportion of the total income. In short, it operates on what is commonly called the star system. There is also a structural excess supply of labour because more people would like to make a living from art than there is demand for their work. And for non-stars, for the journeymen of this market, living standards are anyway likely to be lower than they would be if they worked in a different market, because there are intangible returns and satisfactions that encourage the artist to accept lower wages. This is not an exclusively modern phenomenon. In 1560, there were 300 registered masters of painting and the graphic arts in Antwerp compared with 169 bakers and seventy-eight butchers, while, of the 111 artists who lived in the borough of Campo Marzio in Rome in the mid-seventeenth century, almost 50 per cent were listed as poor.[185] If there is a difference today, it is simply that the modern business techniques employed by successful, commercially minded artists are more sophisticated. Jeff Koons, for example, who worked as a commodity broker on Wall Street before becoming a full-time artist, attracted considerable attention by employing an image consultant.

At Chicago University, home of free market ideology, there are economists who rejoice in the commercialism of such artists as Warhol, Koons and Hirst and who regard the high-mindedness of William Blake and Keynes as absurdly misplaced. David Galenson, one of their number, talks of the 'prudish distaste' exhibited by many art scholars and critics for discussing the nexus between money and art, arguing that the market price is an eloquent verdict on the importance of a work of art:

> Long before Andy Warhol, Théodore Duret [a French art critic] established the principle that prices provide evidence of artistic success. What is disappointing, however, is how poor the quality of the art world's economic discourse remains even in the post-Warhol era. It continues to be fashionable among many critics and scholars to claim that art markets are irrational, and that prices have no value as indicators of artistic importance. These claims are both ignorant and foolish.[186]

I think Galenson has a point about prudishness. There is a genuine reluctance, sometimes bordering on hypocrisy, in the world of art, music and literature to acknowledge the importance of money. The ultimate example of that prudishness is to be found in the novels of Henry James, where business is treated as merely mundane – absurdly so in *The Ambassadors*, where the plot turns on attempts to persuade an errant son to return from Europe to work in a family business in Massachusetts which makes a small object that no one in the novel has the indelicacy to call by name. A lavatorial whiff hangs over the book, almost as elusive as the grin of the Cheshire cat. I also find a degree of preciousness in Keynes's vision of the purpose of capitalism as being to pave the way for the triumph of the values of Bloomsbury, a group with an exceptionally high regard for its talents that failed to produce an artist of the front rank and whose pre-eminent author, Virginia Woolf, produced exquisitely sensitive novels that have always struck me as the literary equivalent of chamber music.

The issue of price and aesthetic value is more difficult. It is true that the art market has sometimes been ahead of the public in perceiving the worth of great paintings, most notably so in the case of the Impressionists. This was Duret's point. Yet at much the same time it delivered verdicts that turned out subsequently to have been ill judged. In the early days of Impressionism, the market was placing much higher values on the works of academic painters such as Bouguereau and Cabanel, who are now to be seen mainly on the walls and in the corridors of French provincial officialdom, having been severely downgraded relative to their more innovative contemporaries. Then there was the extraordinary case of Vermeer, who was well-nigh forgotten after his death in 1675. His paintings fetched very little until the late nineteenth century, after which they rose thousands of per cent in value.

That once again underlines the point that prices of works

of art are driven not by economic fundamentals but by fickle fashion. While there can be no objective definition of aesthetic merit, my personal preference, however elitist, would be to go with the verdict of art historians and critics rather than that of a market whose workings are often questionable. What will become, in a hundred years' time, for example, of Balloon Dog (Orange), a sculpture by Jeff Koons that fetched $58 million at auction in 2013? One of five 'unique' versions, the piece was produced not by Koons's own hand but in a factory.

Art auctions are, incidentally, notoriously susceptible to manipulation, and dealers' ethics often leave much to be desired. The art market, far from being efficient in the economist's sense, is prone to 'herding', reflecting what Robert Hughes identified as a tendency of museums to be slow to identify good contemporary artists and then simultaneously to rush to buy the top five 'hot' artists of the day. Much the same happens with hedge fund managers, who are often heavily reliant on their dealers' advice. Those dealers frequently carry large inventories of the work of the artists they decide to promote and actively seek to massage the market to keep prices artificially high. Indeed, David Galenson himself quotes an editorial in the *New York Times* on Damien Hirst that declared that 'no artist has managed the escalation of prices for his own work as brilliantly as Mr Hirst'. An equivalent allegation in the US securities markets would have more serious consequences. Certainly by the standards of other investment markets, the art market is a singularly murky place, one of the nether reaches of capitalism, and while Robert Hughes may have been exaggerating when he said that the art world was 'the biggest unregulated market outside illicit drugs', he was certainly onto something.

That said, the main buyers of art are big enough to look after themselves, so from a public policy point of view, caveat emptor is the appropriate response. There is no need for vastly increased regulation to protect buyers and sellers, although there may be a case for closer scrutiny of the art market's role in criminal activities such as money laundering and tax evasion. It should also be recognised that the modern art market is more diverse than the very limited one that prevailed at the time of the Italian Renaissance, though the nature of the contemporary art that is produced is still dictated by a relatively small number of influential purchasers. Museum buyers, to a degree, embody the values of William Blake, in that they are not looking to make a profit when they purchase a work of art – though the buying decisions of curators and trustees are inevitably influenced by career concerns, which means that museums do worry about subsequent market verdicts on their spending decisions. Hence the tendency noted by Robert Hughes towards herding.

Looking at the issue more widely, William Blake's wisdom is rooted in a fundamental truth: we can no more measure the value of a Shakespeare play than reckon the utility of Beethoven's late quartets. Much in the arts is inherently unquantifiable in financial terms and where it is quantifiable, the quantity may say nothing about the well-being or aesthetic delight that the art in question imparts. The relationship of the arts with the values of capitalism is thus an awkward one. The Victorian novelist Samuel Butler was, I think, right to say that the sinews of art and literature are money – a neat tweak of Cicero's aphorism on war. But while this is an interesting point to make about art and literature, the important point is that it is not *the* point.

CHAPTER ELEVEN

TAX AND THE DIVISION
OF THE SPOILS

Here, from that great American controversialist H. L. Mencken, is something utterly counter-intuitive. 'Taxation', he says, 'is eternally lively; it concerns nine-tenths of us more directly than either smallpox or golf, and has just as much drama in it; moreover, it has been mellowed and made gay by as many gaudy, preposterous theories.'[187] A similar thought, less colourfully expressed, comes from the economist Joseph Schumpeter:

> The spirit of a people, its cultural level, its social structure, the deeds its policy may prepare – all this and more is written in its fiscal history, stripped of all phrases. He who knows how to listen to its message here discerns the thunder of world history more clearly than anywhere else … The public finances are one of the best starting points for an investigation of society, especially though not exclusively of its political life.[188]

Implicit in both these assertions is the fundamental insight that taxation goes to the heart of the compact between the

individual and the state in the system of democratic capitalism. It is a fraught relationship involving a tension between
people who feel they have a right to keep what they earn and
those who argue that a just society requires the better-off to
provide a safety net to the less well-off through the tax and
benefit system. This boils down to the question of how to distribute the spoils of capitalism.

Given the rising concern about inequality, on which the art
market cast an interesting light in the previous chapter, the case
for redistributive taxation might seem self-evident. Yet the tax
debate has become notably more fraught over the past four
decades, not least in the United States, where government has
been paralysed latterly by a stand-off between Republicans and
Democrats over fiscal policy. Indeed, Republican fiscal fundamentalism came close in 2012 and 2013 to forcing the US
federal government to default on its debt. At the same time, the
Tea Party movement's powerful grass-roots campaign against
what it regards as excessive levels of taxation and public spending has pushed Republican politicians into adopting more extreme positions on this score. So, too, has the anti-tax pledge
drawn up by conservative libertarian Grover Norquist, founder
of the organisation Americans for Tax Reform, which argues
for a minimalist state version of capitalism. Most Republican
politicians are signatories. In Europe, as indicated in Chapter
Eight, the anti-tax protest takes a different form. Northern Europeans are broadly supportive of the social democratic model
of capitalism, but do not want to finance a Europe-wide version
of it. They have encouraged their politicians to impose a fiscal
straitjacket on supposedly profligate southern Europeans and
to resist turning the monetary union into a broader transfer

union where creditor countries come to the rescue of indigent sovereign debtors. This has led to suggestions that the political manageability of democratic capitalism has sharply declined.

Yet this resentment over the demands of the tax authorities merits deeper examination because it is neither unprecedented nor anything like as violent as in earlier centuries. The seventeenth-century civil war in France, known as the *Fronde*, was prompted by a tax revolt when the government tried to recoup some of the costs of the Thirty Years War through increased taxes. It started when a tax levied on the judicial officers of the Parlement of Paris caused an uproar, leading to demands for constitutional reform. Instead of reform, France suffered years of chaos as troops who returned from the Thirty Years War roamed the country in conditions of anarchy. The psychological impact on the young Louis XIV was so powerful that it provided the spur that turned France into the most centralised, absolutist monarchy in Europe.

Louis's finance minister Jean-Baptiste Colbert famously remarked that 'the art of taxation consists in so plucking the goose as to obtain the largest possible amount of feathers with the smallest possible amount of hissing'. Yet, in practice, French kings and their ministers were often too greedy for funds to employ such subtle means. François I boasted that France was a meadow which he could mow as often as he wished. He did a great deal of mowing to finance fine castles and an exceptionally luxurious court, as did his successor Henri II, who also managed to run up a huge national debt. Equally cynical was Cardinal Richelieu, chief minister of Louis XIII, who argued that if taxes were not high, people would not be stimulated into working hard. No surprise, then, that history's most epic popular revolution took place in France. It was a fiscal crisis that prompted a decision in 1789 to call the Estates General – an assembly of the Church, nobles and common people – for the first time since 1614. The failure to reach an adequate constitutional and fiscal settlement set in train the events that led to the French Revolution.

Similar problems had arisen across the Channel. The origins of the English Civil War lay, among other things, in the determination of Charles I to impose taxes without the consent of Parliament. The proximate cause of trouble was 'ship money'. The king's subjects had traditionally been obliged to fit out a fleet in times of national peril. Charles decided that they could pay ship money instead. Having discovered this was a wonderfully handy tax, he insisted on coming back for more when the country was not subject to any serious external threat; also on extending the tax to non-maritime counties. This imposition, together with the fear that Charles was too sympathetic to Catholicism, ultimately led to his beheading. Richard Cobden, the great nineteenth-century liberal, was later to say: 'When a government deals unjustly by the people with respect to taxation, that constitutes the whole matter of account between them. That has been the ground of almost all the revolutions in this country.'[189]

Yet if the English believed strongly in the principle of no taxation without representation, they were not inclined to extend the courtesy to citizens in the colonies. The Boston Tea Party was a classic tax revolt against the English monarchy, which ultimately led to the Declaration of Independence. Not that the American colonialists were entirely free of double standards. As John Kenneth Galbraith has remarked, they were equally hostile to taxation *with* representation, a phenomenon that survives in the Tea Party movement's campaign. And it was not as if the British demands for tax revenue were devoid of all justification. The war waged in the defence of the thirteen colonies by the government of William Pitt on France in North America saddled the mother country with huge debts. Meantime, the colonies were busy trading with the enemy: American merchants, who did not have to worry about maintaining their own army to protect themselves against the French and Native American Indians, provided the French army with most of its supplies.

What is it that makes the burden of taxation intolerable? The contrast between Britain and France is instructive. Through much of English and British history, a process of constant negotiation of taxation in Parliament generated a higher degree of consent. This experience illustrates the importance of trust in economic and commercial dealings. It is much easier to raise tax to enhance the capacity of the state if people feel they can trust their fellow taxpayers and the government to fulfil their obligations. The only alternative, if trust is lacking, is tough or even savage enforcement. Pre-revolutionary France was just such a low-trust environment, in which the fiscal system created greater tensions. The economic historian Martin Daunton points out that the French system left fewer opportunities for bargaining and resolution of conflicts. Sale of offices, use of tax farmers with a private interest in the collection of revenue, exemptions for aristocrats and church, the presence of intrusive internal duties, and the absence of an assembly to negotiate disputes between interests and with the crown – all these things added to the tensions. French 'absolutism', he adds, was therefore constrained by a greater degree of local and sectional opposition to taxation than in Britain, and officials at the centre of the French state had less knowledge of revenues and expenditure than their British counterparts.[190]

The nature of the government that levies the tax is important. Nobody likes paying tax to a state that is controlled by a foreign power. Many people are equally reluctant to stump up where a state is perceived to favour one sectional interest at the expense of others or uses tax revenues inefficiently or corruptly. Take the Belgians, who are notoriously averse to paying tax – and small wonder. They were ruled in the seventeenth century by the Spanish; for much of the eighteenth by the Austrians; from 1795 by the French; and after 1815 by the Dutch. The experience of being taxed by foreigners taught Belgians to regard tax as a tribute to a foreign power and the deep-seated habit of evasion continued, unsurprisingly, after independence, and persists to this day. The problem of legitimacy is exacerbated by the division in the country between the well-off Flemish and the poorer French-speaking Walloons, who inhabit a part of the country that is badly afflicted by industrial decline.

Much the same could be said of the Greeks, who before achieving independence were ruled by Turks under the Ottoman Empire. The Great Powers then in 1833 installed a Bavarian prince as king, along with a rigid Bavarian bureaucracy which the Greeks deeply resented. Latterly, their resentment has been directed at the incompetence and corruption of the Greek ruling class. As a result, there is a widespread perception that only stupid people pay tax, while doctors and dentists who are self-employed pay less tax than their receptionists.

In this, at least, there is some justification in the resentment of northern Europeans towards bailing out southern Europe. Then there is Italy, where a lack of solidarity between north and south and the failure of constant injections of state funds to boost the southern Italian economy undermines the willingness of many Italians to pay up. Resentments of this kind contribute powerfully to the growth of black economies.

Nothing creates greater resentment than intrusive or vicious methods of collecting direct taxes. The English MP Francis Burdett, a proponent of constitutional reform and leading critic of high taxes, told Parliament in 1802:

> The income tax has created an inquisitorial power of the most partial, offensive and cruel nature. The whole transactions of a life may be inquired into, family affairs laid open, and an Englishman, like a culprit, summoned to attend commissioners; compelled to wait like a lacquey in their anti-chamber from day to day until they are ready to institute their inquisition into his property; put to his oath, after all perhaps disbelieved, surcharged and stigmatized as perjured, without any redress from or appeal to a jury of his country ... Sir, the repeal of this tax is not a sufficient remedy for its infamy; its principles must be stigmatised and branded.[191]

Yet English practice was mild compared with what prevailed in much of continental Europe, where tax farming was rife. Ferdinand Grapperhaus, a leading Dutch authority on taxation, has this to say on the privatised system of tax collecting in pre-revolutionary France:

In the seventeenth century the system of tax farming was further extended in France until it became an integral part of French national finances. One third of the income of the state went through the hands of the tax farmers who had united in syndicates, and in particular regions for various taxes at regular intervals, mostly every six years when they concluded or renewed their contracts with the government. The most notorious tax leases were those concerning the duties on salt and tobacco; besides there were less important ones on commodities such as leather, ironmongery, soap. The professional group of tax farmers was the biggest employer (after the army and navy). The majority of employees were armed and in uniform. They had the right to enter, and search on suspicion each house, and confiscate any goods which they thought suspect. The tax farmers were an intricately structured, and financially and economically supreme paramilitary organisation, practically a state within a state. The humane treatment of their own employees was proportional to the heartlessness the taxpayers were faced with. The hate against the tax farmers, many of whom ended up under the guillotine during the French Revolution, was intense. Other countries, too, knew about the leasing-out of taxes, but this was not taken to such extremes as in France.[192]

Tax farming goes back in history at least as far as the early Roman republic and could still be found in twentieth-century Europe. In the strictest sense, tax farming involves the farmer paying the government up front for the right to extract the taxes. But if we include the private collection of taxes in exchange for fees, the practice applied for much of the post-war period in Italy, where banks and private businesses collected taxes for the government until 2006. They made their profit primarily from the interest on the cash float they held between collecting the tax and transferring it to the Treasury. Yet this could be a risky business, especially in southern Italy, where the incidence of non-payment was high, because the tax farmers' contracts stipulated that they had to pay up for uncollected taxes. The definition of tax farming could also be stretched to include pay-as-you-earn forms of income tax collection, where the corporate sector in many developed-world economies acts as an unpaid tax collector for the government.

In the end, high tax rates and excessive burdens are what drive people to distraction. Sidney Smith, the brilliant clergyman who founded the *Edinburgh Review*, wrote at the end of the period of high taxation during the Napoleonic Wars:

The inevitable consequences of being too fond of glory; – TAXES upon every article which enters into the mouth, or covers the back, or is placed under the foot; taxes upon everything which is pleasant to see, hear, feel smell, or taste; taxes upon warmth, light and locomotion; taxes on everything on earth, and the waters under the earth, on everything that comes from abroad or is grown at home; taxes on the raw material; taxes on every fresh value that is added to it by the industry of man; taxes on the sauce which pampers man's appetite, and the drug which restores him to health; on the ermine which decorates the judge, and the rope which hangs the criminal; on the poor man's salt, and the rich man's spice; on the brass nails of the coffin, and the ribands of the bride; at bed or board couchant or levant, we must pay. The schoolboy whips his taxed top; the beardless youth manages his taxed horse, with a taxed bridle, on a taxed road; – and the dying Englishman, pouring his medicine, which has paid 7 per cent, into a spoon which has paid 15 per cent, flings himself back upon his chintz bed, which has paid 22 per cent, and expires in the arms of an apothecary who has paid a license of a hundred pounds for the privilege of putting him to death. His whole property is then immediately taxed from 2 to 10 per cent. Besides the probate, large fees are demanded for burying him in the chancel; his virtues are handed down to posterity on taxed marble; and he is then gathered to his fathers to be taxed no more.[193]

A more enjoyably pithy fulmination from roughly the same period came from a British naval officer: 'It is a vile, Jacobin, jumped-up Jack-in-Office piece of impertinence – is a true Briton to have no privacy? Are the fruits of his labour and toil to be picked over, farthing by farthing, by the pimply minions of bureaucracy?'[194]

This was a not untypical response to William Pitt's income tax of 1798, a 10 per cent levy that is generally regarded as a pivotal point in the development of taxation. The irony here is that, as historian Niall Ferguson has pointed out in his peroration on money and power, *The Cash Nexus*:

The history of Britain's rise to great power status is also, and not coincidentally, the history of a rising tax burden … One reason Britain was able to mount such an effective military challenge to her larger neighbour was her higher rate of taxation. As a percentage of GNP, total taxes were nearly double

what they were in France in 1788 (12.4 per cent compared
with 6.8 per cent). If France had only been able to raise more
tax, her fiscal crisis might have been averted.[195]

In other words, the ability to extract money from the taxpayer
is fundamental to the capacity of the state, as is the ability to
raise debt. And it is striking in the history of capitalism that
democratisation and liberty have expanded with the growth
of the number of income and property taxpayers. In effect,
taxpayers swap a share of their income for participation in the
political process. An equally striking feature of undemocratic
regimes is that they try to maintain sources of revenue that
do not require popular consent. The Prussian monarchy, for
example, held on to its domain revenues tenaciously in the
nineteenth century to bolster its power against the onward
march of democracy, as mentioned in Chapter Four.[196] In the
twenty-first century it remains an unsettling feature of Middle
Eastern politics that ruling families in so many oil states derive
little revenue from direct taxes. The absence of a social contract based on the tax relationship is a key reason they lack political legitimacy. The people are subjects rather than citizens,
living in a state of permanent dependency. They see the ruling
families as providers of patronage in the shape of income, jobs
and opportunities, not as political and public servants who
can be held properly to account.

For much of history, tax revenues tended to come more
from indirect than direct taxes. Since these taxes on things
like alcohol, tobacco and clothing are not fully visible to the
taxpayer, they are a softer option for the taxing authority than
direct taxes. Yet they are regressive, which means that they

bear hard on the poor who have to sacrifice a bigger share of their income than the rich. And as the quotation from Sidney Smith demonstrates, people notice in the end if they are being excessively milked by the indirect route. Direct taxes can also be regressive, as the English well know. The fourteenth-century Peasants' Revolt was prompted by a poll tax, one of the crudest forms of direct taxation, amounting to a shilling per head on everyone aged over fifteen apart from beggars, while Margaret Thatcher's departure from office in 1990 was precipitated in part by her ill-judged introduction of a poll tax called the Community Charge.

A sea change in the workings of taxation came in the twentieth century when income tax, a progressive levy, became the crucial lever of fiscal policy. Yet it is easy to forget how recently income tax took on this central role. In a classic book on the British tax system, Mervyn (now Lord) King and John Kay point out that less than a fifth of the working population in 1939 paid income tax.[197] At that point, most people paid only indirect taxes. The subsequent explosion in tax revenues is explained by the growth of the welfare state. Where previously tax had been regarded chiefly as a means of financing wars, it now provided the wherewithal for health care, education, pensions and infrastructure, as well as defence. This was a cornerstone of the post-war settlement between labour and capital, which included increased welfare and free collective bargaining for workers, together with a political guarantee of full employment underpinned by Keynesian demand management.

The post-war social contract implicitly recognised that the utilitarian ethical basis of capitalism – that is, its ability to deliver the greatest good of the greatest number through the self-interested actions of individuals – involved potential conflicts with social justice. Not only did it help mitigate the rigours of red-in-tooth-and-claw capitalism; it brought about a growing willingness on the part of the electorate to accept the case for individual financial sacrifice for collective goals. Many came to accept the view of the great American judge Oliver Wendell Holmes, who said: 'I like paying taxes. With them I buy civilisation.' It was nonetheless a view based on the assumption that the system was administered by wise and benevolent bureaucrats like the guardians of Plato's Republic. That assumption turned out to be flawed. An intense debate on the relative requirements of economic growth versus social justice became a permanent feature of the political landscape.

The collision of an inevitably imperfect tax system with the growth of public spending became acute as economic growth slowed down in the 1970s. At the same time, politicians acquired the habit of tinkering with the fiscal plumbing by offering tax reliefs to interest groups who might help put them in power. As the British economist Brian Reading pointed out to me when we both worked on *The Economist* in the 1970s, the tax and benefits system increasingly rewarded people not for what they did, but for what they were: pension scheme members, home owners, unemployed and the rest. Increasingly, rival interest groups fought to raise their share of government revenue. This was taken to extremes in the US, where the fiscal system is now riddled with concessions and exemptions won through lobbying and special pleading. The result everywhere is a high degree of complexity and the growth of tax bureaucracies, along with a new form of tax revolt whereby armies of lawyers and accountants exploit avoidance opportunities, often via off-shore tax havens, on behalf of their clients. Their guiding philosophy is the dictum of the British judge Lord Clyde, who said:

> No man in this country is under the smallest obligation, moral or other, so to arrange his legal relations as to enable the Inland Revenue to put the largest shovel into his stores. The Inland Revenue is not slow, and quite rightly, to take every advantage which is open to it under the Taxing Statutes for the purposes of depleting the taxpayer's pocket. And the taxpayer is in like manner entitled to be astute to prevent, so far as he honestly can, the depletion of his means by the Inland Revenue.[198]

In this historically novel environment, politicians are constantly battling to keep a lid on public spending and taxation. Some, like Ronald Reagan in the 1980s, adopted the theories of the economist Arthur Laffer, which suggested that tax cuts would actually generate increased government revenue by encouraging people to generate more taxable earnings – a prime example of H. L. Mencken's gaudy and preposterous tales about tax. In the event, the Reagan tax cuts contributed to an increased government deficit, while much of the impact leaked outside the US via imports thereby diluting the domestic benefit of the policy. And all across the developed world, spending and taxation have shown a marked tendency to creep back up despite efforts to cut back, not least because citizens want more of such public goods as health care and education as they grow richer. In most developed countries the state is an important provider of these services.

The resulting expansion of the taxing and spending state ultimately prompted a challenge from the libertarian right. The intellectual ammunition was provided by Friedrich Hayek's *The Constitution of Liberty*, which contained a frontal attack on the progressive nature of the tax system, declaring that a democracy in which the majority was free to impose a discriminatory tax burden on the minority was unjust and oppressive. Hayek believed that reshuffling income and property rights through interest group haggling was destabilising and coercive. The development of public choice theory in the US likewise challenged the notion of a benign state run by Platonic guardians. James Buchanan and his followers saw the state as predatory, using its monopoly power over the tax base to maximise revenue. On this view, politicians and bureaucrats were 'personal utility maximisers' who needed to be curbed. Such thinking played a part in the Californian tax revolt in the late 1970s that led to the famous Proposition 13 referendum, which put a curb on property taxes.

Now a new challenge has arisen from the left of centre. The French economist Thomas Piketty has advanced a novel theory of capitalist accumulation, backed by a mass of data on income and wealth over three centuries, which asserts that the ratio of capital to income will rise without limit so long as the rate of return on capital is significantly higher than the rate of growth of the economy. Piketty argues that, historically, this is a normal state of affairs. The only deviations from the norm have occurred when much of the return on wealth has been expropriated or destroyed, or when economies have grown exceptionally rapidly, as in the post-war reconstruction of Europe or the catch-up growth now taking place in emerging markets. The thesis is controversial. Not everyone accepts the French economist's definition of normality. In periods when the return on capital is higher than the rate of economic growth, the resulting premium is the amount investors require to compensate for the risk of deviations from the norm that could destroy income and wealth. There can be no scientific guarantee that the return on capital will outstrip economic growth and at the time of writing there is widespread concern in capital markets that the risk-adjusted return on capital is below current rates of growth in the developed world. But should Piketty's assertion turn out to be right, the already extreme levels of inequality in pre-tax income and wealth in much of the developed world would indeed become even more extreme. Hence his case for far higher marginal tax rates on high incomes and a progressive global wealth tax.[199]

If policymakers found his arguments persuasive, that would imply a return to the level of taxation reached in Western democracies in the 1970s – the high water mark in terms of redistribution. Since then, globalisation, the growth of competition between different tax jurisdictions and of tax havens, has restrained the power of governments to tax. Yet reformers such as Margaret Thatcher and Ronald Reagan largely failed in their efforts to shrink the size of the state. And, paradoxically, we now have more taxation without representation on a voluntary basis, because declining turnouts in elections in the US and Europe mean that a growing proportion of the electorate pays taxes but does not vote. At the same time, in the over-indebted countries of the eurozone, citizens are saddled with a system that comes close to taxation without representation because taxing and spending decisions have been substantially dictated by a German-led policy agenda administered by the European Commission, the European Central Bank and the International Monetary Fund.

There are nonetheless some eternal verities in taxation. 'In this world,' Benjamin Franklin famously remarked in 1789, 'nothing can be said to be certain except death and taxes', while the British Liberal Prime Minister David Lloyd George added the macabre but accurate postscript that 'death is the most convenient time to tax rich people'. For his part, the great Irish-born statesman Edmund Burke rightly remarked that 'to tax and to please, no more than to love and be wise, is not given to men'. Yet the deep divisions within the societies of North America and Europe over taxing and spending definitely reflect something new. In the US, the debate over President Obama's health-care reforms revealed, as never before, the nature of the divide. Democrat voters continue to regard a system in which society's winners are taxed to pay for a social safety net as morally superior to the more rugged capitalism that prevailed before President Roosevelt's New Deal in the 1930s. Republicans increasingly feel that to be taxed to support those in need is a moral outrage tantamount to theft, and that they have a right to keep what they earn. The recent polarisation of American politics reflects the fact that there can be no common ground between these views.

In Europe, the divide is between northern taxpayers, who resent stumping up to bail out troubled fellow members of the eurozone, and southern debtors, together with Ireland, who can reasonably argue that their plight is largely a result of the flawed design of the monetary union, which led to huge imbalances between creditors and debtors. Without a readiness on the part of the creditors to pursue more expansionary policies or make fiscal transfers, it is hard to see how the eurozone can survive in its present form. Yet the moralistic view of surpluses and deficits outlined in Chapter Eight prevails. Debtor countries are being required to aim for Germanic balanced budgets, current account surpluses on the balance of payments and low public debt, while Germany and its fellow northern Europeans continue to do the same.

I fear that the divisions in American society and in Europe over the provision of safety nets to the disadvantaged could fairly be characterised as a crisis of democratic capitalism and that such distributional conflicts, exacerbated by the ageing of populations, will remain an overwhelming feature of the political landscape for the foreseeable future. And while today's world looks more threatened by deflation than inflation, the logic of demography points in the direction of renewed inflation in the developed world in due course. This is because voting power lies with the elderly while economic power rests increasingly with a shrinking population of younger workers. There are thus too many potential claimants for too little income.[200] If the democratic system ends up penalising the economically powerful youth, the young will impose an inflation tax on the elderly to secure what they believe to be their rightful share of the spoils of the capitalist system.

CHAPTER TWELVE

CAPITALISM, WARTS AND ALL

Has there ever been a time when people really felt at ease with capitalism? That question was put to me by Richard Lambert, former director-general of the Confederation of British Industry and before that editor of the *Financial Times*, when I explained to him the theme of this book. An interesting light is cast on his question by Johann Wolfgang von Goethe in his great two-part drama *Faust*, written at the start of the nineteenth century when the industrial revolution in Europe was in its earliest stages. *Faust*, Part Two, among many other rich themes, incorporates what amounts to a parable of the costs and benefits of capitalist economic development. It is extraordinarily prescient in relation to current concerns.

In the story, Faust serves as the embodiment of modern man, seeking through science and technology to pursue the materialist goal of domination over nature and to build a rich, earthly paradise. The urge to subjugate the forces of nature comes as he watches what he calls the 'pointless power' of the waves by the sea and says:

> *They swell,*
> *They climb, they tower, they overreach*

> *And topple and their breakers spill*
> *In a long and broad assault up the flat beach.*
> *And that annoys me. Any man*
> *Who values freedom and his rights would feel*
> *By such an insolent presumption*
> *Flung into discontent and turmoil…*
> *I will bar*
> *The masterful sea from coming near the shore,*
> *Set limits on its stretch of wet*
> *And cram it deep back down its own gullet.*[201]

Faust thus embarks on a great land reclamation project, undertaken in partnership with Mephistopheles. In his efforts to push back the sea, the entrepreneurial Faust, epitomising capitalist exploitation, drives his workers furiously to build a dyke that creates the space for his prosperous new realm. To finance the scheme and pay the workers, he uses paper money created by the emperor who rules over the territory.

Where Goethe, who had been finance minister to the Duke of Saxe-Weimar, shows particular foresight is in identifying unintended consequences of capitalist enterprise – consequences that, unlike those associated with Adam Smith's invisible hand, are far from positive. Environmental damage results from the creation of Faust's dyke because he failed to provide an outlet for putrid water. His land consequently becomes a foetid quagmire that has to be drained. His insatiable desire for more land leads him to drive out long-standing residents of the dunes. He asks Mephistopheles and his acolytes to remove Philemon and Baucis – an old couple borrowed by Goethe from Ovid's *Metamorphoses* – from their home. When the couple refuse to leave, Mephistopheles, against Faust's instructions, kills them and burns down the house. The natural beauty of the landscape is subsequently ruined. At the same time, the dyke has been imperfectly put together and needs constant shoring up, prompting Mephistopheles to pass a critical verdict on Faust's hubris:

> *Dam by dam and groyne by groyne*
> *You're laying up for Father Neptune,*
> *The water devil, a fine repast.*
> *This way or that you lose, we and*
> *The elements are in league, we bend*
> *All to nothing at the last.*

In the political economy of Faust's realm, it is striking that ethics are subordinate to economic growth. His port is a haven for pirates with whom Faust has a successful business partnership. As described by Mephistopheles, his business activities even anticipate globalisation:

> *Ships put out from shore, they ride*
> *Fast away on the willing tide.*
> *Admit it now: from this palace*
> *You take the world in your embrace.*

Another important strand of the story concerns the emperor's paper money. When it is first launched, on the advice of Mephistopheles, it is acclaimed by everyone and frees the emperor from excessive debt and economic stagnation. It feels like the continuation of alchemy by other means, with paper turning into valid money in the same way that alchemists aimed to turn lead into gold. Yet in due course the emperor cannot resist the temptation to flood the country with too much paper. In theory, the currency is backed by all the empire's gold that has yet to be mined. But the gold is illusory. The reality is that the emperor presides over a fiat currency – that is, one not backed by precious metal. So an excess of paper currency leads to inflation, financial chaos and social strife, as Mephistopheles explains:

> *The Empire sliding into anarchy the while,*
> *Strife among great and small on every side,*
> *Much brotherly expulsion and homicide,*
> *Burgh against burgh, city against city,*
> *Guilds feuding with the nobility,*
> *The bishop with his chapter and his see,*
> *Eyes never meeting but in enmity,*
> *Murder in the churches, and on the road*
> *No mercy shown to travellers or trade.*

The resonance for a modern audience lies partly in the fact that financial innovation was an important contributory cause of the great financial crisis that began in 2007. Subprime mortgages granted to Americans who were scarcely creditworthy were packaged into complex investment products to which credit rating agencies accorded top ratings – a case of financial alchemy apparently turning subprime lead into triple-A gold. Then, when bubble-inflated US house prices declined across the nation, the value of this ersatz gold shrank, rocking the confidence of banks and precipitating the credit crunch that preceded the Great Recession. For Germans, this passage brings back ingrained memories of the chaos wrought by the Weimar inflation in the 1920s, as well as the turbulent monetary conditions that prevailed after 1945.

That underlines a deep-seated problem with the workings of market capitalism. In contrast with the feudal period, when economic fluctuations were driven chiefly by the forces of nature, war or plague, capitalism introduced regular boom-and-bust cycles. The system is inherently unstable and has become more so as a result of the deregulation of finance since the 1960s. The economist Hyman Minsky provided the best explanation of the dynamics of this instability in the 1980s, arguing that long periods of stability and prosperity breed complacency and encourage risk taking, as outlined in Chapter Five.[202]

Also implicit in Goethe's tale, and a natural consequence of the instability described by Minsky, is what Marx and Engels called the 'eternal insecurity' of capitalism:

The bourgeoisie cannot exist without constantly revolutionising the instruments of production, and thereby the relations of production, and therefore social relations as a whole. By contrast, the prime condition of existence for all previous industrial classes was the unaltered preservation of the old modes of production. The continual upheaval of production, the uninterrupted disturbance of all social conditions, eternal insecurity and movement distinguish the bourgeois epoch from every previous one. All fixed, encrusted relations along with their train of ancient and venerable prejudices and opinions are dissolved, and any new ones are antiquated before they can ossify. All that is solid and established melts into air, all that is holy is profaned, and people are finally forced to view their place in life and their relations to one another with open eyes.[203]

The Faustian obsession with growth is particularly relevant to 21st-century worries. For modern politicians, the rate of increase in gross domestic product remains overwhelmingly important, imposing a yardstick that many feel reduces economic endeavour to banal materialism and to the commodification of human society. The critique is also apposite for countries such as Japan and China, where politicians and business people conspire to ignore the environmental damage that untrammelled industrialisation brings, thereby underlining the shortcomings of the utilitarian ethical justification for capitalism, which emphasises the greatest happiness of the greatest number while relying on self-interest or greed to bring about that end. Here, Goethe anticipates the Ruskinian aesthetic and environmental assault on capitalist political economy referred to in Chapter One. It serves to remind us that managing the environmental consequences of bringing the developing world's population up to the consumption levels of the advanced countries is one of the greatest challenges facing market capitalism. The task is not made easier by a fundamental flaw in capitalism's scoring system, which arises because market prices do not reflect the full social cost of externalities such as the environmental damage produced by global manufacturing. The accounting mechanics of the utilitarian calculus thus become elusive.

In the tale of Philemon and Baucis, meantime, Goethe echoes the lament of Oliver Goldsmith in *The Deserted Village* about the breakdown of community as a result of industrialisation.

And all across the world, problems of shoddy construction and poor safety remain a pressing concern – think only of British Petroleum's disastrous oil spill in the Gulf of Mexico, Tokyo Electric Power's nuclear spill at Fukushima or the loss of life due to faulty trains and tracks in China. Faust, at least, pays a price for his blindness to the wider consequences of his driven entrepreneurial activity. In a moment of high symbolism towards the end of the drama, he is blinded. What all this tells us is that the difficulties of living with capitalism and of the problematic legitimacy of the system were apparent at the very outset of the industrial revolution. Goethe foresaw most of what was to trouble people about capitalism for the next two centuries. He was warning us, in effect, to prepare for endless disappointment with this extraordinarily potent economic system.

It is true that since the Great Depression of the 1930s policymakers have sought to remove the sting from the perpetual revolution identified by Marx through resort to various forms of social spending. Keynesian fiscal and monetary pump priming after the collapse of Lehman Brothers in 2008 ensured that there was no return to soup queues and to acute deprivation. Mercifully, no politician of importance in the US or Europe echoed, in the immediate aftermath, the moralistic injunction of Andrew Mellon, US Treasury Secretary during the Great Depression, who urged the liquidation of stocks, farmers and real estate to purge the rottenness from the system. Competition policy has also sought to address the in-built tendency of capitalism towards industrial concentration. Politicians nonetheless failed to prevent the Great Recession of 2007–09, the worst since the Great Depression, which was accompanied by big losses of output and appalling unemployment.

At the same time, developed-world governments faced a new problem relating to debt. Historically, public sector debt spiralled in wartime, but was paid down during the peace. That changed after 1945 with the growth of welfare spending. And, as Raghuram Rajan, former chief economist of the International Monetary Fund and subseqently governor of the Reserve Bank of India, has pointed out, there is an alternative narrative to the conventional Keynesian one to explain the current predicament of the developed world. Some argue that after the long post-war boom the advanced economies' ability to grow by making useful things went into decline. Simultaneously, governments in the developed world expanded the welfare state on the assumption that the growth rates of the 1950s and 1960s would endure. With growth faltering and government spending continuing to expand in the 1970s and 1980s despite less buoyant tax revenues, central banks financed this fiscal excess. The result was inflation without much addition to economic growth.

While inflation helped reduce the debt, it caused widespread discontent – more shades of *Faust*, Part Two – not least because, as Milton Friedman remarked, inflation is taxation without legislation. So Keynesian policies became discredited and central banks, granted independence from the politicians, focused on low and stable inflation as their primary objective. Yet government deficit spending continued, thereby confirming the homespun wisdom of US President Calvin Coolidge, touched on in Chapter One, who warned: 'Nothing is easier than spending the public money. It does not appear to belong to anybody. The temptation is overwhelming to bestow it on somebody.'[204]

The remorseless rise in public indebtedness was further exacerbated by rising life expectancy and falling birth rates, which made health-care and pension commitments more costly. In the US and several other countries, incomes remained stagnant for the best part of three decades. An illusion of rising living standards was nonetheless maintained, either because households borrowed more against their overvalued homes in a very free credit environment fuelled by a global savings glut, which was the case in the US and the UK, or because governments created unproductive make-work jobs, as in Italy, Spain and Greece. As Raghuram Rajan sees it:

> The advanced countries have a choice. They can act as if all is well, except that their consumers are in a funk, and that 'animal spirits' must be revived through stimulus. Or they can treat the crisis as a wake-up call to fix what debt has papered over in the last few decades. For better or worse, the narrative that persuades these countries' governments and publics will determine their future – and that of the global economy.[205]

Whether the advanced countries would be able anyway to revive innovation and productivity growth is an open question. Northwestern University's Robert Gordon has forecast a slower rate of productivity improvement in the US than in the past because there is nothing in prospect that matches the huge changes wrought by such advances as steam power, railways, electrification, the internal combustion engine, or even such simple things as running water and home sanitation. He argues that the transformative power of the internet is less potent than these earlier innovations. There is also the question of how much productivity growth will find its way into workers' incomes. As long ago as 1964, the British economist James Meade highlighted the difficulty of finding jobs for humans displaced by machines. His vision of the future was bleak:

> There would be a limited number of exceedingly wealthy property owners; the proportion of the working population required to man the extremely profitable automated industries would be small; wage rates would thus be depressed; there would have to be a large expansion of the production of the labour-intensive goods and services which were in high demand by the few multi-multi-multi-millionaires; we would be back in a super-world of an immiserised proletariat of butlers, footmen, kitchen maids and other hangers on. Let us call this the Brave New Capitalists' Paradise.

'It is to me,' he added, 'a hideous outlook.'[206] This chimes with much of our current predicament. Over the past three decades, Marx's notion of the immiseration of the proletariat has acquired renewed relevance as a result of globalisation. Productivity gains have not been fully reflected in rising real incomes in the developed world because the supply of labour in emerging markets, new technology and the decline of trade union power have together put a cap on wage increases. The benefits of increased productivity flow instead to a small minority of highly skilled, elite workers and to shareholders. Meantime, low-end service sector jobs for careworkers and hospital orderlies – today's equivalent of Meade's butlers and footmen – appeal chiefly to unskilled immigrants rather than to a surfeit of university graduates. So many Americans and

Europeans confront a form of genteel immiseration. There is a real question as to where future jobs will come from and whether they will satisfy the aspirations of the workforce of the advanced countries.

To return to the issue of debt, it is clear that public sector debt has reached levels in many countries where it is unlikely ever to be repaid in full. The only question is whether countries will formally default as Greece and Argentina have done or whether the default will be engineered covertly through inflation. Equally questionable is whether a Keynesian response will be possible in any future crisis. In the US, there is no appetite on Capitol Hill for further bank bailouts, and even less enthusiasm on the part of the public. The Dodd–Frank legislation that followed the crisis seeks to outlaw resort to taxpayers' money to finance bailouts. There is thus great uncertainty about what precisely would happen in the event of a systemic financial crisis; but if the privately held debt and equity capital of a failing bank were insufficient to absorb its losses, any shortfall would have to be paid for by an assessment on the banking industry. So, solvent banks would become less solvent as they carried out their rescue mission. That is a very risky expedient, since it has the potential to further undermine confidence as a crisis evolves. Some say that it will never come to that, but in the unstable world of finance, such insouciance often turns out to be Panglossian optimism.

As I argued earlier, the precise shape of a future crisis is always hard to predict, but against this background it seems likely to be very messy. What *is* clear is that any future crisis will be even bigger than the last one because banks are more concentrated as a result of mergers and acquisitions prompted by the 2007–09 debacle. The number of banks falling into the category of 'too big' or 'too interconnected' to fail is thus greater than ever before. Many, in my judgement, remain undercapitalised. Nassim Nicholas Taleb, a devastating critic of the risk management practices of the big banks, presciently observed in 2007:

> Financial Institutions have been merging into a smaller number of very large banks. Almost all banks are interrelated. So the financial ecology is swelling into gigantic, incestuous, bureaucratic banks – when one fails, they all fall. The increased concentration among banks seems to have the effect of making financial crisis less likely, but when they happen they are more global in scale and hit us very hard. We have moved from a diversified ecology of small banks, with varied lending policies, to a more homogeneous framework of firms that all resemble one another. True, we now have fewer failures, but when they occur ... I shiver at the thought.[207]

The position today is the same only more so. It is as if an innate feature of the roller-coaster capitalist system is that it constantly finds both old and new ways of making people uncomfortable. As for the regulatory response to the crisis, it has been inadequate. Indeed, the banks' huge lobbying power ensures that new regulations are constantly subject to attempts to dismantle them. The world economy thus remains hostage to the big banks and it does not require genius to see that another global financial crisis will strike in due course, as suggested in Chapter Three, though I believe we have yet to reach the degree of complacency and leverage required to make the crisis happen.

Alongside the problem of eternal insecurity, creative destruction and boom or bust, there remain all those issues Goethe hints at when pointing to the essentially amoral nature of the political economy of Faust's realm. Capitalism's greatest achievement in recent decades has been to lift hundreds of millions out of poverty in the developing world. The World Bank estimates that the extreme poverty rate – $1.25 in 2005 prices – halved between 1990 and 2010 after adjusting for the purchasing power of the dollar in different countries. That left 21 per cent of people in the developing world living at or below $1.25 a day, down from 43 per cent in 1990 and 52 per cent in 1981.[208] Yet this has not changed a basic truth: even if capital no longer tyrannises over labour in the developed world and even if marked progress has been made in reducing global poverty, the system has not shaped the political economy of a just society.

This goes to the heart of many current discontents about capitalism. The ethical basis of the system is essentially utilitarian, which entails the disconcerting assumption that the individual can be subordinated to collective ends. While capitalism does not incorporate a Leninist-style utilitarian calculus – the notion, say, that thousands should be slaughtered in the broader interest of millions – it nonetheless raises similar questions, not least because economic efficiency is constantly at odds with the conventional notions of morality enshrined in the Abrahamic religions and, to a degree, in Confucianism. At the same time, capitalism's promotion of self-interest at the expense of social solidarity continues to cause offence. The idea that speculation, debt and greed can be socially useful remains troubling for many. Moreover, the constant tendency to excess in the workings of the capitalist system, not least in the form of extreme inequality of income and wealth, erodes its legitimacy.

It is striking that the recent period of financialisation in the US and UK witnessed the highest levels of inequality since the 1920s, when high finance enjoyed a similarly dominant role. A study by the Organisation for Economic Cooperation and Development has shown, for example, that the wealthiest Americans 'have collected the bulk of the past three decades' income gains', a statistic that casts the notion of the US as the land of opportunity in a rather strange light.[209] As mentioned earlier, most of the economic gains have gone to a tiny handful at the top, who are predominantly business people and bankers. Recent research into US income tax returns has shown that executives, managers, supervisors and financial professionals account for about 60 per cent of the top 0.1 per cent of income earners and account for 70 per cent of the increase in the share of national income going to the top 0.1 per cent of the income distribution between 1979 and 2005.[210] In cruder terms, American CEOs earned 20.1 times more than typical workers in 1965. That figure rose to 231 times more in 2011 if the value of stock options exercised in a given year is included in CEO pay.[211] Of course, it is possible to argue with these figures, because they incorporate assumptions about the valuation of stock options that can never be definitive. Yet, however the numbers are done, they invariably reveal that there has been an astonishing increase in the gap between CEO pay and that of the average worker. Only a CEO could believe that CEOs' productivity has been so remarkable over this period as to justify the extraordinary increase in income inequality in the workplace. The US probably constitutes an extreme case, but similar trends in inequality are apparent in Britain and much of the rest of the English-speaking world. Even in continental Europe, income inequality is creeping up in countries such as Germany and Sweden where equality has hitherto been regarded as integral to the social ethos.

All of this reflects a deep imbalance of power in the structure of modern capitalism. Politicians have done nothing to restrain these excesses because business has the whip hand in the political market place. This derives partly from funding power – business's ability to put up campaign finance and sustain expensive lobbying – but also because, in an increasingly complex economic environment, politicians depend on the support of business to offer the electorate the prospect of jobs, investment and prosperity. Indeed, lawmakers depend on business support more than at any time in the past. So the corporate sector enjoys a privileged position in today's democracy.

While global inequality is falling because the likes of China and India are growing faster than rich countries, the developed world economy has thus become polarised between a small group of the super-rich and the rest. The laggards enjoyed rising living standards before 2007, despite stagnant real incomes, thanks mainly to increased borrowing on the security of their homes. The German sociologist Wolfgang Streeck rightly points out that subprime mortgages became a substitute, however illusory in the end, for social policy that was simultaneously being scrapped, as well as for wage increases that were no longer forthcoming at the lower end of a more flexible labour market.[212] Since the crisis, however, American and British home owners have faced a long and deep squeeze on real living standards, while struggling to service an unprecedented level of indebtedness. At the same time, finance has become a mechanism for recycling resources from the rest of the economy into the pockets of a global super-rich elite. It was against this background that President Obama declared late in 2013 that the basic bargain at the heart of the American economy had frayed, as increasing inequality combined with declining upward mobility posed a fundamental threat to the American dream, to Americans' way of life and to what the US stood for around the globe.[213]

Inequality has been further increased by the measures adopted by central bankers to address the aftermath of the financial crisis. Asked in 2012 by the UK's parliamentary Treasury Select Committee to highlight the redistributional impact of its asset-purchasing programme – so-called quantitative easing – the Bank of England explained: 'By pushing up a range of asset prices, asset purchases have boosted the value of households' financial wealth held outside pension funds, but holdings are heavily skewed with the top 5 per cent of households holding 40 per cent of these assets.'

The Bank emphasised its belief that without its asset purchases, most people in the United Kingdom would have been worse off because economic growth would have been lower, unemployment would have been higher and many more companies would have gone out of business. That would have had a significant detrimental impact on savers and pensioners, along with every other group in society. A rise in inequality should obviously be seen in that light. Yet there is no escaping the fact that the rich have been the biggest beneficiaries. In the words of Marc Faber, an influential Asia-based investment strategist, quantitative easing funnels money to the 'Mayfair economy' of the well-to-do and 'boosts the prices of Warhols'.[214]

In continental Europe, the increase in inequality is less pronounced. Yet there is angst in the eurozone about inequality and imbalances between countries. As we saw in the previous chapter, northern Europeans resent a monetary union that has permitted southern Europe to engage in what they see as fiscally profligate behaviour, while southern Europeans and the Irish are required to submit to extreme austerity programmes that exacerbate their sovereign debt problems and keep living standards depressed.

All of this contributes to the widespread feeling that the legitimacy of capitalism is in question, especially since gains reaped by bankers were largely at the taxpayer's expense, and profits on which bonuses were based turned out to be illusory when the financial crisis broke. Concern about inequality cannot, incidentally, simply be written off as a matter of envy. There is a long-standing critique of inequality going back to Aristotle, who argued in his *Politics* that economic inequality could lead to revolution. It was, he thought, both an obstacle to the pursuit of the good life and a threat to the integrity of the community. In Renaissance Italy, Machiavelli in his *Discorsi* argued for limiting inequality of wealth in order to preserve a republic of free citizens. He feared that extremes of wealth and poverty could lead to corruption or revolution. Enlightenment thinkers such as Montesquieu followed Machiavelli in wanting to put limits on economic inequality. The author of *De L'Esprit des Lois* believed this was necessary to prevent undue concentration of power and a consequent threat to liberty.

Today, extreme inequality in the US, UK and other English-speaking countries is not going to cause revolutions or, let us hope, corruption. While incomes have been stagnating, they are still at relatively high levels by historical standards. Few suffer from extreme deprivation. Yet Aristotle's argument in Book Five of his *Politics* that great economic inequality encourages the rich to seek a share of power matching their share of economic resources is an accurate description of what has been happening in much of the developed world – not least in the US, where the Supreme Court doctrine enunciated in the *Citizens United* case that money in politics deserves the protections accorded to speech has given carte blanche to business plutocrats to spend limitless billions in pursuit of their own political ends.

There are big risks inherent in a system where increasingly powerful elites grab an ever larger share of the national pie. One is that when disadvantaged people with low incomes observe that the political agenda has been corralled by the higher-income elite, they conclude that there is little point engaging with the game of politics and feel that taxes are an unfair imposition. In the words of the great American lawyer Louis Brandeis, if democracy becomes plutocracy, those who are not rich are effectively disenfranchised. And it is probably no coincidence that there is a marked trend towards lower turnouts in developed-world elections in countries where voting is not compulsory. Another risk, more apparent in Europe, where the political agenda is dominated by an unrepresentative bureaucratic elite in Brussels, is that people look to extremist political parties to address their problems.

Many economists, including those in official institutions such as the International Monetary Fund and the Bank of

International Settlements, also claim that inequality is bad for economic growth. Indeed, a recent paper from the IMF – not generally regarded as a left-wing body – refers to

> the tentative consensus in the literature that inequality can undermine progress in health and education, cause investment-reducing political and economic instability, and undercut the social consensus required to adjust in the face of shocks, and thus that it tends to reduce the pace and durability of growth.[215]

And it has undoubtedly contributed to anti-business sentiment. Poll evidence suggests that an erosion of trust in business reflects ordinary people's inability to see any moral connection between effort and reward at the top end of industry and commerce.[216] That concern was evident in the Occupy Wall Street movement, with its slogan 'we are the 99 per cent', together with other, similar protest movements around the world.

The debate on how to share the spoils of the system also gives rise to questions at the level of the company. In the Anglosphere, the shareholder-capitalist is seen as the key stakeholder in the system, enjoying the residual right to corporate profits after the claims of labour and all other creditors have been met. This view of the limited liability company was designed for nineteenth-century conditions where capital was scarce and labour plentiful. It allowed the shareholder-capitalist to exercise the control rights over the corporation – that is, shareholders could vote at the annual meeting on issues such as the election of directors, while other stakeholders could not. Whether it is appropriate for the owners of financial capital, which is abundant in a world of excess savings, to have all the control rights in the corporation when the real driver of high growth in the economy is human capital is moot. The human capital of highly skilled executives and employees is often specific to their firm, in that their skills are not transferrable to other firms. Such people are at much greater risk from bankruptcy of their employer than the managers or beneficiaries of widely diversified investment portfolios. Yet the pension scheme trustees and fund managers, who often take a narrowly financial view of corporate performance, retain the control rights.

There is, then, an issue of distributional fairness here. It is conceivable that executives in businesses where human capital is the driver of performance feel no compunction about demanding what others regard as excessive pay because, whether consciously or unconsciously, they sense the inequity in their relationship with shareholders. Certainly there has been a tendency in the US for those running high-tech companies and social network groups to insist on two-tier capital structures on flotation, so that they retain voting control even if they hold only a minority of the equity capital. Social network entrepreneurs such as Mark Zuckerberg of Facebook have shown conspicuously little regard for outside shareholders. However high-handed this may appear, it is not entirely surprising. Facebook had no need of new capital on flotation. In most internet-based businesses, the chief reason for going public is to allow venture capitalists to cash in their chips, not to raise money. This disdainful attitude harks back to the views that prevailed until recently in the bank-dominated capital markets of Germany. The banker Carl Fürstenberg, who ran the

Berliner Handels-Gesellschaft in the late nineteenth and early twentieth centuries, famously remarked: 'Shareholders are stupid and impertinent – stupid because they give their money to somebody else without any effective control over what this person is doing with it, and impertinent because they ask for a dividend as a reward for their stupidity.'[217]

Fürstenburg's first point is relevant to the wider corporate sector today because there is another sense in which quoted companies in the Anglosphere have become dysfunctional. The bonus culture that has come to dominate top pay over the past ten to fifteen years was supposed to help align the interests of management with those of shareholders. Instead, it has introduced systematically distorted incentives into the corporate world. Rewards increasingly take the form of shares or share options and are performance related. The benchmarks for performance are crude measures such as earnings per share, return on equity, or total shareholder return, which consists of capital gains plus dividends paid out over a given period. These are open to manipulation. Managers can, for example, cut back research and development expenditure or capital investment to bring about a short-term increase in earnings. Or they can buy back the company's own shares, which reduces the number of shares in issue and thus increases earnings per share. Evidence from academic surveys of finance directors in the US has shown that companies frequently refrain from profitable investment opportunities in the interests of boosting quarterly earnings figures.[218]

Manipulating the numbers in this way carries a risk, because reduced investment leads to the erosion of a company's market share. Yet it can take a long time for this erosion to happen,

whereas executive rewards are based on relatively short
time periods. Given the choice, many executives in the Anglo-
American world, whose average tenure at the top has shrunk
to very short time periods in recent years, appear to be choos-
ing to invest in share buybacks in preference to plant and machinery. So while bonuses have been going up as these people
seize their brief window of opportunity, business investment as
a percentage of GDP has been on a persistent declining trend
in the US and UK.[219]

This is a travesty of shareholder value, the supposed objective of modern managers who run publicly quoted companies.
It reflects a huge and egregious corporate governance vacuum
– another profound imbalance at the heart of modern capitalism. Institutional investors have done little to prevent a pattern
of behaviour that damages the long-term value of their investments. This is because, as we saw in Chapter Seven, they
are mere proxy capitalists, driven by perverse incentives that
ensure that their own interests are misaligned with those of
the pension fund beneficiaries and other savers they are supposed to serve. Too many fund managers are more preoccupied with minimising their own business risk and protecting
their career capital than with looking after the beneficiaries.
Only a handful of big institutional investors acknowledge the
stewardship role they are theoretically supposed to perform
within the capitalist system by engaging with management
on strategy and holding managers to account. The business
models of many, probably most, fund management groups are
not compatible with the stewardship agenda, which requires
time and money. And a growing band of maverick shareholder
activists is more concerned to ratchet up the share price of

corporate targets through financial engineering – selling off subsidiaries, urging more share buybacks – than improving companies' operating performance and productivity. So the dysfunctionality of a corporate sector that under-invests in plant and machinery is a reflection of dysfunctional corporate governance.

Consider, now, the ethical concern that most exercised John Maynard Keynes, namely the central role of the money motive in capitalism – or, to put it more bluntly, greed. One of the sayings attributed to the great economist is that capitalism amounts to 'the astonishing belief that the nastiest motives of the nastiest men somehow or other work for the best results in the best of all possible worlds'.[220] And that certainly is consonant with the view he expressed – only slightly tongue in cheek, according to his biographer Robert Skidelsky – in his essay 'Economic Possibilities for Our Grandchildren':

> When the accumulation of wealth is no longer of high social importance, there will be great change in the code of morals. We shall be able to rid ourselves of many of the pseudo-moral principles which have hag-ridden us for two hundred years, by which we have exalted some of the most distasteful of human qualities into the position of the highest virtues. We shall be able to afford to dare to assess the money-motive at its true value. The love of money as a possession – as distinguished from the love of money as a means to the enjoyments and realities of life – will be recognised for what it is, a somewhat disgusting morbidity, one of those semi-criminal, semi-pathological propensities which one hands over with a shudder to the specialists in mental disease.[221]

Keynes, says Skidelsky, argued further, in *The Economic Consequences of the Peace*, that the price of economic progress was the cultural deformation of the 'rentier bourgeoisie', who had sacrificed the 'arts of enjoyment' to 'compound interest'.

This economist of protean intellect was, at least until the Great Depression, an instinctive liberal in both economics and politics. He had little time for Marxism. Yet these views come in a direct line from Marx and from Friedrich Engels, who wrote in *The Condition of the Working Class in England Based on Personal Observation and Authentic Sources*:

> I have never seen a class so deeply demoralised, so incurably debased by self-interest, so internally corroded and incapable of progress as the English bourgeoisie ... For it, nothing exists in the world except for the sake of money, including the bourgeoisie themselves, who live for no purpose but to earn money, who know no bliss other than quick profit, and no pain beyond monetary loss. No human relationship is untainted by this avarice and lust for money ... The English bourgeois could not care less whether his workers starve or not, as long as he earns money. All conditions of life are measured by profitability, and whatever does not produce money is nonsense, impractical, idealistic.[222]

I believe that in the earlier stages of the industrial revolution, harsh criticism of this extreme focus on economic means at the expense of ends was largely justified. Dickens's portrayal of Gradgrind, the ruthless employer in *Hard Times*, was addressing nineteenth-century reality. Yet today it is a critique that could more readily be levelled at neo-liberal economists, who see markets as an end in themselves, in the same way that nineteenth-century capitalists saw money as an end in itself. For, as we saw in Chapter Two, the Marxian notion that entrepreneurs are exclusively driven by the desire to accumulate capital is a grotesque over-simplification today and it was certainly an over-simplification in 1930 when Keynes wrote his essay.

Perhaps the most prominent British businessman of the time was Sir Alfred Mond, son of the founder of the chemical company Brunner Mond, which was at the core of the group of companies that came to be known as Imperial Chemical Industries (ICI). In his book *After the Victorians*, the novelist, biographer and journalist A. N. Wilson points out that when Mond was raised to the peerage with the title of Lord Melchett, he felt obliged to counter a denunciation of capitalism made by Philip Snowden in the House of Commons.[223] In a classic defence of liberal capitalism, he talked of his father's risk taking and altruism, of the dangers they had endured to build up a huge business and of the benefits to society that resulted. Father, son and various business partners had, he said, given work and prosperity to thousands, an enterprise which 'could never have been commended under any Socialist system that I have ever known'.

Mond believed that *laissez-faire* was no longer the way to produce general prosperity and strongly opposed confrontational industrial relations. He thought there should be profit sharing, employee shareholding and what would now be called a stakeholder approach to capitalism. Yet as Wilson remarks, while referring also to the immense philanthropy and business success of the car maker Lord Nuffield at around the same time, it is a curious feature of twentieth-century history that the businessmen who created what wealth there was for the majority of the population were automatically lumped together with the villains. Even when an enterprise produced as many jobs and as much money for other people as ICI, a figure like Mond could still be written about as if he were Mr Melmotte, the cunning and entirely fraudulent capitalist of Trollope's *The Way We Live Now*. Wilson also cites 'A Cooking Egg', a poem written just after the First World War by T. S. Eliot, which waxes nostalgic about the chivalric heroes whom the poet will now only encounter in heaven since the world has been given over to business values. He offers this faintly snide quip on the prominent captain of industry:

> *I shall not want Capital in Heaven*
> *For I shall meet Sir Alfred Mond.*
> *We two shall lie together, lapt*
> *In a 5 per cent, Exchequer Bond*[224]

(Perhaps Mond got off lightly, for in the poem 'Burbank with a Baedeker; Bleistein with a Cigar', Eliot manages to combine anti-business sentiment with a heavy quotient of anti-Semitism.)

In the end, much of this boils down to anti-business snobbery, which is odd given that Eliot's father was a businessman from St Louis in the United States and Keynes's family were non-conformists, a group that had for much of its history been excluded from the British establishment and was thus traditionally sympathetic to and engaged in business.[225] Such snobbery has not been helpful to enterprise. Thankfully, it has greatly diminished since the 1930s. Yet attempts over centuries to legitimise

capitalism, to make it respectable and to wish away the contradictions inherent in its ethical underpinnings, have nonetheless
failed. As we saw in Chapter Six, the Enlightenment view of
market activity as a civilising influence on human behaviour and
a force for peace was dealt an overwhelming blow by the First
World War. Meanwhile, the arguments of today's pro-market
ideologues have been severely tarnished as a result of the recent
credit bubble and the subsequent financial crisis. And Dr Johnson's conviction that a man is never so innocently employed as
when making money has been definitively shot to pieces by the
greedy bankers at the heart of the global financial crisis.

In effect, the bankers have hijacked capitalism by exploiting
the corporate governance vacuum to which I have just alluded
and by buying up the politicians wholesale through campaign
finance and intensive lobbying. Their role in causing the financial crisis can be exaggerated, as I argued earlier, because
monetary dislocation was of overwhelmingly greater importance in causing economic disruption than the behaviour of
commercial bankers. Yet the bankers have undoubtedly done
their best to give capitalism a bad name. The extraordinary
scale on which big banks have been rigging interest rates and
foreign exchange markets and ripping off their customers is
almost beyond comprehension, as is the paltry nature of the
penalties incurred by individual bankers.

Note, in passing, that far from being a novelty, the bankers'
current behaviour in the political arena is sadly reminiscent of
the way corrupt Medici bankers bought up both politicians
and the papacy as far back as the fifteenth century. Nor is
the anger aroused by bankers a recent phenomenon. It has
been most virulent in the most capitalistic of countries, the US.

Witness this extract from the official journal of the Farmers' State Alliance in the US in 1896 during the Gilded Age, which also saw remarkably high levels of inequality:

> The banking business is an evil. Bankers are leeches on the business body. When bankers prosper, the people mourn. Banking destroys more wealth than any other business … The banking interest is a money combine that corrupts legislatures, Congress and the Administration, as is now the case, and leads to national disgrace and disaster. The country is now in the clutches of the bank combines and it may require a revolution to extricate it. Down with the banks![226]

That populist anti-bank sentiment was further compounded when the failure of countless US banks in the 1930s inflicted bankruptcy on hapless farmers and small businessmen.

Nor is such hostility now confined to the banks. Capitalism's tendency towards industrial concentration, which has not been fully constrained by competition policy, is giving rise to increasing concern in unexpected places. Maurice Saatchi, the Tory peer who ran the advertising campaign that helped propel Margaret Thatcher to power in 1979 and a former chairman of Britain's Conservative Party, recently ruminated on the possibility

> that after all Marx was right: 'The end result of competition is the end of competition.'
> He [Marx] described the outcome: 'After years of internecine warfare amongst capitalists there would be fewer and fewer capitalists controlling vaster and vaster empires.'

Who can doubt the accuracy of that prediction when considering the banks, the trains, electricity, gas, water, oil, or any other large global industry?

The unintended consequence of globalisation is the creation of global cartels in which there is a huge imbalance of power between the individual customer and the giant corporation; a sense of powerlessness and unfairness that results from a world of global corporations whose governance (and maybe tax payments) are beyond the reach of national governments.[227]

All of this leaves us in an uncertain, uncomfortable world. It is a world still marked by global financial imbalances arising from excess savings. US monetary policy since the financial crisis is morally hazardous in much the same way as during Alan Greenspan's tenure as chairman of the Federal Reserve. Under his successors Ben Bernanke and Janet Yellen, it continued to put a floor under asset prices while encouraging investors to take on more risk. This they did as they searched desperately for income at a time of negative real interest rates. In 2013 and 2014, lending standards in banking were once again declining, much as they did before 2007. Far from shrinking after the crisis, total global debt, according to the McKinsey Global Institute, rose from end-2007 to mid-2014 by no less than $57 trillion to $199 trillion, equivalent to 286 per cent of world GDP.[228] The bulk of the increase stems from the sharp rise in public sector debt in mature economies. This leaves financial markets hostage to a future spike in interest rates, which would be one of many potential triggers for a new financial crisis that will be even bigger than the one we have just experienced, as will the accompanying recession. It also suggests that our ability to mitigate the periodic shocks that are part and parcel of capitalism is now increasingly constrained.

There is no escaping the fact noted by Maurice Saatchi that capitalism feels unbalanced. While incomes have stagnated in much of the developed world, corporate profit margins are astonishingly high. In the US, at the time of writing, they are at their highest recorded level. The role of greed in driving the capitalist money machine seems to have reasserted itself with a vengeance across a corporate sector characterised by a profoundly disturbing depletion of the stock of moral capital. Top executives have succeeded, as suggested earlier, in turning industry and commerce into a cash cow for the global business elite at the expense of pension fund beneficiaries and other investors. By ceasing to offer pensions related to final pay and substituting money purchase pensions where the level of retirement incomes is related to the value of the underlying investments, they have transferred the risk of loss in pension provision from the corporation to employees.

This is also a world of great geo-political uncertainty, in which the capitalist mode of production has brought about the industrialisation of warfare and, in the twentieth century, mass killing on a hitherto undreamt-of scale. In two world wars, the lives of the governed became cheap relative to those of the governing elite, much as labour had become cheap relative to capital through the industrial process. Yet this same dangerous, uncomfortable world is one in which Joseph Schumpeter's famous prediction that capitalism would not survive seems unlikely to be realised. The Austrian-born economist worried that capitalism's tendency to monopolistic gigantism, inequality and the encouragement of envy would, with the connivance of an anti-capitalist intellectual elite, drive the world to state socialism. What has changed since Schumpeter's time is that while those tendencies still exist, there is no longer any systemic alternative to capitalism. Since the fall of the Berlin Wall, comprehensive public ownership of the means of production is discredited. To the extent that systemic choices are available, they lie on a spectrum that runs from the market-driven model of capitalism in the US, via the social democratic models of Europe, to the heavily statist, authoritarian form of capitalism that prevails in China and much of the rest of the developing world – a model nonetheless characterised by extensive exposure to the global trading system.

Does this mean that the general discontent with capitalism will ensure a permanent anti-business climate and policy that is inimical to economic growth? I sincerely hope not. Having pondered these questions over a 45-year career in journalism and in business, I am, with caveats, pro-business and pro-capitalism. For, in the end, it is the efforts of business people working within a market system that have lifted millions from poverty all across the world over the past two and a half centuries. It would take far worse than anything capitalism has inflicted on the world so far to outweigh that enormous benefit on any true set of scales. And I rejoice in the fact that the militaristic code of the European aristocracy, whose land-grab bellicosity inflicted centuries of misery on ordinary people, has been displaced by the capitalist ethos, while regretting that geo-political instability remains a dismal fact of life. Yet I also believe we have lost something by abandoning elements of the wisdom of the ancient Greeks, who were much closer to traditional Jewish thinking on money than to the strictures of St Paul's Christianity. They felt that a good man needed money to help him lead a good life. But they also believed that money should not become an end in itself and that the pursuit of profit was not inherently admirable. Worse, if wealth bred self-indulgence, it would cap the sense of public and national obligation.

It is always dangerous to underestimate the capacity of human beings for technological innovation and for muddling through, as they confront the huge challenges posed by globalised markets, financial instability, inequality and the ageing of populations – though muddling through is no answer to such problems as global warming. And it would be pleasant to conclude by quoting the wisdom of Edmund Burke on the central moral issue. The great political theorist exhibits an altogether mature view of how to address the problem raised in this book:

> The love of lucre, though sometimes carried to a ridiculous, sometimes to a vicious excess, is the grand cause of prosperity to all States. In this natural, this reasonable, this powerful, this prolifick principle, it is for the satyrist to expose the ridiculous; it is for the moralist to censure the vicious; it is for the sympathetick heart to reprobate the hard and cruel; it is for the Judge to animadvert on the fraud, the extortion, and the oppression: but it is for the Statesman to employ it as he finds it, with all its concomitant excellencies, with all its imperfections on its head. It is his part, in this case, as it is in all other cases, where he is to make use of the general energies of nature, to take them as he finds them.[229]

This is a highly relevant policy prescription for today's circumstances. It is, in its way, a call for us all to grow up and seek to remedy the injustices and imperfections of the capitalist system while acknowledging its merits. For people in the developed world, life is, notwithstanding the warts-and-all nature of capitalism, longer, healthier and potentially more fulfilling than ever before. Yet sadly, with politicians in thrall to the business and banking lobbies, the representatives of the people are not only unlikely to turn the money motive to best use; they are most unlikely to curb the excesses of an inherently unstable system through more stringent and coherent regulation. It is worth recalling, too, that the extreme inequality recently experienced in the US was in part a reflection of policy-induced redistribution upwards. Since reform of political funding remains elusive, the best hope is that we do indeed manage to muddle through, while falling back on a concluding insight from another great politician, Winston Churchill. His verdict on democracy applies with equal validity to capitalism: it is the worst form of economic management, except for all those other forms that have been tried from time to time.

NOTES

1   Translated by Benjamin Jowett, http: //classics.mit.edu/Plato/republic.9.viii.html

2   http://classics.mit.edu/Plato/laws.html

3   *Politics*, Book 7, Part 9, http://classics.mit.edu/Aristotle/politics.7.seven.html

4   *Reflections on the Death of a Porcupine and Other Essays* (1925), edited by Michael Herbert, Cambridge University Press, 1988.

5   Arden Shakespeare, edited by John Russell Brown, 1964. Later in the play Shakespeare gives a wicked humorous twist to this same market logic when, after Shylock's daughter Jessica has converted to Christianity and married Lorenzo, Launcelot, the jester, remarks: 'This making Christians will raise the price of hogs: if we grow all to be pork eaters, we shall not shortly have a rasher on the coals for money.' Like much else in *The Merchant*, it is, by today's standards, arrestingly politically incorrect.

6   This and subsequent quotations are from the Penguin Classics edition, edited by Phillip Harth, 1989.

7   *The Life of Samuel Johnson*, James Boswell, Penguin Classics.

8   The first big test of the trickledown theory came with the industrial revolution. Brian Reading of Lombard Street Research points out that while this led to mass production and mass urban employment, the profits from increased productivity went to the factory owners. Neither the workers nor mill owners had sufficient purchasing power to buy all the mass-produced goods they churned out. So they had to look abroad for mass markets. In the nineteenth century, this led to huge current account surpluses on the British balance of payments. The same debate is alive and well today in the light of increased inequality in the US and other advanced economies. Because the rich consume a smaller percentage of their income than the rest of the population, inequality tends to lead to weaker aggregate demand than would be the case if society were more equal.

9   In his *Luxury and Capitalism*, Sombart calls capitalism the 'illicit child of luxury'.

10 Penguin Books, edited by Andrew Skinner, 1979.

11 It is not difficult to find distinguished men of learning who took precisely the opposite point of view. Sir Joseph Banks, the great botanist and president of the Royal Society who travelled on Captain Cook's first voyage, remarked that man was never so well employed as when working for the public good with no expectation of gain. Quoted in Richard Holmes, *The Age of Wonder*, Harper Press, 2008.

12 *Lettres Philosophiques*, Letter 10, Nouveaux Classiques Larousse, 1972. My (probably flawed) translation.

13 Ibid., Letter Six.

14 *The World Economy: A Millennial Perspective*, OECD, 2001.

15 http://www.gutenberg.org/files/26159/26159-h/26159-h.htm

16 On being told this man of famously few words had died, the wit Dorothy Parker asked: 'How could they tell?'

17 http://www.britannica.com/presidents/article-9116867

18 *The General Theory of Employment, Interest and Money* from *The Collected Writings of John Maynard Keynes*, edited by Elizabeth Johnson, Donald Moggridge and Austin Robinson, Macmillan, Cambridge University Press for The Royal Economic Society, 1973.

19 *The Company: A Short History of a Revolutionary Idea*, The Modern Library, 2003.

20 Macmillan, 1895. *Ill Fares the Land* is, incidentally, the aptly chosen title of the historian Tony Judt's powerful recent polemic in favour of a social democratic model of capitalism.

21 http://www.gutenberg.org/files/6798/6798-h/6798-h.htm

22 https://archive.org/stream/forsclavigera04ruskiala#page/n423/mode/2up

23 *The Strange Death of Tory England*, Allen Lane, 2005.

24 Article in the *Times Literary Supplement*, 6 December 2002.

25 Ayn Rand commands the fanatical regard of countless market ideologues in the United States who can be relied on to deluge the author with hostile emails on the basis of this negative literary verdict.

26 *Capitalism, Socialism and Democracy*, Unwin Paperbacks Counterpoint Edition, 1987. This extract is of a piece with what Schumpeter claimed were the three goals of his life: to be the greatest economist in the world, to be the best horseman in Austria and to be the greatest lover in all Vienna.

27 *The Sale of the Century: Russia's Wild Ride from Communism to Capitalism*, Crown Business, 2000.

28 http://www.readbookonline.net/readOnLine/29989

29 'Founders need a bit of grit for the fight', *Financial Times*, 5 November 2013.

30 Nicholas Barbon's father, Praise-God Barbon, or Barebone, was a leather merchant and lay preacher who was a leading member of the parliament nominated by Oliver Cromwell's army in 1653. It was nicknamed the Barebones Parliament because his name conveniently highlighted the small and unrepresentative nature of the assembly. After a few months it was dissolved and Cromwell became Lord Protector.

31 *Notes of Me: The Autobiography of Roger North*, Toronto University Press, 2000.

32 http://quod.lib.umich.edu/e/ecco/004843169.0001.000/1:2?rgn=div1;view=fulltext

33 http://www.gutenberg.org/files/36541/36541-h/36541-h.htm

34 http://classics.mit.edu/Aristotle/politics.7.seven.html

35 Quoted in *The Ancient Economy*, M. I. Finley, Penguin Books, 1992.

36 Francesco da Molin, quoted in *Venice: A Documentary History, 1450–1630*, edited by David Chambers and Brian Pullan, Blackwell, 1992.

37 *I Wouldn't Have Missed It: Selected Poems*, Andre Deutsch, 1983.

38 Hodder & Stoughton, 1989.

39   Figures from 'The Bank and the banks', speech by Andrew G. Haldane, while executive director, financial stability, and member of the Financial Policy Committee of the Bank of England, at Queen's University, Belfast, 2012.

40   Figures from 'Small lessons from a big crisis', a speech by Andrew G. Haldane at the 45th annual conference of the Federal Reserve Bank of Chicago.

41   Figures from 'A Leaf Being Turned', a speech by Andrew G. Haldane given to Occupy Economics at Friends House, Euston, London, 2012.

42   Address at Trinity Church in Lower Manhattan on the first anniversary of the 2001 attacks on the Twin Towers.

43   A notable exception was Eric Knight of the activist fund management group Knight Vinke. He pointed out, in his campaign to improve performance at HSBC, that the underlying return on HSBC's assets was stagnant and that return on equity was a misleading indicator of performance. With hindsight, it has to be said that his choice of target was less than inspired, given that HSBC survived the financial crisis better than most. But his analysis was acute.

44   Jean-Claude Trichet, president of the European Central Bank during the credit bubble, was an honourable exception. He sees the theoretical case for leaning against the wind but thinks the circumstances in which the policy could be embarked on with confidence are likely to be rare. See http://www.ecb.europa.eu/press/key/date/2005/html/sp050608.en.html

45   Remarks at the meeting of the Eastern Economic Association, 20 February 2004.

46   *The City of London, Vol IV: A Club No More*, Pimlico, 2001.

47   'The Art of Central Banking', Working Paper GPB 81–6, Centre for Research in Government Policy and Business, University of Rochester Graduate School of Management.

48   *Banking on the Future: The Fall and Rise Of Central Banking*, Princeton University Press, 2010.

49   'Systemic Banking Crises Database: An Update', Luc Laeven and Fabián Valencia, IMF Working Paper WP/12/163, 2012.

50   Figures from 'Capital discipline', a speech by Andrew G. Haldane given at the American Economic Association, Denver, 2011.

51   'The dog and the frisbee', speech given at the Federal Reserve Bank of Kansas City's 36th economic policy symposium, 2012.

52   *The Great Crash 1929*, Penguin Books, 1975.

53   *Poetical Works*, Oxford University Press, 1967.

54   See *The Road to Recovery: How and Why Economic Policy Must Change*, Wiley, 2013. Andrew Smithers, incidentally, is the great-grandson of the founder of Akroyd & Smithers, a leading firm of stockjobbers in the era before the deregulatory reforms in the City referred to as the Big Bang.

55   Article in the *Financial Times*, 17 September 2013.

56   http://www.marxists.org/archive/marx/works/1867-c1/ch14.htm

57   *An Inquiry into the Nature and Causes of the Wealth of Nations*, edited by Andrew Skinner, Penguin Books, 1979.

58   See Paul Addison's review of *Servants: A downstairs view of twentieth-century Britain* in the *Times Literary Supplement*, 10 May 2013.

59   Quoted by Barry Supple in 'Fear of failing: economic history and the decline of Britain', *Economic History Review*, XLVII, 3, 1994.

60 Remark made to the historian Jules Michelet, recorded in Michelet's *Journal*, edited by Paul Viallaneix, Gallimard, 1959.

61 That is not to say that pastoral life disappeared completely from poetic discourse. It remained a central preoccupation of the Irish poet Seamus Heaney, for example. Yet this was because Heaney's childhood world, which inspired so much of his poetry, was essentially pre-industrial. In rural County Derry, where he was brought up, the farmers still ploughed with horses and their houses had no electric lighting, according to Fintan O'Toole, literary editor of the *Irish Times*.

62 A similar argument is made in relation to music by the writer and journalist A. N. Wilson in his *After the Victorians: The World Our Parents Knew*, Arrow Books, 2006. He suggests that the practical, Benthamite, down-to-earth values of the utilitarian economists and capitalist factory owners silenced the great English musical tradition of Dowland, Tallis, Byrd, Purcell and Handel and that to be seriously musical in nineteenth-century England was to be unhelpfully marked out. Given that Bentham's felicific calculus was indifferent to whether units of pleasure were generated by Bach's *St Matthew Passion* or a pint of ale, this is suggestive. But I suspect that wider cultural and social factors were more important in the drying up of English musical inspiration.

63 *Chartism*, James Fraser, Regent Street, 1840.

64 *Journeys to England and Ireland*, J. P. Mayer, edited by George Lawrence, Arno Press, 1979.

65 Barry Supple, ibid.

66 *The Age of Diminished Expectations*, MIT Press, 1994.

67 Quoted by Richard W. Fisher, president and chief executive officer of the Federal Reserve Bank of Dallas, in his speech 'In the Lap of the Gods', 2 October 2007.

68 These numbers are from successive speeches by Andrew Haldane, executive director of the Bank of England, on the financial crisis.

69 This is the cost of replacing all outstanding contracts at current market prices.

70 *A Short History of Financial Euphoria*, Penguin Books, 1990.

71 BIS Working Paper No. 381, 'Reassessing the impact of finance on growth' by Stephen G. Cecchetti and Enisse Kharroubi, July 2012.

72 *Epistle to Allen Lord Bathurst, Poetical Works*, Oxford University Press, 1978.

73 Richard Bentley, London, 1841.

74 Joint Economic Committee, 'Monetary Policy and the Economic Outlook', 17 June 1999.

75 For an account of Alan Greenspan's frequent changes of position on the bubble, see Frederick J. Sheehan's *Panderer to Power: The Untold Story of How Alan Greenspan Enriched Wall Street and Left a Legacy of Recession*, McGraw-Hill, 2010.

76 http://blogs.hbr.org/2014/01/what-alan-greenspan-has-learned-since-2008

77 'Famous First Bubbles', *Journal of Economic Perspectives*, Vol. 4, No. 2, Spring 1990.

78 *The First Crash: Lessons from the South Sea Bubble*, Princeton University Press, 2004.

79 Ibid.

80 *Reformation of Manners: A Satyr*, http://books.google.co.uk/books?id=oooJAAAAQAAJ&pg=PA76&lpg=PA76&dq=Defoe

81 *Irrational Exuberance*, second edition, Princeton University Press, 2005.

82 See, for example, 'From Efficient Markets Theory to Behavioral Finance', Cowles Foundation for Research in Economics at Yale University, Paper No. 1055, 2003.

83   The title also caused serious concern to academics at the London School of Economics, who feared that it would deter potential sources of funds in the financial sector. Paul Woolley – who had accumulated a fair-sized fortune as a fund manager – made the title an absolute condition of his financing of the centre. The LSE backed down and took the money.

84   *When Genius Failed: The Rise and Fall of Long-Term Capital Management*, Random House Trade Paperbacks, 2000.

85   *Dogs and Demons: The Fall of Modern Japan*, Farrar, Straus & Giroux and Penguin Books, 2001.

86   'Letter from Chicago: After the Blow-up', 11 January 2010.

87   In *Going Off the Rails: Global Capital and the Crisis of Legitimacy*, John Wiley, 2003, I argued that Federal Reserve chairman Alan Greenspan's asymmetric and morally hazardous approach to monetary policymaking, which involved the repeated extension of a safety net to markets, was undermining capitalism's immune system; the use of highly complex financial instruments meant that central banks and bank supervisors were over-dependent on experts in private banks to monitor the plumbing of the system and that supervision had been semi-privatised by default; financial institutions' risk management was fundamentally flawed; financial innovation had failed to come up with any way of hedging against liquidity risk in banking; and the system's pro-cyclicality was being exacerbated by the Basel capital adequacy regime. The book explained that the cycle would end with a credit crunch and system-wide deleveraging, creating severe deflationary pressure. In my columns at the *FT* before the credit crunch of 2007, I elaborated these arguments while highlighting excessive leverage in the system, the decline in bank lending standards and the risks inherent in the fast-growing shadow banking system. I did not, of course, accurately predict the timing of the bursting of the bubble.

88   'Expectations of Returns and Expected Returns', 2012, http://www.hbs.edu/faculty/Publication%20Files/expectedreturns20121020_00760bc1-693c-4b4f-b635-dedoe540e78c.pdf

89   Ibid.

90   http://www.economist.com/node/14165405

91   http://www.johnkay.com/2011/10/04/the-map-is-not-the-territory-an-essay-on-the-state-of-economics

92   Speech to the annual conference of the Institute for New Economic Thinking, quoted by Anatole Kaletsky in the *International New York Times*, April 2014.

93   *Stabilizing an Unstable Economy*, Yale University Press, 1986.

94   *The Time of My Life*, Penguin Books, 1990.

95   The trade-to-GDP ratio is the economy's total trade of goods and services (exports plus imports) divided by GDP.

96   *Politics*, Book 7, Part 9, http://classics.mit.edu/Aristotle/politics.7.seven.html

97   http://classics.mit.edu/Plato/laws.html

98   Quote from Jerry Z. Muller, *The Mind and the Market*, ibid.

99   Quoted in Albert O. Hirschman, *The Passions and the Interests: Political Arguments for Capitalism before its Triumph*, Princeton University Press, 1997. I have drawn extensively on Hirschman's superb essay in this chapter.

100   *The Didascalicon of Hugh of St Victor: A Medieval Guide to the Arts*, translated by Jerome Taylor, Columbia University Press, 1961.

101   *An Inquiry into the Nature and Causes of the Wealth of Nations*, ibid.

102   *Roxana: The Fortunate Mistress or, a History of the Life and Vast Variety of For-
      tunes of Mademoiselle de Beleau, afterwards called the Countess de Wintselsheim
      in Germany Being the Person known by the Name of the Lady Roxana in the time
      of Charles II*, Oxford University Press, 1996.

103   This and subsequent quotes from *De L'Esprit des Lois* are taken from *The Passions
      and the Interests: Political Arguments for Capitalism before Its Triumph* by Albert
      O. Hirschman, who translates from the Pléiade edition of the *Oeuvres Complètes*,
      Gallimard, 1949.

104   Richard Cobden, *Speeches*, London, 1870, vol. I.

105   www.poetryfoundation.org/poem/174629

106   Norman Angell, *The Great Illusion: A Study of the Relation of Military Power in
      Nations to Their Economic and Social Advantage*, G. P. Putnam's Sons, 1910.

107   *The Times*, 5 January 1920.

108   Quote from volume two of Skidelsky's *John Maynard Keynes*, ibid.

109   *The Breaking Of Nations: Order and Chaos in the Twenty-First Century*, Atlantic
      Books, 2003.

110   Amartya Sen, forward to *The Passions and the Interests*, ibid.

111   See, for example, *Mutual Assured Production: Why Trade Will Limit Conflict be-
      tween China and Japan*, Foreign Affairs, July/August 2013, by Richard Katz. He
      argues that money may ultimately tip the balance of forces in China and Japan
      towards those who can prevent war and put these countries' conflicting territorial
      claims back on the shelf.

112   Robert J. Shiller, *Finance and the Good Society*, Princeton University Press, 2012.

113   Quoted in 'China's Holdings of US Securities: Implications for the US economy', a
      report by Wayne M. Morrison and Marc Labonte of the Congressional Research
      Service, 19 August 2013.

114   *The Bill From the China Shop: How Asia's Savings Glut Threatens the World
      Economy*, co-authored with Diana Choyleva, Profile Books, 2006.

115   *The Great Convergence: Asia, the West, and the Logic of One World*, Public Af-
      fairs, 2013.

116   Quoted in *Don't Blame The Shorts* by Robert Sloan, McGraw-Hill, 2010.

117   *Karl Marx*, Fourth Estate, 1999.

118   Kynaston, ibid.

119   Macmillan, 1999.

120   In reality, the lender of shares sells them to the short seller and buys them back
      in due course, so the standard terminology used by market practitioners on stock
      lending and short selling is at odds with the contractual legal position.

121   Ibid.

122   *Alexander Hamilton*, Penguin Group, 2005.

123   *Financial Times*, 16 May 2009.

124   Content.ksg.harvard.edu/.../jeff_frankels.../commodity-prices-again;

125   See Robert Sloan, ibid., for an excellent, more detailed account.

126   This is just one in a splendid Dickensian line of portentously named companies
      that includes such gems as the Anglo-Bengalee Disinterested Loan & Life Insurance
      Company in *Martin Chuzzlewit*. (The disinterested life insurance company has, of
      course, yet to be invented.)

127   Penguin Classics, edited by Mark Ford, 1999.

128   *Where Are the Customers' Yachts? or A Good Hard Look at Wall Street*, Simon & Schuster, 1940.

129   Quoted in Robert Sloan, ibid.

130   This verdict may be a little hard on Kerviel. He argues that the bosses at his bank were happy to turn a blind eye to his unauthorised trades when he was making a profit, but turned on him when he lost money. The bosses deny this, but then they would.

131   Ibid.

132   See *A History of Interest Rates*, S. Homer and R. Sylla, fourth edition, John Wiley & Sons, 2005.

133   *The Ancient Economy*, Penguin Books, 1992.

134   *Paper Promises: Money, Debt and the New World Order*, Penguin Books, 2011.

135   *The Complete Works*, edited by Peter Alexander, Collins, 1951.

136   See *John Milton: A Hero of Our Time*, David Hawkes, Counterpoint, 2010.

137   *No Stone Unturned: A History of the British Land Company, 1856–2006*, John Weston Smith, British Land PLC, 2006.

138   http://www.gutenberg.org/cache/epub/4087/pg4087.html

139   ftp://ibiblio.org/pub/docs/books/gutenberg/1/2/0/5/12050/12050-8.txt

140   Savage wrote in a letter from Bristol Newgate prison: 'One day last week Mr Dagge, finding me at the Door, asked me to take a walk with him, which I did a mile beyond Baptist Mill in Gloucestershire; where, at a public-house, he treated me with ale and toddy. Baptist Mill is the pleasantest walk near this city. I found the smell of the new-mown hay very sweet, and every breeze was reviving to my spirits...' This proof of amazingly humane prison keeping comes from Richard Holmes's *Dr Johnson & Mr Savage*, Hodder & Stoughton, 1993.

141   Quoted in 'The Pathology of Europe's Debt' by Benjamin M. Friedman, *New York Review of Books*, 9 October 2014.

142   *The Theory of Economic Development*, Oxford University Press, 1934.

143   Ibid.

144   *Saving Capitalism from the Capitalists: Unleashing the Power of Financial Markets to Create Wealth and Spread Opportunity*, Crown Business, 2003.

145   *The Oxford Book of Literary Anecdotes*, edited by James Sutherland, Oxford University Press, 1975.

146   *Political Discourses*, www.davidhume.org/texts/pd.html

147   From Remark Q in Mandeville's commentary on the text of his *Fable*, ibid. In his *General Theory*, Keynes suggests that Mandeville owed this perception to Nicholas Barbon, the multi-talented entrepreneur who featured in Chapter Two.

148   It is of course usually possible to find a precedent or aphorism in the Bible for almost anything in the modern world. Proverbs 11.24 appears to fit the problem of under-consumption rather well: 'There is that scattereth, and yet increaseth; and there is that witholdeth more than is meet, but it tendeth to poverty.'

149   The quote is from *The Memoirs of Herbert Hoover: The Great Depression 1929–1941*, Macmillan, 1952. It reads in full: 'Two schools of thought quickly developed within our administration discussions. First was the "leave it alone liquidationists" headed by Secretary of the Treasury Mellon, who felt that government must keep its hands off and let the slump liquidate itself. Mr. Mellon had only one formula:

"Liquidate labor, liquidate stocks, liquidate the farmers, liquidate real estate." He insisted that, when the people get an inflation brainstorm, the only way to get it out of their blood is to let it collapse. He held that even a panic was not altogether a bad thing. He said: "It will purge the rottenness out of the system. High costs of living and high living will come down. People will work harder, live a more moral life. Values will be adjusted, and enterprising people will pick up the wrecks from less competent people."' Some have questioned whether Mellon really said that. We only have Hoover's word for it and he was writing years later and was in need of a scapegoat.

150 Ibid.
151 In fairness to the Germans, I should point out that some American economists have been known to be moralistic about the crisis. After the giant bailout of the insurer AIG in 2009, Austan Goolsbee, a former adviser to President Obama and now a professor at the University of Chicago's Booth School of Business, said of AIG's senior executives: 'It's almost like these guys should have gotten a Nobel Prize for evil.' This quote comes from Gary B. Gorton's *Misunderstanding Financial Crises: Why We Don't See Them Coming*, Oxford University Press, 2012. The title of Gorton's book is breathtakingly sweeping given how many people did see the crisis coming, but it provides a coherent explanation why so many mainstream economists, working with mathematical models, condemned themselves to a kind of myopia.
152 'The Debt We Shouldn't Pay', *New York Review of Books*, 9 May 2013.
153 Ibid.
154 *The Battle of Bretton Woods*, Princeton University Press, 2013.
155 'Banking on the State', presentation delivered at the Federal Reserve Bank of Chicago twelfth annual international banking conference, 2009.
156 *The Rise and Fall of the Great Powers*, Unwin Hyman, 1988.
157 Reputedly from a speech delivered at Harvard University in 1998.
158 *Memoirs of Sir Thomas More*, Vol. II, edited by Arthur Cayley the Younger, Cadell and Davis, 1808.
159 *The Greek Experience*, Signet Paperback, 1959.
160 *The Faerie Queene*, Book Three, Canto IX, Everyman's Library, Dent.
161 Translation from the sleeve notes of Sir Georg Solti's Decca recording of *Das Rheingold* with the Vienna Philharmonic Orchestra.
162 http://www.gutenberg.org/files/4200/4200-h/4200-h.htm#link2H_4_0087
163 Ibid.
164 These numbers come from 'On the Measurement of Zimbabwe's Hyperinflation' by Steve Hanke and Alex Kwok in *Cato Journal*, Vol. 29, Spring/Summer 2009.
165 *German Ideology*, www.marxists.org/archive/marx/works/1845/german-ideology
166 Keynes's antagonism towards speculation in works of art was most clearly set out in an article on art and the state in *The Listener* magazine in 1936.
167 *The Philosophy of Andy Warhol: From A to B and Back Again*, Harcourt Brace Jovanovich, 1975.
168 *Financial Times*, 3–4 March 2012.
169 www.multimedialibrary.com/articles/kazin/alfredblake.asp
170 en.wikisource.org/wiki/Author:Samuel Johnson_(1709–1784)

171   *The New Grove Dictionary of Music and Musicians*, edited by Stanley Sadie, Macmillan Publishers Limited, 1980.

172   This information comes from the broadcaster Peter Day, who explored the ledgers at the Bank of England while making a radio programme for the BBC.

173   Margot and Rudolf Wittkower, 'Born Under Saturn', *New York Review of Books*, 2007.

174   Ibid.

175   Andy Warhol and Pat Hackett, *POPism: The Warhol Sixties*, Harcourt Brace Jovanovich, 1980.

176   http://sacramentalsocialists.wordpress.com/2010/12/18/capitalism-as-religion

177   *Art on the Edge*, University of Chicago Press, 1983.

178   I have gleaned this from Angus Trumble's review of 'The British as Art Collectors' by James Stourton and Charles Sebag-Montefiore in the *Times Literary Supplement*, 5 July 2013.

179   Joan Miró, *Selected Writings and Interviews*, Da Capo Press, 1992.

180   See Christopher Stace in 'A devotion to figures', *Times Literary Supplement*, 14 October 2011.

181   Ibid.

182   www.amien.org/forums/showthread.php?38-Art-amp-Money-by-Robert-Hughes

183   See 'Art and Money', William N. Goetzmann, Luc Renneboog and Christophe Spaenjers, NBER Working Paper 15502, 2009.

184   For a more detailed account of this episode, see my book *That's the Way the Money Goes*, André Deutsch, 1982.

185   Margot and Rudolf Wittkower, ibid.

186   'Artists and the Market: From Leonardo and Titian to Andy Warhol and Damien Hirst', NEBR Working Paper 13377, 2007.

187   *Prejudices, A Selection*, edited by James T. Farrell, Vintage Books.

188   'The crisis of the tax state' in *International Economy Papers*, No. 4, 1954 edited by A. T. Peacock, R. Turvey, W. F. Stolper and E. Henderson.

189   Quoted in H. C. G. Matthew, 'Disraeli, Gladstone and the politics of mid-Victorian budgets', *Historical Journal*, 22, 1979. The reference for this quote came from Martin Daunton's *Trusting Leviathan: The Politics of Taxation in Britain 1799–1914*, Cambridge University Press, 2001.

190   Daunton, ibid.

191   Daunton, ibid.

192   Ferdinand H. M. Grapperhaus, *Tax Tales from the Second Millennium*, International Bureau of Fiscal Documentation, 1998.

193   Daunton, ibid.

194   Quoted in B. E. V. Sabine, *A History of Income Tax*, George Allen & Unwin Ltd, 1966. Also a reference from Daunton.

195   *The Cash Nexus: Money and Power in the Modern World 1700–2000*, Allen Lane/The Penguin Press, 2001. The phrase 'cash nexus' comes from Thomas Carlyle, who used it in *Chartism*, 1840, and *Past and Present*, 1843.

196   See *Gold and Iron: Bismarck, Bleichröder and the Building of the German Empire*, Fritz Stern, Vintage Books, 1979.

197   *The British Tax System*, Oxford University Press, 1978.

198   Remarks from Ayrshire Pullman Motor Services *v.* Inland Revenue, 1929.

199   *Capital in the Twenty-First Century*, Harvard University Press, 2014, translated by Arthur Goldhammer.

200   I owe this insight to Brian Reading of Lombard Street Research.

201   Penguin Classics, 2009, translation by David Constantine. All subsequent quotes from Goethe are from the same source.

202   *Stabilizing an Unstable Economy*, Yale University Press, 1986.

203   'Manifest der Kommunistischen Partei' in *Marx-Engels Werke*, Vol. 4, Berlin, 1969. Translation by Jerry Z. Muller.

204   This was attributed to Coolidge in the *Reader's Digest* of June 1960, but I have been unable to find the original source.

205   http://www.project-syndicate.org/commentary/a-crisis-in-two-narratives

206   See *Efficiency, Equality and the Ownership of Private Property*, Harvard University Press, 1964. I was alerted to this by Benjamin M. Friedman's thought-provoking article '"Brave New Capitalists' Paradise": The Jobs?' in the *New York Review of Books*, 7 November 2013.

207   *The Black Swan: The Impact of the Highly Improbable*, Random House, 2007.

208   http://www.worldbank.org/en/topic/poverty/overview

209   *Divided We Stand: Why Inequality Keeps Rising*, OECD, 2011.

210   See Jon Bakija, Adam Cole, and Bradley T. Heim, 'Jobs and Income Growth of Top Earners and the Causes of Changing Income Inequality: Evidence from US Tax Return Data', Department of Economics Working Paper, Williams College, Williamstown, MA, 2012.

211   Figures from Lawrence Mishel of the Economic Policy Institute of the US, see http://www.epi.org/publication/ceo-pay-231-times-greater-average-worker

212   'The Crises of Democratic Capitalism', *New Left Review*, September–October 2011.

213   Remarks at THEARC, Washington DC, 4 December 2013.

214   'What did QE achieve, apart from boosting the price of Warhols?', *Financial Times*, 19 October 2013.

215   *Redistribution, Inequality and Growth*, Jonathan D. Ostry, Andrew Berg, Charalambos G. Tsangarides, 2014.

216   See the annual Edelman Trust Barometer for 2009 and 2011.

217   Quoted by Martin Hellwig in 'Economics and Politics of Corporate Finance and Control' in *Corporate Governance: Theoretical and Empirical Perspectives*, edited by Xavier Vives, Cambridge University Press, 2000.

218   See 'The Economic Implications of Corporate Financial Reporting', John R. Graham, Campbell R. Harvey and Shivaram Rajgopal, *Journal of Accounting and Economics*, 2005.

219   This phenomenon of perverse incentives, which I discussed in 2003 in my book *Going Off the Rails*, has been persuasively explored at much greater length by the economist Andrew Smithers in his *The Road to Recovery: How and Why Economic Policy Must Change*, Wiley, 2013.

220   Attributed by Sir George Schuster, *Christianity and human relations in industry*, The Epworth Press, 1951.

221   http://www.econ.yale.edu/smith/econ116a/keynes1.pdf

222   Marx-Engel Werke, Berlin, 1970, translated by Jerry Z. Muller.

223   Arrow Books, 2006.

224   *Collected Poems 1909–1962*, Faber & Faber, 1974.

225   Maybe non-conformist values could not have been expected to survive an Eton and Cambridge education of the kind enjoyed by Keynes.

226   Quoted in Gary B. Gorton, ibid.

227   From an article in the *Mail on Sunday*, 20 October 2013.

228   'Debt and (not much) deleveraging', Richard Dobbs, Susan Lund, Jonathan Woetzel and Mina Mutafchieva, 2015.

229   http://www.econlib.org/library/LFBooks/Burke/brkSWv3c3.html#firstpage-bar

INDEX

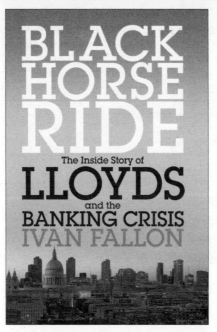